JB JOSSEY-BASS

ASPHALT JESUS

FINDING A NEW CHRISTIAN FAITH
ALONG THE HIGHWAYS OF AMERICA

Eric Elnes

Foreword by
Diana Butler Bass

BICENTENNIAL
1807
WILEY
2007
BICENTENNIAL

John Wiley & Sons

Published by Jossey-Bass
A Wiley Imprint
989 Market Street, San Francisco, CA 94103-1741   www.josseybass.com

Wiley Bicentennial logo: Richard J. Pacifico

Jossey-Bass books and products are available through most bookstores.
To contact Jossey-Bass directly call our Customer Care Department within the U.S.
at 800-956-7739, outside the U.S. at 317-572-3986, or fax 317-572-4002.

Jossey-Bass also publishes its books in a variety of electronic formats. Some content
that appears in print may not be available in electronic books.

All photographs by Scott Griessel.

Library of Congress Cataloging-in-Publication Data
Elnes, Eric.
  Asphalt Jesus : finding a new Christian faith along the highways of
America / Eric Elnes ; foreword by Diana Butler Bass. — 1st ed.
      p. cm.
  Includes bibliographical references.
  ISBN 978-0-7879-8608-7 (cloth)
  1. Christianity—United States—21st century. I. Title.
  BR526.E56   2007
  277.3'083—dc22   2007013595

Printed in the United States of America
FIRST EDITION
HB Printing   10 9 8 7 6 5 4 3 2 1

CONTENTS

FOREWORD

Diana Butler Bass

I FIRST MET ERIC ELNES, pastor of Scottsdale Congregational United Church of Christ, by telephone in early 2004 when I was researching vital mainline Protestant churches. At the time, I was working on a book about vibrant liberal congregations—spiritual communities that many Americans do not know exist. Another pastor recommended Scottsdale Congregational as a possible study site for my project, noting its innovative worship, its commitment to social justice, and its practice of hospitality. The congregation's Web site told the story of an open, optimistic, imaginative, and risk-taking sort of church.

In that first phone meeting, Eric became very excited about my project and thought that Scottsdale Congregational would offer much as a study church. However, he was about to go on sabbatical and thought it best that I wait to include the church upon his return. The congregation seemed a perfect fit for the research, and I liked Eric immensely, so I was willing to wait.

When Eric came back from sabbatical, he shared with me that an idea had come to him—an idea that he could not shake. It was more than just an idea, a vision really. He sensed that Christianity was on the verge of a "new Reformation," and he felt that God was calling him to walk across the United States spreading the word of a "more joyful, inclusive, and compassionate Christian faith."

I was tempted to dismiss Eric's story—it is not often that progressive Christians talk about visions from God—and wondered if I knew a therapist in Scottsdale to recommend! But I remembered a quip from a friend of mine who works as a spiritual director: "When God talks to a liberal, pay attention." I paid attention. For almost an hour, Eric unfolded a process of intuition, discernment, and prayer indicating that he should organize a walk across the country for progressive Christianity. As the conversation came to an end, he (more likely the Holy Spirit) had convinced me. Eric had not yet shared this with his congregation, and he asked me to pray for his further insight and courage to share with his church community.

Asphalt Jesus begins by recounting this discernment process, taking readers on the internal walk-before-the-walk, and then traces the actual journey: "CrossWalk America." Six walkers, materially and spiritually backed by Scottsdale Congregational and several companion organizations, left Phoenix on Easter Sunday 2006. Their way would not be that of big cities and major highways, nor of hotels and restaurants. They were not spiritual tourists. Instead, they became pilgrims, winding through America's back roads and rural towns, dependent on the hospitality and kindness of strangers in unknown small churches. They set out to proclaim the message of progressive Christianity. They quickly discovered that their journey was not to tell others what to believe. Instead, they learned to listen, to share stories, and to find God in unexpected places. Their journey of proclamation turned into a journey of transformation.

What they found in places like Springerville, Clovis, Hereford, and Podunk Corner make up the stories of discovery in *Asphalt Jesus*. The walkers discovered a more unified American community than they anticipated—a surprisingly loving form of Christianity in the churches and people they encountered. More important, however, the walkers discovered more love within themselves, more openness, and more of Jesus. In this pilgrimage tale, the outer journey of the walk across America merges with an inner journey of the walking pilgrim, pointing toward the hopeful possibility that we can escape our prejudices and find grace in every cranny of our nation and our own souls.

Eric invites you to join him and his friends on Crosswalk America's journey, to meet the quirky, down-to-earth, good folks they met, and learn the lessons they learned. As you mark their steps, both your heart and mind will be challenged, opened, and enlarged. Ultimately, *Asphalt Jesus* is a journey to the unexpected, an experience of finding God on American back roads and country churches, and of taking risks to walk with Jesus wherever he leads. If you are a liberal Christian, you will be surprised by the sincerity and honesty of the conservative Christians who befriended the walkers. If you are a conservative Christian, you may well be amazed at the spiritual insight and biblical depth of the progressive Christians in this book. With each step, stereotypes of the "other" recede to be replaced by a compassionate conversation about what matters to people of faith.

So, strap on your pedometer and start walking. Welcome to the journey. You will not return home the same.

Diana Butler Bass
Author, *Christianity for the Rest of Us: How the Neighborhood Church Is Transforming the Faith*

PREFACE

THIS BOOK OFFERS a glimpse of Christianity at the grass roots in America that is quite different from what is portrayed in the media or by popular religious leaders. Indeed, it reveals a view that neither I nor my companions quite expected to find as we walked across America in the spring and summer of 2006. The picture is both surprising and encouraging for those of us who have been critical of the excesses of Christian fundamentalism and the sterility of liberalism.

The picture you will find in these pages is of nothing less than the emergence of a new form of Christian faith at the grass roots that transcends traditional labels and stereotypes. This faith is more concerned with honesty than morality, more with embracing difference than with judging others, and more with pushing boundaries than with creating them. The story of this emerging faith is not always pretty. It is frequently funny. It is sometimes irreverent, occasionally devastating, and often astonishing. Hints of Easter abound.

This glimpse of Christianity, so overlooked by the media and national leaders, would not have been revealed were it not for nearly two and a half years of hard work on the part of ordinary people who volunteered their time, talent, and much of their treasure to becoming the dynamo known as CrossWalk America. Through their efforts, a six-member core walk team, a guest "houseless, not homeless" walker, an RV support driver, and a two-member film crew traveled 2,500 miles, staying in homes, church basements, seminaries, and campgrounds along the way and meeting face to face with over eleven thousand people.

To all these hardworking CrossWalk America volunteers, financial supporters, and the individuals, churches, seminaries, and organizations who sponsored us, I offer my most sincere thanks. I also wish to thank those who contributed directly to the quality of this book, most especially the walkers themselves who contributed numerous comments and corrections; Sheryl Fullerton, Joanne Clapp Fullagar, and Bruce Emmer, my editor, production editor, and copyeditor respectively, who saved me from much rambling and embarrassment; and Scott Griessel, who very generously made his amazing photos available to giveyou a direct glimpse at the world as we saw it in the spring and summer of 2006. Finally, I wish to thank the patient families of the volunteers, most especially my own— Melanie, Arianna, and Maren. My hope is that this book, which reveals a vital, emerging Christian faith, will serve in part as a gift of gratitude I offer back to you.

Three practical notes about this book are in order. First, in addition to stories from the road, you will find reflections in each chapter keyed to the Phoenix Affirmations. The Phoenix Affirmations were created in 2005 by pastors, laypeople, biblical scholars, and theologians from around the country representing all of the major mainline Christian denominations (Presbyterian, Methodist, Lutheran, Episcopal, United Church of Christ, and Disciples of Christ) and a number outside these fellowships. The Affirmations seek to articulate what the path of Jesus looks like in the modern world, following the principles Jesus himself identifies as central: love of God, love of neighbor, and love of self. The Phoenix Affirmations have rapidly gained popularity in and outside the United States largely because they articulate what a great many Christians in and outside churches believe about the true nature of Christian faith yet either had no words to express or were afraid to express. Each chapter highlights one of the Affirmations for special reflection. If you are reading this book as part of a group or would like to form a study group, a discussion guide is provided at the end of this book to facilitate conversation. Also helpful in this regard is my previous book, *The Phoenix Affirmations: A New Vision for the Future of Christianity* (San Francisco: Jossey-Bass, 2006). A number of resources may also be found on the CrossWalk America Web site at http://www.CrossWalkAmerica.org.

Second, you will find that this book contains quite a number of interesting conversations with people we met on our journey. You may wonder how I was able to reproduce all these conversations in such detail. My ability to reproduce conversations was greatly assisted not only by a pocket digital recorder I started carrying with me but also by the film crew from Creatista Productions that accompanied us each and every day of the walk. While many of these conversations are in fact reproduced word for word, there have also been instances where I have reproduced the essence of conversations for clarity's sake. In these cases, I have sent advance copies of the manuscript to my conversation partners seeking their feedback to ensure accuracy.

Finally, in a couple of instances—notably conversations with "Debbie" and "Don" at Cross Creek United Church of Christ in Chapter Twelve and with "Sue" and "Nathan" in Chapter Thirteen—these individuals actually represent a composite of a number of people and many discussions boiled down into representative conversations. They are in no way fictional, as they accurately represent the statements and attitudes of a great number of people we met at a specific location (Debbie and Don) or along the whole CrossWalk route (Sue and Nathan).

I now invite you to come along with us on our walk across America and into the fascinating world of twenty-first-century Christianity.

*This book is dedicated to
You, the reader;*

*The spiritually homeless, spiritually
uncomfortable, and spiritually exuberant
who appear in these pages;*

*And God, toward whom these pages
endeavor to point*

THE PHOENIX AFFIRMATIONS

VERSION 3.8

The public face of Christianity in America today bears little connection to the historic faith of our ancestors. It represents even less our own faith as Christians who continue to celebrate the gifts of our Creator, revealed and embodied in the life, death, and resurrection of Jesus Christ. Heartened by our experience of the transforming presence of Christ's Holy Spirit in our world, we find ourselves in a time and place where we will be no longer silent. We hereby mark an end to our silence by making the following affirmations:

As people who are joyfully and unapologetically Christian, we pledge ourselves completely to the way of Love. We work to express our love, as Jesus teaches us, in three ways: by loving God, neighbor, and self.

(Matthew 22:34-40 // Mark 12:28-31 //Luke 10:25-28; cf. Deuteronomy 6:5; Leviticus 19:18)

CHRISTIAN LOVE OF GOD INCLUDES:

1 Walking fully in the Path of Jesus without denying the legitimacy of other paths that God may provide humanity.

2 Listening for God's Word, which comes through daily prayer and meditation, studying the ancient testimonies which we call Scripture, and attending to God's present activity in the world.

3 Celebrating the God whose Spirit pervades and whose glory is reflected in all of God's Creation, including the earth and its ecosystems, the sacred and secular, the Christian and non-Christian, the human and non-human.

4 Expressing our love in worship that is as sincere, vibrant, and artful as it is scriptural.

CHRISTIAN LOVE OF NEIGHBOR INCLUDES:

5 Engaging people authentically, as Jesus did, treating all as creations made in God's very image, regardless of race, gender, sexual orientation, age, physical or mental ability, nationality, or economic class.

6 Standing, as Jesus does, with the outcast and oppressed, the denigrated and afflicted, seeking peace and justice with or without the support of others.

7 Preserving religious freedom and the church's ability to speak prophetically to government by resisting the commingling of church and state.

8 Walking humbly with God, acknowledging our own shortcomings while honestly seeking to understand and call forth the best in others, including those who consider us their enemies.

CHRISTIAN LOVE OF SELF INCLUDES:

9 Basing our lives on the faith that in Christ all things are made new and that we, and all people, are loved beyond our wildest imagination—for eternity.

10 Claiming the sacredness of both our minds and our hearts and recognizing that faith and science, doubt and belief serve the purpose of truth.

11 Caring for our bodies and insisting on taking time to enjoy the benefits of prayer, reflection, worship, and recreation in addition to work.

12 Acting on the faith that we are born with a meaning and purpose, a vocation and ministry that serve to strengthen and extend God's realm of love.

ASPHALT
JESUS

Eric Elnes walking in Phoenix.

1

THE IDEA THAT
WOULDN'T GO AWAY

LISTENING TO GOD

IT STARTED WITH A THOUGHT—an image, really, that flashed through my mind's eye for just a moment and was gone. I laughed out loud, finished dressing, and left to meet with colleagues who were on retreat with me. I'd like to say the whole thing started more dramatically, that the rain-soaked clouds parted over the Oregon retreat center, a shaft of sunlight shined brightly on my face, and a booming voice revealed how my life would very shortly be turned upside down. But all I had was a simple mental picture that made me laugh.

The picture was of a group of people sitting around a table drafting a set of basic principles of Christian faith—a more inclusive, joyful, compassionate Christian faith than had been proclaimed in the media by certain Christian leaders. I saw the group take these principles in hand and walk them across the country, nailing them to a church doorway in Washington, D.C., much as Martin Luther had done with his Ninety-Five Theses five hundred years earlier in Germany.

That image made me laugh for several reasons. First of all, I'm not a walker. As a Boy Scout I once hiked eighty miles across Washington State's Olympic Mountains, but since high school days I've done little more than walk to my car and back.

Second, I walk funny. People are always telling me I look like I'm walking on my tiptoes. I don't know exactly what it means, but someone once said that my stride looks like a combination of Big Bird and the Baltimore Orioles mascot.

Finally, I had only recently returned from a three-month sabbatical in northern Ethiopia and southern India to my Scottsdale, Arizona, congregation. I could just see my congregation saying to me as their senior pastor, "What? You've just come back and you're already looking for an excuse to leave again?" They might tell me to leave and not come back. Even if by some small stretch of the imagination they actually granted the time off, my leave would certainly be without pay, and I had no financial resources to fall back on.

For the rest of the morning and throughout the day I joked with my retreat colleagues about my funny mental image. A week later I was no longer laughing. In fact I was pretty grumpy. The idea had not left me. It returned morning after morning during my prayers and meditations like a new friend anxious to get to know me better. During the day it stayed close by my side like a hungry child pulling my pant leg asking for food. At night the idea would cuddle up like lover prodding me awake.

That's when I got scared. "Am I going crazy?" I wondered. "Please, God," I said one morning in prayer, "don't let this become a serious idea. Take it out of my life and give me some peace. Even if I could physically handle the journey, which is doubtful, there's no way I can ask the congregation for more time off." Day after day this was the essence of my prayers.

Yet day after day, while my mind was spinning with apprehension and denial, somewhere in a remote corner of my anxious inner landscape a quiet, peaceful voice was whispering. My gut intuition remained calm, even a bit gleeful, as though saying, "Relax. Although this project is way too big for you to handle on your own and your parishioners will be shocked when they first hear of it, neither you nor they will be alone. You have powerful help, and the members of your congregation have been praying for a way to change the face of Christianity."

I already knew about that last part. In a sense my congregation was entirely ready for something crazy like this. When I returned from sabbatical in the fall of 2004, the parishioners were in turmoil. Their turmoil wasn't caused by my absence. In fact they had excellent pastoral and lay leadership while I was away. The cause of the upheaval was one too many straws breaking one too many backs with respect to the way Christian fundamentalism was influencing American culture, politics, and religion.

As I related in *The Phoenix Affirmations: A New Vision for the Future of Christianity*, a congregation member encapsulated the feeling best when she said, "I'm tired of being a Christian, but . . ." and I thought she said "Christian butt."

She clarified: "I'm tired of the fact that when I meet new people and it comes out that I'm a Christian, I might as well have told them I'm radioactive. I'm sick of always feeling like I've got to qualify who I am saying, "I'm a Christian, *but* I don't think homosexuals are evil. . . . I'm Christian, *but* I believe women are equal to men . . . *but* I'm concerned about poverty . . . *but* I care about the earth . . . *but* I don't think people who believe differently from me will fry in hell for eternity. . . ."

People from a wide variety of perspectives politically and theologically were wondering, "Are we destined to live as embarrassed Christians for the rest of our lives?" Emotionally, they were on the same page as Howard Beale in the film *Network* when he screams, "I'm mad as hell, and I'm not going to take it anymore!"

Eventually, I realized that my congregation might resonate with the *idea* of walking across the country to change the face of Christianity, but I remained certain that people would become as grumpy as I was if the vision turned to action. So I prayed, "God, I am going to actively resist this idea. From here on out, I'm going do everything in my power to get rid of it and move on. If you really want this vision to become a reality, then you'll have to either tap someone else on the shoulder or hit me hard over the head with a spiritual sledgehammer to make me believe it."

One morning I spontaneously walked twenty miles, figuring the physicality of walking would shake something loose and return me to my senses. Instead, by the time I finished walking, I was so pumped up about the idea I could have kept going another ten! I thought to myself, "This wasn't supposed to happen this way!"

Finally, in an act of utter desperation to be rid of the idea and move on, I pulled my "A-bomb" approach to killing ideas. I selected a handful of friends and swore them to secrecy. Then I talked about the idea with them incessantly—night and day, as much as humanly possible. I know from experience that if an idea has no real substance, I and the people around me will soon get bored and move on to other things.

Instead, what happened was that I suddenly found myself with a handful of people who couldn't get the idea out of their heads either!

One of those people was Tom Glenn. Years earlier Tom had helped me with a large, complicated project at my church that called for someone with a particularly good ability to sort through myriad details without losing sight of the forest for the trees. Professionally, Tom once helped craft the merger between Honeywell and Allied Signal. In other words, Tom has both a keen mind and an excellent eye for spotting potential design flaws. I sat him down over lunch one day, secretly hoping he'd shoot holes in the walk idea. Instead, Tom exclaimed, "This idea sounds crazy, but it just might work. Even if Christianity budged just a little bit in a more progressive direction, that would be huge." Tom grew pensive for a moment and then added, "Given the fact that what happens in America ends up affecting the world—for better or worse—this walk could actually change the world!"

"Great," I thought. "How is this going to help me get rid of the idea?"

The next morning came a call on my cell phone from Tom's wife that sent me into a panic.

"Eric? This is Rebecca." Thick tension filled her voice. "I need to speak with you *in private,* preferably today or tomorrow."

"Oh, no," I thought. "Tom's told Rebecca, and now she's on the warpath! This is going to leak out to the congregation, and I'm going to be crucified for an idea I never even wanted to have in the first place!"

I scheduled an afternoon appointment with her, figuring I'd better run "damage control" right way.

We met at a coffeehouse a couple of miles from church. As Rebecca approached the table, my stomach was in knots. Her brief smile when she first saw me did little to put me at ease. Neither did her first comment: "Eric, I have to admit, last night Tom spilled the beans about this walk idea of yours."

Trying to remain as casual-sounding as possible while dreading what she'd say, I replied, "Yes, I figured."

What came next hit me out of the blue. It falls squarely into the "truth is stranger than fiction" category.

"You know my work history," she started. I did. She had spent many years as a high-level information technology officer at Motorola and was currently working as the IT VP for an insurance company.

She continued, "I guess you could say that these jobs have always been meaningful to me on an intellectual level. I've found them challenging and rewarding on a whole lot of levels. But what's been troubling me for some time is that my vocational path isn't really mattering to me in here," pointing to her heart. "Ever since I attended that prayer retreat a few years ago and began praying regularly, I've grown increasingly discontent with working so hard at something that doesn't matter on a soul level.

"I've been thinking of quitting my job for some time, but I haven't found anything that really moves me. I'd like to hear more about your idea about the walk because, frankly, when Tom told me about it last night, it hit me like a ton of bricks. I thought, 'This could be what I've been looking for.'"

After discussing the idea with Rebecca for the next hour or so, she said, "Don't hold me to this, but if this walk idea pans out, what would you think if I were to quit my job and work full time on it as a volunteer?"

My jaw nearly hit the table. "Holy cow! Let me ponder this for a nano-second and get back to you," I thought to myself. Instead I responded,

"That would certainly be something we could both pray about. Remember, though, even if you become convinced that this walk is a good and right thing, I'm still wrestling personally with it. And even if I become convinced, it's not clear how this would fly with the congregation. So pray not only for yourself but for me and for everyone. I'll pray for all of us, too. If we both end up agreeing that this is a true calling, then we're going to have one heck of a lot of work to do and one heck of a process to go through with the congregation."

Not even a week had passed when Rebecca told me, "I'm convinced that this needs to be done and that I need to be a part of it. I'm in if you are." The very next day, one of the handful of friends from my "A-bomb" group, Scott Logan, pulled me aside at our church's Thursday evening jazz coffeehouse, saying, "Eric, I wanted you to know that I just sold my company. I'll have to work again eventually, but I figure I've got about a year I could devote to working as a full-time volunteer on the walk if you'd be interested."

It wasn't long afterward that I finally hoisted the white flag of surrender in my morning prayers. "OK, God, I give up! You win. From this point on, I'm going to assume that this crazy walk thing is your will. I'm hugely scared about losing my job over this, but I'm going to take some little steps in faith to pursue the idea. All I ask is that if I'm on the wrong path, you push me off of it, and if I'm on the right path, keep giving me assurance and I'll keep going."

An enormous feeling of relief suddenly fell over me, like I'd just thrown an eight hundred pound gorilla off my back. After that, not once did I ever sense that I was on the wrong path. Yes, I cursed the path more than once. I cried a number of times, when the pressure became too great to handle. And I panicked fairly regularly, wondering how we would ever pull the walk off on schedule or raise the funds to finance it. But from the moment I let go of my fear of the idea and surrendered to its draw, the deepest waters of my soul were at peace. I knew that I would one day be standing with a group of friends in Washington, D.C., posting a yet-to-be-written document that might change the future of Christianity in the United States and possibly beyond.

Listening to God

When people pray, does God answer? The second Phoenix Affirmation emphasizes the importance of daily prayer and meditation, and the story I've just told indicates my own personal experience. But to me, the critical question is not "Does God answer prayer?" but "If and when God does answer, will I be listening in such a way to hear and respond?" Spiritual discernment has been an important piece of the Christian path since the beginning. Indeed, it is a key component of the faith and practice of each of the major world religions, including Buddhism, which does not formally acknowledge a God. Yet the practice of spiritual discernment, which varies widely the world over, is surprisingly foreign to most American Christians.

AFFIRMATION 2

[Christian love of God includes]
Listening for God's Word, which comes through daily prayer
and meditation, studying the ancient testimonies which we call
Scripture, and attending to God's present activity in the world.

If you do not believe that God answers prayer to begin with, you may find the practice of spiritual discernment a bit naive or quaint. But permit me to make one observation that you may not expect from a Christian minister who spends thirty to sixty minutes in contemplative prayer and meditation every day: it really doesn't matter to me whether you believe that God answers prayer or not, and I don't think it matters much to God either.

Why? Back in the fourth century, Saint Augustine said it well when he observed that the path to knowing God and the path to knowing oneself are one and the same path. If you follow some basic principles to knowing God better, you will come to know yourself better in the process. If you have no belief in God or believe that God is silent and yet follow some basic principles for getting to know your deepest self better, you will come to know God better in the process.

In classic Christian and Jewish theology, human beings are believed to be created in the image and likeness of God. If this is true, then God and self are connected at the very deepest levels. The deeper we plunge into our inmost being—our intuitions and gut feelings, our very soul—the closer we move into sacred space. For the rest of this chapter I'm going to trace the outlines of a path that may lead believers, agnostics, and atheists alike to "hearing" their true self better. If you believe, as I do, that God does answer prayer, then you may not only come to understand yourself better but may very well hear God's voice more clearly than you have before and respond to it with greater confidence. Before getting to some practical listening principles, though, it's helpful to bear in mind something Jesus observed about etiquette around a dinner table.

A Place at the Table

Jesus once advised his followers to sit at the lowest place at the table when invited to someone's house to eat. In his day, his advice would have struck people as odd. In the ancient world of Jesus, the pecking order around the table (actually often a carpet on the floor) was established by a common code of honor. Those with the highest honor in the community sat closest to the head of the table. Those held in lowest esteem sat farthest away.

Jesus advises his followers to take the place of lowest honor when invited as a guest "in case someone more distinguished than you has been invited by your host and the host who invited both of you may come and say to you, 'Give this person your place,' and then in disgrace you would start to take the lowest place" (Luke 14:8–9).

To avoid this embarrassment, Jesus advises, "go and sit down at the lowest place, so that when your host comes, he may say to you, 'Friend, move up higher'; then you will be honored in the presence of all who sit at the table with you." Jesus adds, "For all who exalt themselves will be humbled, and those who humble themselves will be exalted" (Luke 14:10–11).

Given Jesus' feelings on the subject, where do you suppose he chose to sit when invited to dinner? Unless Jesus was a hypocrite, chances are he sought the lowest place at the table, moving higher only if the host insisted. I get the feeling that Jesus wasn't giving this advice or acting this way because of some early "Miss Manners" impulse. Jesus both spoke and lived in parables. His external behavior pointed to inward realities.

Each day, whether aware of it or not, you and I set a table inside ourselves. Around this table sit a number of people, or at least their voices. Some are voices we have invited, and some are uninvited but are there nonetheless. All of these are the voices that help us make the decisions that guide our lives.

If I am trying to discern whether or not to accept a particular job offer, for instance, a number of voices will weigh in with their opinion. There's the voice of the *conscience* (which sounds suspiciously like my parents), advising me on whether or not this job is appropriate or respectable enough. There's the voice of the *pragmatist* asking about the financial package and benefits and whether or not the job will help me climb the vocational ladder. The voice of the *pessimist* also weighs in, offering a dismal evaluation of how long I'll be happy in this job and how long my employer will be happy with me. The *free child* voice gives his take on whether or not the job will be any fun. The *hero* voice asserts an opinion on how much good my service will do for the community. The voice of the *adversary* may tell me I'm an arrogant jerk for even entertaining the thought that I'm good enough to fill the position in question. Or it may tell me the employer is a jerk for not offering me a high enough position.

Where is the voice of Jesus at my internal table? Exactly where he says he'll be: at the lowest end, farthest away from where I can see his face or hear what he has to say. He's willing to move higher, naturally, but not until I invite him to, and then only if I'm pretty insistent.

Much of the time, the other voices are trying so hard to get my attention, assuming that *they* should hold the highest honor, that I forget that Jesus is down there to begin with. And Jesus rarely if ever protests. I don't hear him shouting above the din, "Hey, fellah, what about me? I'm not getting any respect down here!" Instead, he seems content to be left to himself, quietly eating while the other voices talk my ear off. He's not uninterested. He just wants to protect my free will. He doesn't want to influence me unless I really want him to.

If you're nervous about my referring to Jesus speaking at my inner table, feel free to call this voice something else. Parker Palmer does an excellent job at describing this voice in secular yet spiritual terms in his book *A Hidden Wholeness*. In it, he describes the voice by referring to the soul, or our deepest voice:

> The soul is like a wild animal.
>
> Like a wild animal, the soul is tough, resilient, resourceful, savvy, and self-sufficient: it knows how to survive in hard places. . . . Yet despite its toughness, the soul is also shy. Just like a wild animal, it seeks safety in the dense underbrush, especially when other people are around. If we want to see a wild animal, we know that the last thing we should do is go crashing through the woods yelling for it to come out. But if we will walk quietly into the woods, sit patiently at the base of a tree, breathe with the earth, and fade into our surroundings, the wild creature we seek might put in an appearance. We may see it only briefly and only out of the corner of an eye—but the sight is a gift we will always treasure as an end in itself.[1]

The half hour or so I spend in prayer every morning is my time to get quiet, listen to the voices around my internal table, and then silence all of them enough to allow the possibility that Jesus—this wild animal of a soul—will come into the clearing. If he does, I make some room next to me, hoping he may step close enough to let me hear him breathe. At the end of my formal prayer time, I ask that voice to remain near me throughout the day. I promise to try as hard as my imperfect self will allow to keep listening to what it might whisper.

How do I know this is the voice of Jesus and not the pessimist, the pragmatist, the free child, or even the adversary whispering to me? It's not a perfect science, which is why I pray each day and continue to ask for confirmation every time I put a foot forward to follow where I believe I'm being led. One of the basic checks-and-balances mechanisms I use to gauge whether or not I'm on track is to ask if whatever I'm feeling led to conclude or do "looks like Jesus." This is not quite the same as asking, "What would Jesus do?" (often abbreviated WWJD). After all, Jesus might do a lot of things I'm not specifically called to do. I ask, instead, "Does the action I'm feeling called to take look like something that Jesus, as revealed in Scripture and in my experience of his ongoing presence (the risen Christ) would do?" If not, the red flags start waving mightily.

I also recognize that sometimes the voice of Jesus has been whispering to the other voices, influencing what they have to say. Jesus may even take the form of one of these voices, but again, only to advocate something that "looks like Jesus."

My good friend and mentor, Bruce Van Blair, describes what it sounds like to hear the wild animal/soul/Jesus voice when he notes, "This voice thinks differently from the others—and concludes from beyond your capacity to understand. It is quiet-like—peace with power—and it says very beautiful and sometimes very strange things. And sometimes it asks hard, almost impossible favors without any apology or embarrassment. 'Of course I know it is hard—but it needs doing.'"[2]

Over the years, I have found some basic principles to help sift through the voices to arrive at something of substance. Based on my reading of Christian mystics and my experiences, I distilled them into ten principles for discerning the voice of God at my internal table. Perhaps they will help you in your journey:

1. Be willing to hear God and willing to move in whatever direction God leads. (This is the hardest part!)

2. Avoid, as much as humanly possible, being in a rush to decide whether some thought is from God or not. Also avoid like the plague any notion that one must be in a hurry to make a decision based on what one has heard in prayer. This is one of the easiest ways to get tripped up ("You must decide right this moment or all

is lost . . ."). Remember: very small errors can have very large consequences when we are in a rush. God rarely desires or needs us to rush.

3. When God is trying to move us in a particular direction, that direction is *always* marked by a sense joy or profound peace, even if the direction involves extreme difficulty, pain, or even death.

4. God never asks us to do anything that is against our true self-interest and never asks us to do anything that runs counter to our benefit, even if we are asked to do what the world calls a "selfless act."[3]

5. God normally asks us to move in small steps that may cumulatively be quite large but may seem so small individually as to be insignificant. God rarely asks us to take a giant leap of faith without moving us to the edge of the precipice in very small steps. (The only exception I can think of is when we stumble into a situation that endangers us and God works to "get us out quick.")[4]

6. Our intuition is generally sharper than we give it credit for. Provided we're staying open to God's voice (rather than fixating on our fears and prejudices), if we consistently have a "bad feeling" about something, generally it's accurate. Similarly, if our gut consistently fills with peace and joy—a deep sense of contentedness or of being freed from excessive burden—we are often on the right track.

7. Once you've taken a step forward believing it's where God is calling you, don't keep second-guessing yourself. Tell God, "I'm going to move with confidence in this direction until or unless you start sending me signals to change course." Then stay open to those signals in case they come. God normally starts throwing us confirming signals when we've made a good decision and warning signals when we've misjudged, though they may not come in the forms we expect.

8. God does not use "strange coincidences" as signs nearly as often as God uses gut hunches, "aha!" moments, deep intuitions, mental images, and plain old logic. (Be careful with this one, though; God's bidding often defies logic, at least until one has the benefit of hindsight.)

9. Asking "What would Jesus do?" doesn't get us very far. God is concerned about what *you* should be doing. Although God will not call you into un-Christ-like action, the mere fact that Christ did something long ago does not mean that God is necessarily calling you to do the same thing. Don't, for example, feed the poor just

because Christ did. Do something if you sense God calling you to do it and if it does not contradict Christ-like behavior.

10. The fact that you have accurately discerned where God is leading you does not guarantee the success of whatever it is God is calling you to achieve. Because God respects human free will, God's purposes *can* be thwarted by others, in the short-run anyway. Sometimes even God has to switch to plan B (and C and so on). Also, be aware that God may have a different end result in mind than you do.

Walking the Walk and Talking the Talk

Statistically, chances are high that you do not pray for a half hour or more per day. Since the publication of *The Phoenix Affirmations: A New Vision for the Future of Christianity,* a number of ministers have approached me confessing that not even they pray this long each day. Many have told me they used to, but over time they let the exigencies of parish life persuade them that they are "too busy." A number of them have thanked me for reminding them how powerful their prayer lives used to be and have since taken it up again in earnest. Indeed, studies of prayer disciplines shows that the threshold amount of time that leads to even moderate satisfaction in prayer is a half hour. Those who pray for twice this long report the highest degree of satisfaction with their prayer life. This makes sense, doesn't it? After all, if you are waiting in the woods for a wild animal to appear, it's not a quick thing.

Why not give it a try? If you find a daily practice that suits you well, you will not only find yourself more connected to God but also more connected to yourself. You will likely join the great cloud of witnesses throughout the centuries who have found that the busier a person is, the more helpful it is to spend time in prayer.

If you're not in the habit of praying for more than a few minutes a day, I suggest trying the following thirty-minute recipe for "basic prayer." Like the "basic bread" recipe in *The Joy of Cooking,* you can use this template to create seemingly infinite variations to suit your particular taste and style. Just try this approach until you get the hang of it, and gradually branch out if you feel the need. If it is helpful, play some soothing instrumental music during this time.

A RECIPE FOR BASIC PRAYER

1. *Clearing (5 minutes).* Use this time to relax and let your soul catch up with your body. Take a series of deep breaths, letting them out slowly. As you do, try to clear away any obstacles you may have

brought with you to experiencing God's presence. Some people like to ring a bell at the beginning, letting go of thoughts as the bell's reverberations fade away.

2. *Focusing (5 minutes).* You may wish to read a few verses from Scripture or another writing you consider sacred. Whatever it is, it should be a kind that tells your intuitive self, "I'm now actively preparing to listen to the voices around my table, especially the voice of God." You may also wish to bring a particular question to the table. If you do, be open to the possibility that this may not be the subject God wants to talk about (trusting that whatever God wants to talk about is in your best interests to hear).

3. *Listening (10 minutes).* Pay attention to thoughts and voices that enter your head. Don't decide too quickly that they're not of God. Instead, try to gently trace the origins, paying careful attention to your gut feelings about them. Do they make you scared, angry, anxious, calm, joyful? If you are exploring a particular question you've brought to the table, it is often helpful to intentionally ask, "What is my free child saying?" "What is my pessimist saying?" and so forth. There are normally a number of voices who show up regularly at your table. Who are they, and what are they saying?

4. *Asking (5 minutes).* When most people pray, asking is all they do. They offer God their laundry list and then wonder why God never seems to get around to it. The truth is that God does want you to ask for things in prayer. However, God wants you to ask from your truest self. Chances are good that whatever is in the best interest of your truest self (not your paranoid self or your scared self or your "I just want to get ahead" self) is of more interest to God than it is even to you.

5. *Thanking (5 minutes).* The mystics have always known that grati- tude is one of the most powerful spiritual forces there is. Just like a child who asks and takes without ever thanking her parents rarely benefits from what is given, so an adult who never focuses on giving rarely receives. End your prayer time with gratitude. It is the surest way to set yourself up for continuing to invite Jesus to the head of your internal table throughout the day.

Two youths celebrating Easter Sunrise walk kickoff.

2

PHOENIX RISING

HAVING LOST MY WRESTLING MATCH with God about walking across the country, one of the first tasks before me was to create a document outlining a vision of a more generous and affirmative Christian faith to share with the public—a list of essential principles. I knew that the best list would emerge in conversation with others, but I decided to take a stab at the first draft myself as a way of clarifying what I considered to be the essence of my own faith.

That first draft was nineteen pages long! When I shared it with others, they liked it but all told me it needed to be shortened—radically.

"How radically?" I asked.

Nearly everyone said the same thing: "To a single page."

"Yikes," I thought to myself. "How on earth can you get the whole Christian faith onto a page without dumbing it down beyond recognition?" Yet I realized that what was needed was not a theological textbook. Sometimes less is more. Jesus' Sermon on the Mount can fit on a single page, after all.

As a way of weighing the relative importance of each principle I'd listed, I tried an exercise that led to unexpected results. I asked myself, "What sacrifices would I be willing to make to protect or preserve this principle if I felt it was threatened?"

I started by considering what principles I would be willing to give a sizable portion of my income to preserve or protect. There were many.

Then I asked, "What principles would I be willing to do something amazingly challenging for—like walk across the country?" The list shortened.

"Which principles would I sacrifice my job or vocation over?" The list condensed further.

I kept ratcheting up the sacrifices and narrowing down the list until I hit this question: "Which principles would you be willing to die for?"

I wasn't sure about asking that question—was it too "over the top"? But then I realized that if I and others were going to walk across the country, there was a chance that we could actually die in the process. A car might hit us by accident, or some lunatics could decide we were Satan's spawn (as it turns out they did) and take us out (thankfully, they didn't). This question was therefore no parlor game. I had to think hard. Are there principles that are so essential to life's happiness and freedom that I would be willing to die on their behalf?

Several months earlier in worship I had interviewed a couple soldiers from the National Guard who were also members of my church. They were being sent to Kuwait, so we wanted to wish them a proper farewell. In the process, I asked them essentially the same question I was now asking myself: "What principles are so important that you would give your life for them on the battlefield? Freedom? Justice? Democracy?" They shook their heads at each one. To my surprise, they insisted that there are absolutely *no* principles worth dying for!

"But you're in the military, and you're being shipped into a war zone," I responded. "What are you fighting for, then?"

"We fight to protect *each other*. We die for our comrades, not our principles."

Their words reminded me of Jesus' own statement about what's worth dying for. He said, "No greater love does a person have than to . . ." Do you remember the rest of the line? He doesn't say "to lay down one's life for the principle of love" or "to protect democracy." He says there is no greater love than "to lay one's life down for one's friends" (John 15:13). Jesus doesn't ask us to sacrifice for principles or ideas but for *people*. That's what the soldiers were saying, too.

Seen from this perspective, I realized that I would gladly die for my two daughters or my wife. I would also give my life to protect members of my congregation or my friends. I would probably even give my life to save a perfect stranger from being hit by an automobile. "This is getting a bit 'over the top' again," I thought to myself. "My friends and family aren't in mortal danger, and I'm not going to walk across the country in order to find people to save from moving vehicles! Is there nothing worth walking for if it means I might die in the process?"

Yes, there was.

I'm going to tell you what I'd give my life for, but first I have to confess that I feel rather uncomfortable doing it. For to do so, I have to tell you a story that I almost never tell others, and certainly not before getting to know them quite well. While I am hesitant, I am doing so because it not only clarified why I would walk but also pointed me to certain critical understandings of Christian faith. To avoid telling this story would thus be disingenuous. I'd have to pretend that there were other more important reasons for walking, but there weren't, at least not for me. So here goes.

My Unforgettable Encounter

It happened in late May 1981. I was a junior in high school. I had a friend named Becky (not her real name) who was going through a very difficult situation. Recently, as she was walking home along a dimly lit road at dusk, someone in a ski mask tried to rape her. Somehow she managed to struggle free and fled without being physically harmed. I say she was *physically* unharmed, but *emotionally* she struggled, especially since it happened in her neighborhood. She had no idea who the perpetrator was.

Adding to her distress, she had only two weeks earlier been visiting her grandfather in the hospital who was undergoing cancer treatment. Her grandfather's immune system had been compromised, so the hospital was allowing only close family to visit, and then only if completely healthy.

The morning after Becky visited her grandfather, she woke up with a terrible sore throat. A couple of days later, her grandfather fell ill and died. In Becky's mind, she had killed her grandfather! She was racked with guilt.

One evening we were at my home talking about all this. I told her that I had around six months earlier discovered a powerful way to deal productively with my own struggles. I told her I'd learned to pray. Specifically, I'd learned how to pray in a way that didn't simply offer a wish list to God expecting that everything would come out all right. I had learned to be silent, to simply dwell in God's presence, and let whatever happens happen.

I wasn't trying to evangelize Becky. She was already a Christian, and I wasn't into converting people anyway. I was simply baring my soul to her, telling her of something I'd found helpful in my journey that might help her, too.

That got us into a deep conversation about God that lasted well into the evening. My mother finally came into the living room and told me it was time to take Becky home. We drove to her house and parked outside still deep in conversation. At one point while Becky was speaking, a thought entered my head. It concerned her grandfather and the guilt she was feeling about him. The thought was simple: "Tell Becky, 'It's OK.'"

We weren't talking about her grandfather at the moment, so I let the thought go and continued to listen. The thought came back: "Tell Becky, 'It's OK.'" I didn't. The thought returned several more times. Each time I pushed it out of my mind and continued listening. The thought became more insistent: *"Tell Becky, 'It's OK!'"* Finally, I could hardly concentrate on anything but this thought. It had grown so strong that I was even picturing her grandfather in my mind saying this over and over. So I broke in and, feeling rather stupid, said, "Becky, I think there's something I should tell you with respect to your grandfather: *It's OK.*"

What happened next defies explanation. In fact, though I have tried at certain times in the last twenty-five years to describe it logically, metaphor is the only way that actually works. What I'm about to tell you didn't physically happen, but it gets more to the point than anything I can describe through other means.

It was like a giant explosion suddenly took place. The car filled with the light of ten thousand suns. Time utterly stopped in its tracks and we were filled with the greatest sense of God's presence and love we'd ever experienced. God was right there. In the car! Only there was no longer any "there" or "car." There wasn't really even an "us." All was simply God. And God was simply Love. Pure love. This Love was fully aware of who we were, aware of everything we'd ever done or left undone, aware of every cell and sinew in our bodies, aware of every breath. It was so intense that if we were to add up all the love we'd ever experienced in our entire lives and multiplied it hundreds of times, it still wouldn't come close to the love we felt in that moment. We felt this love for ourselves and for all people. *All* people, no matter who they are, loved beyond their wildest imagination. We wept uncontrollably at the majesty of the awareness.

How long did this experience last? I wouldn't have a clue if I had not looked at my watch after the awareness subsided. It was 11:30 P.M. The last time I'd looked at my watch, before the encounter, it was 11:00 P.M. If I hadn't been wearing a watch that evening, I wouldn't have been able to tell you even moments after the experience whether it lasted a minute or several hours.

We sat back in our seats, mostly in silence, for the better part of an hour trying to catch our breath. "What on earth just happened?" Becky asked. I had no answer. Our heads were spinning. Our hearts were pounding so fast it was as though we'd just run a marathon.

I guess I should clarify a couple of things at this point. There was no physical contact between Becky and me; we were just friends in a completely platonic relationship. Nor had we consumed any mind-altering substances or eaten or drunk anything out of the ordinary. We'd simply talked.

Eventually, Becky got out of the car and went inside, and I drove home in a daze. When I arrived, I went into my parents' bedroom to tell them I'd returned, as was the custom. They were asleep. I awakened my mother by saying, "Mom, I've just had an intense spiritual experience with Becky."

She mumbled, "That's nice," and I left the room. A few minutes later there was a knock on my bedroom door. My mother entered, asking, "What did you just say?"

For the next several weeks, Becky and I lived as if we were three feet off the ground. We were totally high on God and wanted to share our experience with the whole world. We just had to let everyone know of this amazing Presence that surrounds us at all times, that is totally aware of us and loves us beyond what we can know.

We spoke to people in our family and our churches. We shared our experience with teachers, friends—anyone who would listen. Most people reacted the way you might expect: "Huh?" Others instantly seemed to "get it." They spoke excitedly of experiences they'd had that resonated with ours on various levels. Some of them related quite dramatic, mystical experiences that they felt were from God. Others had come into an awareness of God's love more subtly and gradually.

Those who were most interested in our experience tended to be fairly conservative religiously. They even had a term for our experience: "born again." So for a brief time we both drifted away from our mainline churches (I had attended a United Church of Christ, and Becky was Lutheran). We started hanging out with fundamentalists. This didn't last long, however. Even though many spoke of knowing the kind of love we'd experienced, few acted like it. We were especially dismayed that there wasn't much of a sense that God loves *everyone* this way. Many people claimed that God's love is reserved only for those who affirm that Christ is Lord and Savior. Further, they claimed that people who didn't have a "born again" experience would burn in hell for eternity.

"*You* are saved because you've been born again," they assured us, inferring that we had special status. Yet in no way did our experience even remotely suggest that some people are saved and others are not. It was absolutely clear to us that God's love is for all people, regardless of whether they know of God or Jesus.

We both returned to our mainline churches. While we were a bit frustrated that fewer people in them could relate to our experience, we were content at least to know they didn't condemn others who didn't believe the way they did. And they didn't condemn us either for having had an experience they couldn't relate to.

That's my story. Over the years, I've tried time after time to rationalize the experience. I've thought about the fact that we were young, and that we were both in an emotional state that might trigger certain unusual feelings. I've also considered that the brain is influenced by chemicals that occur naturally and that perhaps certain ways of thinking may trigger the effect. At times I have wanted with all my heart to deny what happened or explain it away or just plain forget about it. Sometimes the pain created by the chasm between the reality of this immense love and the reality of the world has seemed too great to bear. But I've never been able to explain it or wish it away. Twenty-five years later, this encounter continues to be more real to me than any other experience in my life.

This is what sent me to Princeton Theological Seminary to become a minister instead of a solar energy research scientist. This experience was responsible for my essentially devouring every book I could read while at Princeton when I discovered that Christians (and non-Christians!) for thousands of years had come into a similar awareness of God's love and were better at articulating it than I was. Some even wrote of encounters that were astonishingly like the one Becky and I had had.

My experience is also what kept me in theological education for another six years to earn a Ph.D. I just couldn't drag myself away from learning how others had dealt with their awareness of God's love and had found ways to put it into practice in their everyday lives. This awareness is what eventually led me, like so many before me throughout Christian history, to evaluating everything I'd ever learned about life, faith, the Bible, Christian tradition—everything—against the standard of God's unconditional love. It led me to affirm certain beliefs and practices in Christianity and to reject others.

Finally, my experience is also what answered the perplexing question about what I'd be willing to die for if that should happen on the walk across America. I realized that I wouldn't be willing to die for a principle or even a set of principles no matter how threatened they are, but I would indeed be willing to die for a *relationship*. As I considered all the people in our country who are being told by representatives of my own faith that they are outside the circle of God's love or being told that God will burn them in hell for all of eternity unless they act or believe in a certain way, I realized that there are many, many relationships worth dying for.

Each and every day in America, people are literally dying because of what they've been taught by their churches. Homosexual youth, for instance, commit suicide at a rate three times higher than that of their heterosexual peers. Is it any wonder when so many are told that they are possessed by the devil or that they are lost beyond hope? Straight people, too, are dying, killing themselves with alcohol or narcotics, trying to self-medicate away the "lessons" they were taught about who God loves and who God does not. (If you have any doubt, just attend an Alcoholics Anonymous meeting sometime and ask people about their experiences with Christianity.) And aside from death, millions of people—six in every ten Americans in fact—have become part of the "spiritually homeless" of our country. These are people who identify themselves as Christian but feel so alienated from the faith community that they no longer actively participate in one.

"Yes," I thought to myself, "I'd give my life if necessary to help just one or two people truly understand that they are loved, not hated, by God. It would be worth it if just one or two people came to know that they are not alone and that they are loved beyond their wildest imagination. There are millions out there. I'll walk for that and for them."

The Phoenix Affirmations

To me, the Phoenix Affirmations represent far more than a set of principles. They represent a relationship—actually, a set of relationships: our relationship with God, with each other, and with ourselves. The Affirmations are the result of pastors, laypeople, biblical scholars, and theologians from around the country and across denominational lines working together to express the essence of what it means to discover that one is loved beyond one's wildest imagination and then to order all of our relationships around this discovery.

Because the Phoenix Affirmations are meant to point beyond themselves and to a set of relationships, they keep evolving. Like any good relationship, they change over time in light of new awareness. Because the Phoenix Affirmations point to God's love for *all* people, they are *not* meant to act as a new creed by which people who agree are deemed acceptable or worthy and those who disagree are not. The Affirmations have nothing to say about who is or is not a Christian. They are simply principles by which some people have chosen to live and love in a manner that to them "looks like Jesus."

One of the truly amazing things I discovered in the two years it took to develop the Phoenix Affirmations, create CrossWalk America, and plan and carry out the walk is that when you step out in faith in the name of loving God, neighbor, and self, you do not walk alone. Opposition may—and does—arise (see Chapters Three and Five especially), but so does support. I am still dumbfounded by how many people came forward offering enormous amounts of time, talent, and treasure. Many of these people had little time or treasure to offer but did so with astonishing abandon. Most also thought they had little talent to contribute, yet they excelled in jobs they'd never had the slightest experience doing—public relations, Web site development, fundraising, walk logistics, and so forth.

Support came not only from Christian liberals and moderates but also from certain Christian conservatives. (Some did not agree with all twelve of the Phoenix Affirmations but agreed with the spirit of them.) It came from Jews, Hindus, Buddhists, and Muslims as well. It also came from agnostics and atheists. I was particularly intrigued by this last group—atheists supporting a Christian organization helping us spread the news of God's love! Who says God doesn't have a sense of humor?

Much to my relief and delight, support also came—robustly so—from my congregation. After the vision was announced from the pulpit one Sunday, my parishioners entered a forty-day period of prayer and discernment. Meet-up groups and forums were scheduled to discuss the pros and cons, both with and without me present. At the end of the forty days, in a packed congregational meeting, they voted by a landslide to grant me a five-month leave of absence (after having returned from a three-month sabbatical less than a year earlier) in order to walk across America. They also volunteered in droves to assist with the planning and implementation of the vision. One congregation member summed up the feelings of many when she observed, "This is a new Reformation. I'm glad to be a part of it. Let's do whatever it takes!"

As a result of energetic support like this, involving hundreds of people working for over a year and a half to plan and finance the walk, dream became reality. At sunrise on Easter Sunday (April 16), 2006, six "core walkers," two documentary filmmakers, and one RV support vehicle driver stood before a large crowd of worshipers and media people at a Phoenix park ready to embark on what would prove to be the adventure of a lifetime. Each person on the crew had quit a job, taken a leave of absence, or left another significant commitment to make the 2,500-mile journey to Washington, D.C. The crowd, which included a crew from Bob Abernethy's *Religion and Ethics Newsweekly* program on PBS, accompanied the walkers for the first mile of the walk at the conclusion of the service.

A surprise "guest walker" also joined us. We had heard that he might be coming, but none of us could quite believe it would happen. A "voluntarily houseless but not homeless" man, as he described himself, named Mark Creek-Water arrived, having walked nearly nine hundred miles from Oakland, California, to Phoenix, crossing the Mohave Desert in the process, in order to join us on Easter and continue for the entire journey! (Mark is the focus of Chapter Eleven.)

In my sermon that morning, I spoke of empty tombs, empty churches, and an ocotillo bush. The ocotillo (pronounced "oh-cuh-TEE-oh") is a tall shrub in the Southwest desert with clumps of straight, thorny, whip-like stalks covered with little green leaves and no branches. Much of the year, the ocotillo's leaves are absent and its thorny stalks are ash gray. It looks utterly dead. In other words, the ocotillo appears a lot like many churches you may know: dry, lifeless, and liable to stick you if you're not careful. However, the ocotillo is not dead. It's just waiting for God to "water the weary land." After even a modest amount of rain, the ocotillo's tiny green leaves suddenly pop out, covering the stalks from top to bottom. Brilliant clusters of red flowers shoot straight out of the tip of each stalk like fireworks. The ocotillo is vibrantly alive!

So it is with many of God's churches across the nation. They may appear dead, but they're not. Rather, they are filled with people waiting to be called into action by a bold vision of God's radical, inclusive love. Throughout that spring and summer, the walk provided such a call, both to churches and to the "spiritually homeless" of America. Leaving Phoenix, we had no idea what we were getting into—neither the level to which this vision would excite people and churches across the country nor the level to which it would incite certain others.

The Way of Love

Two thousand years ago, Jesus was asked what he felt was the single most important principle of his faith. Jesus did not hesitate: "'You shall love the Lord your God with all your heart, and with all your soul, and with all your mind.' This is the greatest and first commandment."[1] Then Jesus added, "And a second is like it: 'You shall love your neighbor as yourself.' On these two commandments hang all the law and the prophets."

Throughout all the years I've heard people refer to Jesus' concise summary of what's most important, I've been surprised by how many miss a full third of it. They say, "Jesus felt that the most important thing to do is love God and love your neighbor."

Is this what Jesus says? In addition to loving God, does not Jesus say to love your neighbor *as yourself*? If my arithmetic is correct, Jesus identifies not two but three Great Loves: God, neighbor, and self.

PREAMBLE TO THE
PHOENIX AFFIRMATIONS

The public face of Christianity in America today bears little

connection to the historic faith of our ancestors. It represents

even less our own faith as Christians who continue to celebrate

the gifts of our Creator, revealed and embodied in the life, death,

and resurrection of Jesus Christ. Heartened by our experience of

the transforming presence of Christ's Holy Spirit in our world,

we find ourselves in a time and place where we will be

no longer silent. We hereby mark an end to our silence

by making the following affirmations:

As people who are joyfully and unapologetically Christian,

we pledge ourselves completely to the way of Love.

We work to express our love, as Jesus teaches us,

in three ways: by loving God, neighbor, and self.

(Matthew 22:34–40, Mark 12:28–31, Luke 10:25–28;

cf. Deuteronomy 6:5, Leviticus 19:18)

Some people believe that loving themselves is narcissistic or egotistical. Of course, it can be. Yet according to Jesus' own words, one cannot properly love one's neighbor if one has no love for oneself. In fact, if one has no love for oneself, then according to Jesus one cannot adequately love one's neighbor.

Love of self is egotistical or narcissistic only if it is abstracted from simultaneously loving God and neighbor. Jesus did not refer to these three Great Loves only to conclude that following "two outta three ain't bad." They must function together in order to function at all.

Loving God and neighbor without also remembering to love oneself may seem like a minor oversight, but it actually amounts to the difference between being truly loving of others and just going through the motions. If a boyfriend of one of my two daughters, for instance, were ever to claim, "I do it all for you, baby," I'd advise her to slap him upside the head and, if he doesn't come to his senses, to break off the relationship as quickly as possible. Why? Because either the guy is a liar and a manipulator, which is likely, or he has no clue about how to sustain a meaningful relationship. If the guy isn't in the relationship as much for himself and his own benefit as he is for that of my daughter, why is he in it at all? Out of pity?

I find the same dynamic at work in faith communities. My church regularly receives refugees from other churches who tell the same basic story: "I came to church seeking a relationship with Jesus, and all anyone did was put me to work on a committee." Such churches tend to see themselves as bright, shining beacons of light in their communities. They claim they exist solely *for others*. They understand the work they do, and the time, talent, and treasure they invest as being "for those who cannot help themselves." In reality, a church that only ever exists *for others* soon becomes no good to anyone. The churches become patronizing, as the phrase "those who cannot help themselves" suggests.

In fact, I'd gladly swap ten parishioners who see themselves as only ever "helping others" for a single one who seeks primarily to meet her own needs through helping others. Why? Because this person will work ten times harder than one who does not consider her needs in service to the community. Further, she will complain about her work a lot less, be far less self-righteous about it, and be markedly happier in the process.

When my parishioners geared up to support CrossWalk America, many surprised even themselves by how much time, talent, and treasure they so willingly devoted. Though the work could be excruciatingly difficult and time-consuming, we hardly ever heard a complaint. Even during the toughest periods, there was plenty of laughter and good feeling to go around. People quietly marveled at what a privilege it was to increase their discipleship. Even though the walk was about spreading word of God's compassionate, inclusive love to the nation—to people they'd never met, living even thousands of miles away—those behind the project clearly saw how the message benefited them personally. It helped them integrate the message more deeply into their everyday faith and practice, and they all longed for a day when being known as "Christian" in society would stand for something positive and gracious, not negative and judgmental. They threw themselves into their tasks with abandon because it was focused on loving God, neighbor, and self *together*.

I've also seen plenty of refugees from churches whose focus is only on loving God and self to the exclusion of their neighbor. These people share horror stories of how "Jesus and me" turns out to be about just this— Jesus and *me*, never Jesus and *us*. Everything is reduced to one's personal walk with Jesus, never the corporate walk. These churches tend to be the ones who do not bat an eye when they proclaim that Jesus loves them and in the same breath claim that the four-fifths of the world who aren't Christian will burn in hell for all of eternity. During the walk, a protester showed up in Saint Louis bearing an antigay placard; he claimed to agree with our assertion that God loves all people beyond their wildest imagination *for eternity* (Affirmation 9), even though he believed that homosexuals would be cast into a lake of fire to burn forever. "God still loves them even when they're burning in hell," he claimed. What an easy claim to make if you have little love for those whom you believe are burning.

In the words of 1 John 14:20, "Those who say, 'I love God,' and hate their brothers or sisters, are liars; for those who do not love a brother or sister whom they have seen, cannot love God whom they have not seen.'"

Our society regularly suffers when one of the Three Great Loves is left out of the equation. When the rich are content to love God and themselves apart from loving their neighbor, they become content to keep "God's abundant blessings" for themselves without concern for those who are less fortunate. Indeed, their "blessings" often come at the expense of the poor. When married heterosexuals love only God and themselves, they easily become content to ignore the earnest desire of homosexuals to maintain long-term, committed relationships, or worse, some claim that their marriages are threatened by the marriages of others and seek to prevent them.

Yet when society focuses only on loving God and neighbor to the exclusion of self, it also breaks down. Personal accomplishment and hard work fail to be rewarded and are subsumed instead under the exigencies of a giant welfare state. Creativity, individuality, and personal freedom are sacrificed on the altar of the cult of "mediocrity for the masses."

Of course, many Christians believe that the biggest problem in society is leaving not neighbor or self out of the equation but God. While there is a degree of truth to this observation, one must bear in mind that nineteen of every twenty people in America believe in some form of God, mostly the God of Jesus. Presumably, most of these harbor some degree of love for the God they believe in. Often, therefore, the claim that others do not love God—besides being highly judgmental—is actually rooted in a difference of opinion or belief regarding *how* God is to be loved or which God.

When we walked through Morgantown, West Virginia, for instance, we encountered a conflict over the removal of a portrait of Jesus from outside the principal's office of a public school. "Atheists are taking God out of the schools!" certain Christians exclaimed with great emotion. Yet those who supported the removal of Jesus' portrait were primarily people of faith. Some were followers of other religions concerned that Christianity was being made to appear as the "official" religion of the school. Others were Christians themselves who believed that loving God includes respecting the diversity of love for God among people of faith and were thus no more interested in promoting one faith over another than their non-Christian neighbors.

Sadly, the Morgantown case over Jesus' portrait, which developed into a full-scale lawsuit, was not resolved by the various sides coming together and agreeing on a way to balance love of God with love of neighbor and self. Rather, the suit was dropped after an intruder entered the school late one night and stole the portrait. To me, this result was as poetic as it was unfortunate. It seems that Jesus always turns up missing when the love of God, neighbor, and self are not practiced together.

Two popular Christian radio talk shows in Los Angeles and Detroit challenge the walk as soon as it leaves Phoenix.

3

HELLFIRE, DAMNATION, AND GARBAGE DUMPS

"IN MY BOOK you're a universalist, you're a gay church, [and] you're doing a publicity stunt from Phoenix to Washington to get attention in an election year to try to redefine the Democratic platform in religious language. That's what I think you're doing. I'll let you respond when we come back."

So much for the "friendly interview" I was promised the day after leaving Phoenix with CrossWalk America! These are the words of Frank Pastore, host of the largest Christian radio show in Los Angeles. His producer, Pat, called after we started walking to inquire about my being a guest on Frank's show, which would air to a hundred thousand listeners during their evening commute. Pat explained that the interview would consist of a fifteen-minute focus on who we are and what we're doing, followed by fifteen minutes of questions.

"Frank will challenge you on a couple of points—the ones you'd probably expect," Pat explained, "but it will all be *friendly fire.* We really love what you're doing!"

Pat was so warm and enthusiastic, I was nearly convinced that what he was telling me was true. But twenty minutes before my scheduled appearance, I tuned into Pastore's show over the Internet to get a feel for where he was coming from. What I heard suggested that our interview might not be so warm and fuzzy.

Pastore was advocating for the United States to bomb Iran because of its insistence on moving ahead with its nuclear energy program. He outlined each kind of bomb that could be deployed, by precise name and explosive power. He insisted that the whole operation could be wrapped up and victory assured in forty-eight hours.

"Hasn't Frank heard about Iraq?" I thought to myself. "Can he really believe the whole thing would be wrapped up in two days? And what do any of these actions have to do with Jesus? Who would Jesus bomb, anyway?"

Before I knew it, I was on the air. Pastore gave me two minutes to explain in my own words what CrossWalk America was about. This was followed immediately by a fifty-eight-minute all-out attack on CrossWalk America, the Phoenix Affirmations, and me personally. So much for "friendly fire."

Two days later, I was a guest on a larger Christian radio show in Detroit. The host, Bob Dutko, is the former press secretary for the Christian Coalition and advertises himself as "Fearlessly defending the faith." His logo on the station's Web site depicts a shield with a cross on it overlaid by a sword. I was told there would be two hundred thousand people listening—twice the audience of Pastore's show.

Given my experience with Pastore, I was prepared to be attacked relentlessly by Dutko. In fact, I figured that Dutko might make Pastore seem like a member of the CrossWalk America Fan Club by comparison! Much to my surprise, however, Dutko was different—or so I thought.

Although Dutko objected to some of the theological stances taken by CrossWalk America, such as openness to other faiths, separation of church and state, and the full equality of lesbian, gay, bisexual, and transgendered people, he was polite. In contrast to Pastore, Dutko allowed me to complete my sentences and gave me ample time to comment on his responses. When I hung up the phone, I remarked to Scott, our film director, who had taped the interview, "He was nothing like Pastore! We actually had an intelligent, respectful conversation. Who would have guessed?"

Several minutes later, I called my mother, who was recording the show over the Internet. "You'd better get back to your computer and listen in," she told me. "You're getting hammered right now!"

Sure enough, Dutko was taking call after call from irate Christians insisting that I was luring people onto a slippery slope to hell. And Dutko was encouraging them!

"Yes, I'm afraid you're right," he was saying. "He sounds like a nice enough guy, and I don't want to sit here and bash him behind his back or any of that kind of stuff, but you know, this is such a concern to me that this is going on. . . . I mean, the guy's got a Ph.D.—a Ph.D. in biblical studies! He's a senior pastor of this church in Arizona! And I'm not just picking on him. There are countless people, uh, biblical scholars across this country who are pastors of churches who are buying into this same theology. . . . It's hard to believe that someone with a Ph.D. in the Bible could be so misguided. . . . It has to be a spiritual-veil-over-the-eyes kind of thing because no one can be that illogical!"

One particularly vehement caller asserted, "You hit the nail on the head when you said that when somebody preaches another gospel, let him be accursed, and that was another gospel if I ever heard it. This guy is leading people to hell."

"Yeah, I agree. I have to agree."

"That doesn't mean he's not doing it in a nice way," the caller continued.

"Right."

"He was cordial, but we have to cordially and nicely say with all due respect that you're headed over a cliff!"

Why all this venom? Why all the accusations about luring people to hell, spiritual veils, and being accursed? Although both Pastore and Dutko voiced concern with CrossWalk America's stance on homosexuality, neither found this to be the most contentious point of difference. Both men started their interviews by raising the issue of homosexuality, but both soon set it aside, saying something to the effect of "Now what *really* concerns me is not homosexuality so much as your stance on *salvation*."

Neither Pastore nor Dutko could believe that any self-respecting follower of Jesus would ever hold that God's love and grace extends beyond those who claim Jesus as Lord and include all people—including those of other faiths—for eternity, as Phoenix Affirmations 1 and 9 imply.[1]

"We would break fellowship over this one," claimed Pastore.

"God is a jealous God," Dutko insisted to his audience after I was off the air. "How could God be jealous of other gods and yet let their followers into heaven?" With respect to those who don't hold the same understanding of Scripture as his, Dutko concluded, "Jesus said there will be many who think they are Christians, they'll say 'Lord, Lord, we did all these wonderful things in your name,' but Jesus will say, 'I never knew you.'"

Ironically, Dutko uses Tom Petty's song "I Won't Back Down" as his theme music—specifically, the part where Petty sings, "You can stand me up at the gates of hell, but I won't back down."[2]

In the context of Petty's song, this line serves as a critique of those who would condemn others who don't believe or act exactly like them. Yet on Dutko's show it's used to say, in effect, "Never back down from condemning those who believe or act differently than you"! This isn't the only example of a line being taken out of context to make it say the opposite of its intent. This is a tendency that is quite common in certain Christian visions of salvation and damnation.

For instance, some Christians quote Jesus' statements about hell in the Gospels as a way of supporting their beliefs that non-Christians will burn in a lake of fire for all of eternity unless they accept Jesus as Lord. But they don't acknowledge that in nearly every instance where "hell" appears in Jesus' words, the underlying Greek word is Gehenna, from the Hebrew *gey hinnom*, "Valley of Hinnom." The Valley of Hinnom was a literal place in the Bible. In Jesus' day, it was a garbage dump on the outskirts of Jerusalem. When Jesus' listeners heard reference to this place, they would not have understood him to mean a place of everlasting torment. The Valley of Hinnom did have a horrifying history, however. The place had once been used by worshipers of the god Molech to burn their children as sacrifices. When King Josiah ascended to the throne late in the seventh century B.C.E., he was appalled by this practice. As part of a sweeping reform movement, Josiah turned the Valley of Hinnom into a garbage dump and set up an eternal flame where the sacrificial altar had once been so that garbage would be burned there continuously. The purpose was to ensure that the Valley of Hinnom would never again serve as a place where children would be sacrificed to a deity.

Yet in our day certain Christians want to reverse what Josiah did and make it infinitely worse. The Valley of Hinnom—Gehenna, or "hell"—has once again become a place where children are burned. Only it's not Molech but the Christian God who is not just burning God's children but torturing them eternally in the fire!

To give you a feel for the difference between translating Gehenna as "the garbage dump" and translating it as "hell," I invite you to consider the following saying of Jesus:

> All who exalt themselves will be humbled, and all who humble them-
> selves will be exalted. But woe to you, scribes and Pharisees, hyp-
> ocrites! For you lock people out of the kingdom of heaven. For you do
> not go in yourselves, and when others are going in, you stop them.
> Woe to you, scribes and Pharisees, hypocrites! For you cross sea and
> land to make a single convert, and you make the new convert twice as
> much a child of *the garbage dump* as yourselves [Matthew 23:12–15].

In other words, Jesus is telling those who sit in condemning judgment of others, "Your theology is absolute garbage!" Here's another passage to consider, one that was quoted to me on the radio:

If your hand causes you to stumble, cut it off; it is better for you to enter life maimed than to have two hands and to go to *the garbage dump,* to the unquenchable fire. And if your foot causes you to stumble, cut it off; it is better for you to enter life lame than to have two feet and to be thrown into *the garbage dump.* And if your eye causes you to stumble, tear it out; it is better for you to enter the kingdom of God with one eye than to have two eyes and to be thrown into *the garbage dump,* where [the] worm never dies, and the fire is never quenched [Mark 9:43–48].

To be sure, Jesus' words here are difficult. No one wants to understand themselves or others as cast into a dump to be burned up as trash. Yet there are two important points to be made here. First, garbage dumps are not eternal torture chambers. They simply burn up what has become useless. Trash does not burn forever. The *flame* may burn forever, as it did in Gehenna, but the garbage burns only until it's gone. Second, if one reads the two verses that immediately follow this passage, the message changes still further, as Jesus concludes, "For *everyone* will be salted with fire. Salt is good; but if salt has lost its saltiness, how can you season it? Have salt in yourselves, and be at peace with one another."

In other words, the fires of Gehenna are not meant for torture but for cleansing! They burn away what has become useless and burdensome, allowing only what is helpful and godly to remain. ("Have salt—fire—in yourselves, and be at peace with one another.")

Jesus' statement here comports well with several other statements made about fire in the Gospels. For instance, when John the Baptist speaks of Jesus, he refers to him as baptizing people "with the Holy Spirit and fire. His winnowing fork is in his hand, to clear his threshing floor and to gather the wheat into his granary; but the chaff he will burn with unquenchable fire" (Matthew 3:11–12; Luke 3:16–17). According to John, Jesus is the one who removes what is dead and useless from us, leaving behind what nourishes and sustains life. Jesus himself observes, "I came to bring fire to the earth, and how I wish it were already kindled!" (Luke 12:49).[3]

Fire may not be a pleasant metaphor for what God does with our chaff, but neither is it anything but a healing one. Even if one understands God's fire as a form of discipline, Scripture still insists that it acts for our good, not our harm. The author of the letter to the Hebrews writes, "Do not regard lightly the discipline of the Lord, or lose heart when you are punished by him; for the Lord disciplines those *whom he loves,* and chastises every child whom *he accepts.* . . . [God] disciplines us *for our good, in order that we may share his holiness*" (Hebrews 12:5–6, 10).

As CrossWalk America passed through Arizona, we pondered why it is so threatening to believe that hell may not be a place where God encases the vast majority of the world's population in an eternal torture chamber for failing to confess that Jesus is Lord. If grace, by definition, is something we receive quite apart from anything we do or deserve, why would it seem so blasphemous to assume that God's grace extends beyond our immediate faith community, especially when there are so many scriptures that point in this very direction?

The answer to that question lay in one of the things Frank Pastore said during our interview. "So Eric, why the incarnation, then? I mean, if God's grading on a curve and you just sort of try hard and everybody's in, then why an incarnation, why the Christmas story, why celebrate the resurrection, why Christianity, why be a Christian?"

"I'd be curious to hear *your* answer to that," I responded. I wasn't avoiding his question. I was countering his avoidance of an earlier one.

Pastore responded rapidly, as if reading something off a card. "John 14:6: 'I am the way, the truth, and the life. No one comes unto the Father but through me.' Those saved in the Old Testament that know God were looking forward to a Messiah. Those saved following the earthly ministry of Jesus Christ rely on his saving work on the cross. It was finished on the cross, and if you believe that he was the propitiation for your sin, then you're in."

"You say 'if.' You're putting a big 'if' in there, right?"

"Yes. Theoretically, I have a high view of free will."

"What about Romans 5:18?" I asked. "'Therefore just as one man's trespass led to condemnation *for all,* so one man's—Jesus'—act of righteousness leads to justification and life *for all.*' What part of *all* do you not want to hear?"

"That's the classic universalistic line on Romans 5:18, and that's why we reject it, though," Pastore countered, as if any scripture may be rejected if it supports a notion of universal salvation.

I continued, "'For Christ also suffered for sins once *for all,* the righteous for the unrighteous.' That's 1 Peter 3:18."

"Right. Christ died for the unrighteous—that would be *all* of us, but you take that to mean that everyone's in even if they don't want to be."

Ignoring the attempts to put words in my mouth, I continued, "'With all wisdom and insight [God] has made known to us the mystery of his will, according to his good pleasure that he set forth in Christ, as a plan *for the fullness of time,* to gather up *all things* in him, things in heaven and things on earth.' That's Ephesians 1:8–10."

"Triple 8, 995-KKLA. Let's go to Joe out on the I-10. Your question for Eric Elnes . . ."

It seems sometimes that those who quote Scripture to support their views get a bit nervous when they encounter others who can quote Scripture back at them. Pastore countered by trying to label me a "universalist," as if the label is so obviously flawed that it could end all debate. "Universalist" and "universalistic" refer to any theology that assumes that ultimately all people are saved by God. Some universalists, though not many, believe that this happens quite apart from human free will, which is why Pastore made reference to his "high view" of free will. Few universalists I've ever met or read, however, claim that we have no free will in the matter of salvation—that we are saved even if we don't want to be saved. Rather, most believe that now, or in eternity, we will all eventually *desire* what God has freely given us. They assume that God has more patience than we do.

Despite being tagged with the universalist label, I am sympathetic to the universalists' views but do not agree with all of them. For example, while I don't presume to know what happens when we die, I suspect that God honors our free will to the point that if we choose with our entire will not to live within God's love and grace (now or in eternity—I have no idea), God will let us. What God has created, God uncreates. Whatever happens, it makes no sense to me at all that a loving God would take a person who has so decided and torture this person forever.

Some people object, "If everyone who wants to is going to be with God, why bother with Jesus at all?"

The implication in this question is that if Jesus did not come to save us from damnation, then he's of no use to us. If you happen to think that Jesus is of no use at all unless he keeps you from frying in hell, then I invite you to reconsider your love and respect for Jesus. As I believe and as the Phoenix Affirmations suggest, Jesus is not about saving us from eternal damnation after we die but saving us for living in this world as people who trust that God loves us and all people for eternity.

As we walked into the mountains of Arizona's high desert, we continued to mull over the radio interviews. Some of the walkers were curious about how these radio hosts (and listeners who agree with them) could be so sure that some people are going to be eternally punished when they die. I explained in a Bible study one night that the scriptures do not speak with a single voice with respect to heaven, hell, and salvation. Just as I could cite a number of passages to support my understanding that God's grace and love extends to all people, forever, they could cite scriptures back to me to support their views. Thus biblical interpretation is an art, not a science. You cannot simply assume that just because one passage or even a cluster of them supports one point of view, this is the only position that may be called "biblical." Seeking a "biblical perspective" on a certain matter of faith means setting any passage or set of passages against the whole backdrop of Scripture—what is asserted throughout the whole of Scripture about God's nature and character, God's love and grace, God's anger and wrath. One must ask, "Does my understanding of one particular passage or set of passages comport well with the entire witness of Scripture?"

To my mind, as I told my walking companions, the popular understanding of hell and eternal damnation doesn't stand up well against the whole of Scripture.

"Then why do so many people insist on believing it?" someone asked.

"They run the odds," I responded. "Many believe they're being wise gamblers."

By that I meant that since Scripture speaks with more than one voice with respect to salvation, and even though passages that could be interpreted to support a view of eternal damnation are distinctly in the minority, any rational person would have to acknowledge that there's a chance we could be wrong. We may believe that God loves all people eternally and therefore does not choose to cast us into eternal damnation, but what if we're wrong?

"What if there's a ten percent chance that we're wrong and that people who don't believe a certain way really are cast into eternal damnation?" I asked. "What if there's a five percent chance? What if there's even a one percent chance? People are quite aware that eternity is a very long time! So they run the numbers. Consciously or otherwise, they think, 'If there's even a small chance that I, or people I love, may burn in hell for eternity, I'd better play it safe. I'm going to place my faith in the worst-case scenario. That way if I'm proved wrong after I die, I'll be no worse for it. But if I were to place my faith in God's grace and am wrong about it and then I die and discover I'm wrong, what happens?"

"The person is toast," someone responded.

"Yes, worse than toast. This kind of odds-making is what can cause the most compassionate people in the world to do horrible things to others."

The walkers looked puzzled.

"What I mean is that if you honestly believe that there is a reasonable chance that someone you love is going to land in hell for eternity because he or she doesn't believe in Jesus at all or in the same way as you do, then if you have any compassion at all, what will you do?"

"Try to convert the person," Meighan responded.

"Yes, by hook or by crook. After all, even if you've gotten people to have faith in Jesus and they get into heaven because of it, they'll thank you for it, won't they? We should be doing anything and everything in our power to get them into heaven if we have any compassion at all. Why do you think people were tortured into making confessions of Christian faith during the Middle Ages? People thought it was more compassionate to create Christians through torture than to let them die as non-Christians and be condemned to hell. Really, saving people from eternal damnation should be our highest priority in life, according to this view."

The following Sunday, two of the walkers, Rebecca and Merrill, found themselves by accident in a fundamentalist church. The pastor stood before his flock brandishing a large Bible in his hand, claiming, "My job as a pastor is not to help you become a better Christian. My job isn't to help you become nicer or wiser or happier or more ethical or a better parent or spouse. And *yours* shouldn't be either. As Christians, we have only one job. That's to get people on the lifeboat. The job of a Christian is to make more Christians. Period! What job could be more important than that? When people are dying and going to hell every day, do we really have time to waste on these other things? They're distractions, people! And the devil loves to distract us from our job."

Rebecca left with a stomachache.

I tried explaining that her reaction could be due to the fact that she's one of the eternally damned, but she wasn't laughing.

"I don't see why people would ever want to convert to Christianity if this is all they have to look forward to."

The apostle Paul made much the same point in his letter to the Romans. If you replace the word *Jew* with *Christian*, his point stands out well for modern-day Christians:

> You can get by with almost anything if you front it with eloquent talk about God and his law. The line from Scripture, "It's because of you Christians that the outsiders are down on God," shows it's an old problem that isn't going to go away.[4]

Indeed, it isn't going away anytime soon.

AFFIRMATION 9

[Christian love of self includes]
Basing our lives on the faith that in Christ all things
are made new and that we, and all people, are loved
beyond our wildest imagination—for eternity.

Eternity

Some people object that if God loves all people beyond their wildest imagination, they will have no incentive to change, to try to follow God and Jesus more faithfully. But love actually has quite the opposite effect. If you have doubts, then try to find any honest expression of love—any truly loving relationship on earth—that does not provoke deep change in those involved in it, whether they initially believed they'd be changed or not. Consider, for instance, how the extravagant love and grace of a parent can transform a prodigal child's life (Jesus told a parable about this in Luke 15:11–32). Personally, I became persuaded that God loves me this way twenty-five years ago, and it completely changed the course of my life.

True love does not just affirm. It also convicts. But it does even more than that. It provokes a turning from not loving. Indeed, it is love that saves, not fear.

Because love is not based in fear, it also inspires those caught up in love to take risks—risks for the purpose of expanding love. For instance, because we cannot be assured with absolute and final certainty that we are not wrong about God's extravagant love and grace, living by it involves implicit risk. It involves *faith,* which is another word for trust. We have to trust God enough that we refrain from playing the game of odds—or at least from playing it totally safe. Living by Affirmation 9 means that we choose not to assume or act as if people may be damned for eternity "just in case." We assume and act as if we are all loved beyond what we can know.

Jesus knew well the kind of risk involved in living and loving this way. He knew also that people would instinctively want to play it safe rather than take risks with God's love. His advice to would-be risk averters is told well in a parable of a master who entrusts three servants with large amounts of money before leaving town for a while. Two servants take risks with the money, investing it and turning a profit for the master. The third servant plays it safe, digging a hole and burying it so it wouldn't be lost. Upon his return, the master generously rewards the first two servants and is furious with the third. "Master," says the third in self-defense, "I knew that you were a harsh man, reaping where you did not sow, and gathering where you did not scatter seed; so I was afraid, and I went and hid your talent in the ground. Here you have what is yours."

The master replies, "You wicked and lazy slave! You knew, did you, that I reap where I did not sow, and gather where I did not scatter? Then you ought to have invested my money with the bankers, and on my return

I would have received what was my own with interest." The master then instructs his servants to take the money from the third servant and give it to the first, who had turned the largest profit, concluding, "For to all those who have, more will be given, and they will have an abundance; but from those who have nothing, even what they have will be taken away. As for this worthless slave, throw him into the outer darkness, where there will be weeping and gnashing of teeth" (Matthew 25:14–30).

In this parable, the master stands for God. The money given by the master represents the only kind of currency God deals in: love. What Jesus is telling us is that God wants us to take risks with God's love. After all, taking risks involves having faith in God's love and grace. When we have such faith, God's Realm grows and prospers. The parable also serves as a warning. In Jesus' understanding, it is actually more dangerous to play it safe with God's love than to take risks with it.

In the end, could we be mistaken in our faith that God loves all people beyond their wildest imagination, for eternity? Yes. And if so, we will be guilty of extending *too much love* to others on God's behalf. Yet what if our faith in God's love is correct but we choose to "play it safe" by insisting that people who don't believe the way we do will be tortured in hell for all of eternity? Personally, I would rather be found guilty of giving away too much of God's love than giving away too little.

Jesus First Baptist Church.

4

JESUS FIRST BAPTIST CHURCH

SOME PEOPLE HAVE a hard time believing that Jesus rose from the dead. I can relate. Resurrection is a pretty big miracle to wrap one's mind around. But I'm a believer. I don't believe just because the Bible says so but because of my experience. The Bible makes a number of historical claims that I do not hold. I believe because Jesus keeps showing up in my life, frequently unannounced, in situations where I least expect to find him. I just can't seem to make him go away even when I would like nothing better. For me the question is not how can I believe but how can I *not* believe? One surprising and unforgettable encounter with Jesus happened two weeks into our walk.

We were passing through a part of northeastern Arizona so religiously conservative that we could not even find support in traditionally mainline churches. As we walked into Springerville, the conservatism of the area was amply demonstrated by a billboard advertisement. It read "Jesus First Baptist Church." Two American flags adorned either side of the name where one might expect to see crosses or other religious symbols. As we walked by Jesus First in the neighboring town of Eagar, we found a large American flag posted prominently on an exterior wall.

Since the coming Sunday would be the only one on the entire walk on which none of us had a speaking engagement, I told the group, "I'd like to visit Jesus First Baptist on Sunday."

"Why?" came the universal response.

"It has been a long time since I've worshiped in a fundamentalist church," I replied, "and I'd like to hear what the people have to say. After all, we'll be encountering a lot of fundamentalists on our walk, especially as we go through the Bible Belt." Since I'd just had run-ins with Frank

Pastore and Bob Dutko on their conservative Christian radio shows (as re-counted in Chapter Three), I had a special incentive to listen.

"Plus," I said, "they may introduce visitors in their service. If they do, I'd like to stand up and tell them exactly who I am, what I'm doing, and why I'm walking. I'll say, 'I'm walking to proclaim that you can be a lover of Jesus and love people of other faiths; you can be a lover of Jesus and love the earth and its ecosystems; you can love Jesus and love the poor; you can love Jesus and love gay, lesbian, bisexual, and transgen-dered people—or be one; you can love Jesus and read the Bible nonliter-ally, affirm the separation of church and state, and affirm that faith and science can be allies in the pursuit of truth.'"

"Don't do it!" they replied. "You're just asking for a fight!"

"No, I don't want to fight. I just want to see how they respond." I fig-ured the worst thing that might happen is being ignored.

"Who'd like to come with me?"

Dead silence. I looked around patiently, hoping someone might vol-unteer. They were all looking at their navels.

Finally, Meighan Pritchard, our walker from Seattle, spoke a bit sheep-ishly: "I'll go with you." Clearly, Meighan was stepping outside her com-fort zone by volunteering. One of the big fears she was trying to overcome on the walk was of speaking about her faith with people who disagree with her. Meighan explained that she wanted to observe and learn from the experience at Jesus First, hoping that watching what happened to me might give her some pointers for later on.

"Great!" I said.

Our filmmaker, Scott, added, "I'd love to film that! Would you mind if I called the pastor to tell him you're coming and see if I can bring a video camera?"

"Go right ahead."

Scott placed the call. Much to Scott's surprise, not only did he receive permission, but the pastor invited us to attend a Bible study an hour be-fore the service started on Sunday. Scott gave the pastor the CrossWalk America Web address so he could check us out further.

At ten o'clock Sunday morning, Meighan and I showed up at Jesus First Baptist along with Scott and our cameraman, Chris. While we weren't really expecting much drama, we believed we had prepared our-selves for anything that might happen. As we soon discovered, we hadn't!

Pastor Larry Rhodes greeted us at the door. We introduced ourselves and gave him our complete press packet containing information about our walk and a copy of the Phoenix Affirmations, which, we explained, were the theological platform on which we were walking. Pastor Rhodes received us warmly and invited us to take a seat. He then went back to his office to look over our materials as a lay leader conducted the Bible study.

Before it began, the lay leader noticed that Meighan and I were new and asked us to introduce ourselves to the group. "This will be interesting!" I thought to myself.

I stood up, took a deep breath, and introduced Meighan and myself in the manner I described, adding that part of our purpose in walking was to meet with people who believe differently than we do, to try to transcend the polarization taking place in our country between Christians, and to find common ground even as we delineate our differences. The lay leader nodded, and we took our seats.

For the next hour, Meighan and I listened to the lay leader go over the ins and outs of various theories on Christ's Second Coming in the book of Revelation. He reminded the participants that their church reads the Bible literally. He explained how people like them will be taken up to heaven in a sudden "rapture"; after that, a period of a thousand years would commence in which nonbelievers who are "left behind"—including Jews, people of other faiths, atheists, and Christians without "true" faith (presumably people like Meighan and me)—would have a chance to convert before the final judgment.

We listened quietly. As the lay leader went over the scriptures one by one, I tried to find as much common ground as possible between us. "What can I affirm here?" I asked myself. Nothing. I wasn't buying any of it. In fact, I found myself disagreeing with pretty much everything he was saying about the Bible and his interpretation of it!

At the same time, much to my surprise, I found myself also thinking, "I kind of *like* this guy." He struck me as a kind, honest, sincere person of faith. He didn't seem malicious or angry at anyone. Rather, he seemed more like someone who had learned the answer to the final exam—say, it's 12—and he was trying to help us understand how $2 + 7 + 11 + 42$ could equal 12 so that we could pass the final exam.

"I don't believe any of your answers," I thought to myself, "but I do believe what your heart is trying to convey." His sincerity and genuineness were preaching much better than his words.

At the conclusion of the Bible study and before the service began, a woman who had perked up during our introduction when I mentioned that Meighan was from Seattle came over and introduced herself as someone who had once lived in Seattle. She wanted to know what kind of church Meighan attends. Knowing full well what kind of church Meighan attends—a United Church of Christ that is "open and affirming" of gays, lesbians, bisexuals, and transgendered people—I wondered what Meighan would say. Would she play it safe, or would she mention anything that might provoke the exact kind of confrontation she was most nervous about encountering?

Meighan glanced at me nervously and then smiled and told the woman exactly what kind of church she attends and how happy she is to be a part of it. She spoke directly and honestly, conveying how much her church's decision to go "open and affirming" years ago had changed the very nature of her faith community, making it a more joyous, energetic, and welcoming place to be.

The woman was no longer smiling. Instead, her face became quite serious. She told Meighan that her church welcomes such people, too, but that it does not believe in letting people "continue in their sin."

"What do you mean by that?" Meighan asked.

"I mean that we welcome gay people fully in our church, but after a while—maybe a year—if they haven't acknowledged their sin and tried to turn from it, we would have to ask them to leave."

Before Meighan could respond, Pastor Rhodes stepped to the front of the sanctuary, signaling the beginning of worship.

"We have some special guests with us this morning," the pastor announced. "They're walking across this country to promote Christian faith." Those who had recently arrived looked around to see who the visitors might be. "Pastor Elnes, would you mind standing up to tell us a little about your group?"

Once again, Meighan glanced at me nervously as I stood and launched into my "You can be a lover of Jesus" introduction.

As I was speaking, Scott was watching people's body language. As I listed the loves, he noticed that people were tightening up. Their smiles and nods disappeared. They were crossing their arms and looking at one another. When I got to the part about desiring to meet people who believe differently and to do as much listening as proclaiming, finding common ground within difference, the body language loosened up again. Arms uncrossed. Smiles returned.

As I took my seat, a song leader appeared, leading us in an opening prayer in which she thanked God for "our courageous visitors who are walking for Jesus," a preamble to a half hour of praise music. About twenty minutes into our singing, the song leader did something surprising. She paused momentarily, clasped her hands, and said, "You know, I think our next song seems like a CrossWalk America song. Eric, Meighan, would you two mind stepping up to the front? Let's gather around them in a big circle, join hands, and sing 'Shine Jesus Shine' together for Cross-Walk America!"

In a matter of moments, Meighan and I found ourselves at the front of the sanctuary holding hands with a crowd of fundamentalists. Their faces beamed with delight as we sang together "Shine Jesus Shine" on behalf of CrossWalk America.

We were flabbergasted.

After returning to our seats and singing another ten minutes, Pastor Rhodes stepped forward to deliver his sermon. I was keenly aware of the fact that he was perusing our materials during the Bible study. "What will he say?" I wondered. "Will he bring up anything he's read in his sermon?"

He did. At least three times he mentioned CrossWalk America as he preached. Only he didn't denounce us but affirmed us! While he did not bring up any of the affirmations that might be especially controversial to his congregation, he did speak of commitment to the faith, putting faith into action, and having the courage to speak up joyously in the name of Jesus. And he was having a great time doing it, full of smiles and approving nods.

"These people are not the enemy," I thought to myself. "We may disagree on some critical issues, but they themselves are not the enemy."

At the end of his sermon, Pastor Rhodes paused. He cocked his head to the side, put his hand on his heart, choked up a bit, and announced, "Friends, I feel the Holy Spirit upon me. I feel that the Holy Spirit is telling me that we need to take up a love offering for these CrossWalk America folks. I tell you what. Can we pass the offering plates right now to help them out on their walk? And if we don't make, say, two hundred and fifty dollars, would anyone mind if we take it out of the church treasury?"

"Fine!" "Absolutely!" we heard from the congregation.

My head was spinning. "What on earth is happening?" I asked myself.

At the conclusion of the service, people were quick to introduce themselves, congratulating us on our walk. The woman who had turned so stern when Meighan mentioned her church's stance on homosexuality brought her husband and two teenage daughters forward—beaming—to introduce each one to us.

When the crowd thinned out, I rushed out to our van, took out a copy of my book, *The Phoenix Affirmations: A New Vision for the Future of Christianity,* and signed it over to Pastor Rhodes. Placing it in his hands, I said, "Sir, I'm sure you'll find some things we disagree with in this book, but I'm also sure you'll find we share a lot of common ground."

Pastor Rhodes nodded, looked me straight in the eye, and said, "Son, at the base of the cross, it's *all* level ground. God bless your journey."

"Amen," I said, shaking his hand.

That afternoon I spent several hours reflecting on our "truth is stranger than fiction" experience at Jesus First Baptist Church, trying to figure out what had just happened to us and what it could mean for the future of the walk. I concluded that what had happened was this: We all gathered that morning in Jesus' name. After we'd figured out a little about who each other was, knowing full well that we disagreed on some important matters, we each worked as best we were able to get our egos out of the way. And we did it! We got our egos out of the way just enough so that Jesus could actually show up. And he absolutely confounded us all.

Jesus First

Contrary to what many people assume, the vast majority of Christians in the United States believe that God may be found in other faiths. Even among evangelical Christians, an August 2005 *Newsweek*/BeliefNet poll found that nearly seven in ten evangelicals affirm that a person from a different faith can go to heaven. A full nine in every ten Catholics make the same claim. In my own denomination, the United Church of Christ, the percentage likely hovers around 95 percent or greater. Oddly enough, the majority of Christians seem to feel that their fellow believers think exactly the opposite. Many therefore keep silent when certain Christian leaders claim that Christianity is the "only way." Some even feel a bit guilty for believing differently.[1]

At the more liberal end of the theological pool, there is somewhat less silence or embarrassment. Among some Christians, one is not repri-manded but applauded for loving other faiths. These Christians eagerly read the sacred writings of Hinduism and Taoism. They participate in Native American sweat lodges and burnt-sage rituals. They recite the poetry of Islamic Sufis and practice Buddhist meditation. Indeed, when it comes to other faiths and religious practices, they are accepting and affirming.

AFFIRMATION I

[Christian love of God includes]
Walking fully in the Path of Jesus without denying the legitimacy of other paths that God may provide for humanity.

However, if you ask some of these same Christians to comment on more conservative forms of Christianity, particularly Christian funda-mentalism, that's another story. Ironically, it is far easier for some Christians to affirm that God may be found in other faiths than it is to make the same affirmation about parts of their own faith.

I must admit, I relate to this sentiment. For instance, I am often more comfortable talking about faith with a Buddhist than with a fundamentalist Christian. And I can read Zen *koans* seemingly for hours, whereas I find fundamentalist commentaries on the Bible hard to endure for more than a few minutes.[2] Many of the commentaries simply bore me. No matter what book of the Bible, it seems like I read the same questions brought to the text, the same answers taken from it, the same ideology lurking behind it, and the same implications drawn for faith and practice.

Nor do I agree with many fundamentalist teachings (for example, on human sexuality, particularly as it relates to lesbian, gay, bisexual, and transgendered people).[3] I also find their theological and social rigidity disturbing and their absolute certainty in matters of faith and public life reckless and frequently arrogant. When certain Christians celebrate the increasing tensions in the Middle East, eagerly anticipating World War III because they feel it will hasten Jesus' return, I believe they actually obliterate the path of Jesus, who himself said that only God is able to know when the end will come. When these Christians condemn people who disagree with them to hell for eternity, I believe that the name of Jesus, who castigates his followers for merely calling others "fools," is trod upon. When certain leaders seek to tear down the wall of separation between church and state, creating a Christian theocracy, I find this one of the surest ways to kill the faith Jesus espoused.

In fact, I am inclined to agree with a statement made recently by Bishop Carlton Pearson, a former fundamentalist preacher who lost all but two hundred of his five thousand–member congregation within a year after starting to preach that salvation has been given in Christ to *all* people. Pearson claims that "the greatest threat . . . to world civilization is not a nuclear bomb or a holocaust. The greatest threat to human civilization is religious fundamentalism, in any sect, particularly the Abrahamic faiths: Christianity, Judaism, and Islam."[4]

Yet while I agree with this statement, I must also admit that the future of Christian faith in America and around the world does not lie in the hands of Christian liberals and moderates. It lies in the hands of Jesus. And because it lies in Jesus' hands, the path forward likely involves a lot more line-crossing than we would prefer if left to our own devices. It will mean crossing lines between friend and foe, between liberal and conservative, between Republican and Democrat, and between red state and blue state. It will require a strong dose of humility, which itself demands a willingness to find common ground even as we delineate our differences (indeed, *because* we delineate our differences). We will have to allow ourselves to be confounded when Jesus shows up, unannounced, in the strangest of places. As the late William Sloan Coffin, former pastor of Riverside Church in New York City, once observed:

> The Church, of all the institutions in society, interprets the memory
> and proclaims the message of the coming kingdom. The Church may
> distort Jesus into a white middle-class pillar of American respectability;
> it may pervert his image into that of a religious Babbitt pushing the
> cult of successfulness; it may distort and pervert his image, but the
> Church cannot forget Jesus. And in spite of its best efforts to domes-
> ticate that Jesus, the Church knows and frequently fears that his mes-
> sage will be rediscovered. The Church cannot help but keep the name
> in circulation, and where the name is remembered there is hope.[5]

Why do I raise issues regarding Christians' acceptance of other Christians in talking about Affirmation 1, which implies an openness to other faiths? I do so because we really can't begin to speak with honesty about being open to God's activity within other religions—religions in which we may not have been raised, whose scriptures and other sacred writings we may not have spent years studying, whose worship and spiritual practices may appear entirely foreign to our own—if we can't turn to those foreign beliefs and practices in our own faith and affirm that God is great enough, and powerful and creative enough, to be at work where we do not necessarily have eyes to see or ears to hear.

If religious fundamentalism truly is as great a threat to the future of human civilization as Carlton Pearson claims it is—and I agree with him more with each passing day—then Christians cannot afford *not* to be in dialogue with their fundamentalist sisters and brothers. The future of the world is at stake, yet we're so busy condemning each other that we've caught ourselves up in the trees while the whole forest has become endangered.

"Sure," we say, "but those people aren't interested in talking. They see us as Satan's spawn and preach fire and brimstone at us." Yet we must remember that when Jesus said "love your enemy," he was talking about *real* enemies, not fake ones. "Do good to those who *hate* you; pray for those who *persecute* you."

What we found on the walk is that *in general,* fundamentalist Christians are much more willing to dialogue than one might think, particularly when one is willing to do as much listening as talking. This is one of the great lessons learned from interfaith dialogue over the years: that each faith needs to be shown respect and dignity if it is to work at all. It's time to take this same principle and apply it to *intrafaith* dialogue, whether between Christian denominations, between churches, or between individuals chatting in a coffeehouse.

Jesus can be for us, in effect, a modern-day Rosetta Stone, that ancient stele inscribed with the same passage of writing in two Egyptian language scripts and in classical Greek that allowed people to understand Egyptian for the first time. Even though liberals and conservatives, mainliners, evangelicals, and fundamentalists speak the language of Jesus in our own particular tongues and traditions, it is possible to find common ground and build on it because we're all looking at the same person. And this person is not dead. He is alive and able to confound us all.

Of course, we are not called to affirm the entirety of any faith perspective, even our own. What we are asked to do is affirm that God is larger than our preconceived ideas about God. God can and does work creatively within belief systems that are quite foreign to us and may even appall us. To forget this is to forget an important avenue of understanding.

Now, having cleared the air a bit on this sensitive subject, I can turn to the subject of other faiths, and do so (I hope) more honestly.

More Than One Way?

Even though the majority of Christians believe that a person from another faith can find God or be "saved," a great number feel there is little support for their belief from within the Christian faith itself. They feel they're not being a "good Christian" for respecting and valuing the faiths of others. As we moved across the country, we found that where objections to Affirmation 1 were raised, those who raised them almost invariably cited a particular passage from Scripture in support of their position: John 14:6 (the same passage Frank Pastore quoted to me in our radio interview): "I am the way, the truth, and the life. No one comes to the Father except through me." So the question becomes, How can we affirm both what Jesus says here and Affirmation 1?

This passage is found in the Gospel of John, which is quite different from the other three Gospels (Matthew, Mark, and Luke). Whereas the latter three were written between approximately 60 and 80 C.E. and reflect a degree of interest in Jesus as a historical figure, the Gospel of John was written much later, with different interests. Scholars typically date John between 90 and 100 C.E. John's Gospel is less concerned with Jesus as a figure of history than with Jesus as a present reality. That is to say, the Jesus of this Gospel speaks less as the Jesus of history, who died in the early 30s C.E., and more as an eternal voice.

To illustrate the difference concretely, think about when each Gospel writer considers that Jesus became the Christ or Messiah. In Mark's Gospel—the earliest of the four—Jesus is revealed as the Christ at his baptism, when the Holy Spirit descends on him and God announces, "You are my Son, the Beloved; with you I am well pleased" (Mark 1:11). Yet in the Gospels of Matthew and Luke, each written after Mark's, the revelation of Christ's identity is pushed back much earlier—to his birth. Mark's Gospel doesn't even contain a birth narrative. Yet in the Gospel of John, Jesus does not become the Christ at his baptism or his birth. Rather, Jesus is Christ "in the beginning"—that is, in the beginning of all Creation: "In the beginning was the Word, and the Word was with God, and the Word was God. He was in the beginning with God. All things came into being through him, and without him not one thing came into being. What has come into being in him was life, and the life was the light of all people" (John 1:1–4).

When Jesus speaks in the Gospel of John, therefore, it is not Jesus the man speaking so much as Jesus the Cosmic Christ, who was and is and ever shall be and apart from whom nothing came into existence. This is why, for instance, Jesus is always talking about himself as Son of God in this Gospel whereas in the others he almost never refers to himself this way, preferring Son of *Man* and even actively discouraging people (and demons!) from identifying him as Son of *God* (see Mark 3:11–12, for example).

Thus when we read of Jesus' saying, "I am the way, the truth, and the life, and no one comes to the Father except through me," it is not the historical Jesus who makes this claim so much as the Christ through whom all things came into being. Over the centuries, many Christians have understood Christ to be present in other faiths because they have understood Christ to be present in *all* things ("apart from whom nothing came into existence").

Jesus himself indicates as much four chapters earlier in John's Gospel, verses 10:14–16, where Jesus says, "I am the good shepherd. I know my own and my own know me, just as the Father knows me and I know the Father. And I lay down my life for the sheep. I have other sheep that do not belong to this fold. I must bring them also, and they will listen to my voice. So there will be one flock, one shepherd." John 14:6 must be read in light of John 10:4–16.

Although I discuss this passage in *The Phoenix Affirmations: A New Vision for the Future of Christianity*, it is important enough to the subject at hand that it bears repeating here. So forgive me if I cite my own book on the subject!

Some people believe that Jesus is calling here for the conversion of those of other faiths to Christianity. Yet Jesus refers to adherents of other faiths ("other sheep that do not belong to this fold") who *already* belong to him ("I *have* . . ."), who *already* know him ("I know my own and my own know me"), and therefore can be expected to respond to him when he calls, as sheep respond to the familiar voice of their shepherd ("they will listen to my voice"). Jesus is not calling for sheep of different folds to change shepherds. Jesus is simply asking his disciples to recognize that the God they know in Christ is also the God of others. Ultimately, the human family is one flock, with one shepherd.

It is important to understand what Jesus is *not* saying here as well as what he *is* saying. What he's decidedly not saying is "different strokes for different folks." Nor is he saying that anyone can worship the god of one's choice, and it's all good, no matter whom or what one worships. Rather, Jesus is asserting that a number of faiths ultimately worship the same God. Which faiths? They aren't identified. We may surmise, however, that faiths that truly follow the "one shepherd" actively promote the love of God, neighbor, and self, as Jesus did. Jesus does not seem to think that people walking in the path he reveals should be spending all their time worrying about which other paths are watched over by the same Shepherd and which are not. He demonstrates much more enthusiasm throughout the Gospels for his disciples to concentrate on walking their own path and offering hospitality to those they meet along the way.[6]

Jesus' understanding resonates in the depths of his own Jewish faith. When we dig a little deeper and understand the original context for what Jesus says in John's Gospel, we can hear what he says with different ears, the way someone back in his day might have heard it. In doing so, we can understand how God may create other legitimate paths to God besides Christianity.

The Israelites and Their Faith

Contrary to what most Christians (and Jews) believe today, the Israelites did not believe in the existence of just one God (monotheism). They believed in the existence of many gods besides Yahweh, their God. They did not believe that these other gods were actually demons, either, as certain Christians today claim.

Yet the Israelites were not polytheists either. Polytheists not only believe in the existence of other gods but also that the will of one god may supersede or circumvent the will of another. Thus, for instance, the

Babylonian god Marduk may not necessarily get his way if the Assyrian god Asshur doesn't want him to (or vice versa).

Throughout most if not all of the biblical period, the Israelites were neither monotheistic nor polytheistic. Instead, they acknowledged the existence of other gods but ascribed all true power to only one God. The other gods were thought to be completely subservient to the will of their High God. Proof of this Israelite belief system comes not only from extra-biblical inscriptions unearthed in Israel in the past hundred or so years where the existence of other gods is assumed but also from the Bible itself. Take the book of Genesis, for instance.

In the very first chapter of Genesis we find God creating human beings saying, "Let *us* make humankind in *our* image, according to *our* likeness" (Genesis 1:26). Who is the *us*, who is the *our*? Many attempts have been made to explain this plural reference within the confines of monotheistic belief. Some attempts are more strained than others.

One thought is that God is simply speaking to God's own Self, as when we speak of ourselves using words plurals such as *we, our,* and *us* even though there's only one of us. Another thought is that God is speaking in what is known as the "plural of majesty," as when a person of unusually high status and power tells a subordinate, "We are not amused," even though the "we" is really an "I."

Still another thought, one quite popular with Christians but understandably less popular with Jews, is that the passage reflects God speaking as the Trinity of Christian belief—Creator, Christ, and Holy Spirit. As attractive as this idea is to many Christians, it seems a bit odd that a Jewish author, writing six centuries before Christ and nearly a millennium before Christianity itself officially asserted a belief in God as Trinity, would be writing from a Trinitarian perspective.

Far more likely, the author and his audience knew exactly what he was talking about. He believed that his High God presided over a Divine Council in which other gods were seated. Unlike his ancient Near Eastern compatriots, however, the writer did not believe his High God, Yahweh, could have his will thwarted by the others. "Let us create humankind in our image, according to our likeness," commands Yahweh. No deliberation is recorded.

We could turn to other instances in the Bible, but the point is that all kinds of passages in the Hebrew scriptures, from Genesis through the Psalms and prophets, indicate that Yahweh was considered not the *only* god but the *highest* God, even as Yahweh was considered the *only* God for Israel.[7] The underlying assumption in the Hebrew scriptures is that each nation has been assigned its own particular god. Confirmation of this divine scenario is found in several other passages in the Hebrew scriptures, one of the most interesting of which is Deuteronomy 32:8.[8] The text of Deuteronomy 32, commonly called "The Song of Moses," is thought by many scholars to be among the oldest texts in the entire Hebrew Bible. The words are said to have been sung by Moses himself as he stood on Mount Nebo overlooking the Promised Land before the Israelites entered it in the thirteenth century B.C.E. In verse 8, Moses sings about the early beginnings of Israel and the surrounding nations: "When the Most High [that is, Yahweh] apportioned the nations, when he divided humankind, he fixed the boundaries of the peoples according to the number of the gods;[9] Yahweh's own portion was his people, Jacob [Israel] his allotted share." Note that Yahweh is referred to as the "Most High" God. There's no such thing as a "Most High" God unless there are other, less high gods.

If you mention this to a biblical literalist, she will likely refute the notion that the text acknowledges the existence of other gods. Likely she'll cite a passage or two that speak of Yahweh being the "only God, beside whom there is no other." Since, according to a literalist, one part of the Bible must agree with all other parts or the whole thing is bunk, she will insist that the Bible cannot speak of the actual existence of other gods. However, aside from the highly problematic assumption that every passage must agree with every other passage in the Bible, there is strong evidence to suggest that not even claims that Yahweh is the "only God, beside whom there is no other" stems from a strictly monotheistic understanding. Many scholars today agree that such statements were commonly made with respect to Israel but not other nations. The original authors were stating that there are no other gods *for Israel*.

We are so used to hearing that Israel was monotheistic and that the aim of every good Christian is to convert the world to worship of the one and only true God that we often block out anything that contradicts these notions. A Christian reading Genesis 1 often assumes that *us* and *our* refer to the Trinity without looking for other explanations. And why not? That person likely has never heard of the Divine Council or that certain ancient biblical authors believed in the existence of other gods.

It is time to put away the blinders and preconceived notions and look to our foundational texts with new eyes. Looking at them in this way undermines neither the authority of the texts nor the authenticity of our faith. Rather, the opposite occurs. It opens the scriptures up, revitalizes faith, and makes both more comprehensible (and thus more capable of being lived out) in the modern world. With respect to Genesis 1, for instance, we need not force a later, Trinitarian view on the text. Instead, we may now understand how the ancient author ascribed other gods—and thus other faiths—a degree of legitimacy from the very beginning of things. It does not make the Jewish and Christian God any less powerful. It simply relieves us of the burden of having to prove that all other faiths are illegitimate and frees us to discover inherent relationships among and between different faiths.

On this note, we now may return to Jesus, where we started in the first place. Taking a second look at the passage from John 10, we find that Jesus stands solidly within the Jewish tradition when he observes, "I have other sheep that do not belong to this fold," and that these other sheep ultimately belong to one flock and one Shepherd. Jesus recognizes that legitimate paths exist in other faith traditions. He also recognizes that above and behind all these paths is one Good Shepherd whose will reigns supreme. This is a far cry from saying "whatever floats your boat." Recognizing "other sheep" from other folds is not the same as recognizing "all sheep" from any fold. Which folds are connected to the Good Shepherd and which are not? Jesus does not say. He's speaking to his own disciples, not the whole world. His concern is to teach his disciples about their own fold, not that of others, signaling that they may be less concerned about judging other faiths and more concerned with loving their own.

This brings us again to the "problematic" John 14:6, where Jesus tells his disciples, "I am the way, and the truth, and the life. No one comes to the Father except through me." There are two ways to understand this passage in light of our discussion. According to the first interpretation, one notes that Jesus is talking to *his own disciples,* not Buddhists, Taoists, Muslims, or Hindus. Jesus is making an exclusive claim with respect to *his own* disciples. For those of us who follow Jesus as Christ, Christ himself is the way, the truth, and the life; Christ is the Path to God. There is no other. Other sheep may belong to other folds. We belong to Jesus Christ.

A second line of interpretation stresses that Jesus is making this claim as the Cosmic Christ and second member of the Trinity, who "was and is and ever shall be." In this sense, he is making the same claim that was made in John 10 in a different way. Just as Christ is the Good Shepherd who ultimately cares for the sheep of many folds in John 10, so Christ in John 14 serves as the ground on which many paths tread to reach the same mountain peak. Those who ascend the mountain may take very different paths and use vastly different methods to reach the peak. On their way up, they may or may not be aware of the existence of other paths or even that Christ is the ground on which each one treads, yet no one who reaches the peak does it without Christ's aid. "No one comes to the Father except through me."

In many respects, this second interpretation comports well with the Hebrew scriptures even if the underlying belief in John 14 is monotheistic. Just as the Hebrew scriptures acknowledge the existence of many gods who ultimately serve Yahweh's will, so Jesus in John 14:6 represents the incarnation of God's will itself. He is "the Word," which is "from the beginning," "through whom all things were created" and apart from whom "nothing was created." To claim that "no one comes to the Father except through me" is to claim that Christ is a part of all legitimate paths willed by God, whether they bear the name of Jesus or not.

One may object that this second explanation may not appear satisfactory to those of other faiths. They may feel we are claiming them to be "anonymous Christians"—people who follow Jesus but just don't know it yet. Rightfully, they might find such a claim offensive and belittling of their own religion. Yet to claim that the eternal Christ is the ground of any legitimate path is not the same as claiming that the Jesus of history is that ground. The Jesus who lived and died two thousand years ago is not the Path. He points his followers to the Path, which is the Path of Christ, the eternal Word or will of God. The Path of Christ, therefore, transcends Christianity just as much as it transcends Buddhism, Taoism, Hinduism, or Islam.

In the Gospel of Mark, Jesus makes an observation that I believe summarizes everything we've been considering. The disciples are upset that someone who is not a follower of Jesus is casting out demons in Jesus' name. Jesus tells them to calm down, stating, "Whoever is not against us is for us" (Mark 9:40).

What if Christians accepted and embodied this attitude—that whoever is not against us is for us, that whoever does not stand against the love of God, neighbor, and self is on Christ's Path no matter what their religion? If we would do this simple thing, we would be taking seriously the message that Christ *really does* have other sheep who are not of the same fold, that they *really do* know him on some level, and that they *really do* respond to his call in the various ways it comes to them. Then we might *start* to understand what is meant by Jesus' observation that there is ultimately one flock, one Shepherd.

A reporter with the *Clovis News Journal*, Clovis, New Mexico, speaks with Rebecca Glenn and Eric Elnes.

5

THE TRICKSTER SHOWS UP—
AGAIN!

IT STARTED WITH a rejection by the very people we thought would support us. It ended in celebration—one of the high points of the walk, actually—thanks in no small part to people we were certain would reject us.

Our experience in Clovis, New Mexico, like that in Eagar, Arizona, (see Chapter Four), became for us a wake-up call that our stereotypes about people, particularly Christian liberals, moderates, and conservatives, would need to be systematically dismantled if we were to hear what the walk was trying to tell us about faith in America. It also gave us a new appreciation and respect for a frequently overlooked aspect of God: God the Trickster.

The Trickster is a well-understood motif in Native American cultures. In the lore of the Southwest desert, for instance, the coyote often plays the role of Trickster. Like Trickster figures in other Native American traditions, the coyote "alternately scandalizes, disgusts, amuses, disrupts, chastises, and humiliates. . . . He is also a creative force transforming their world, sometimes in bizarre and outrageous ways, with his instinctive energies and cunning." The Trickster is also a "creator of order out of chaos and a destroyer of order which represses creative energies."[1]

In the Jewish and Christian tradition, God the Trickster is at work throughout the Bible, confounding and dumbfounding the faithful and unfaithful alike. For instance, Abraham and Sarah are told that Sarah will bear a son despite Sarah's greatly advanced age and previous barrenness. When Sarah laughs, God commands her to name her son Isaac—"he laughs" in Hebrew! God the Trickster later commands Abraham to sacrifice Isaac on a mountain altar—no laughing now. Yet when Abraham raises the knife to accomplish the deed, God commands Abraham to release Isaac, providing a ram as an alternative sacrifice. In the New Testament, it is God the Trickster who anoints Jesus, the poor carpenter's son, "Savior of the World." This Jesus antagonizes members of the religious establishment, calling them a "brood of vipers" and slyly announcing that prostitutes are better suited to God's Realm than they are. He turns water into wine; he breaks Sabbath laws. Jesus renames Simon "Peter" ("rock") shortly after Peter tries to walk on water but sinks like a rock instead. "Upon this rock I will build my church," he says (Matthew 16:18). And when the world seeks to do away with Jesus by nailing him to a cross, God the Trickster goes to work once more at the site of an empty tomb. Since that time, God the Trickster has shown up regularly throughout two thousand years of Christian history, including during our walk through Clovis, New Mexico.

Clovis

As CrossWalk America moved across the country, we kept our costs low and our human contact high by arranging in advance with individuals, churches, and other organizations for food and lodging as well as speaking engagements. Over the course of our 141-day walk, we were hosted by 150 churches, stayed in 200 homes, and met face to face with over 11,000 people. I can't even tell you how many potlucks we attended! Facilitating all the complex logistical details—minus the potlucks—were Phoenix-based volunteers assigned to each state. A community college professor, Dean Stover, was our logistics coordinator for New Mexico.

A month before the walk started, and two months before arriving in Clovis, New Mexico, Dean contacted the head of the local ministerial alliance, seeking support. The leader was a Presbyterian minister. "Good," Dean thought, "he'll probably be thrilled to lend support. It's got to be a bit lonely for mainline, liberal denominations in the Bible Belt."

Dean e-mailed the minister, providing background information on CrossWalk America, the Phoenix Affirmations, and support for "6–8 walkers for two nights and/or to hold an event/forum at the church to discuss the Phoenix Affirmations and CrossWalk America." The next afternoon, Dean received the minister's reply. He thanked Dean for his invitation to assist with the project but turned him down flatly, claiming that no pastor in the Clovis Christian Ministerial Alliance would be interested in hosting a group like ours. He suggested that we try seeking help in Portales, twenty miles away. He closed the note stating, "I did log on to your Web site and read the Phoenix Affirmations. Some of your points

I can agree with, *but when it comes excusing behavior that God has clearly condemned as sin, I must agree to disagree*" [emphasis mine].

A bit dumbfounded by the minister's dismissal of any possibility of support in Clovis, a town of just over 36,000 people, Dean asked me for some ideas on how to proceed. I decided to write the gentleman myself, speaking minister to minister, explaining in greater detail what we're about, what was needed, and why he could feel good about supporting us. What follows is my exact e-mail, minus his name.

> Dear Reverend,
>
> My name is Eric Elnes, co-president of CrossWalk America and senior pastor of Scottsdale Congregational United Church of Christ. I just received your response to one of our Logistics Team members, Dean Stover, and wanted to write personally to you for two reasons:
>
> (a) I want to clarify that we are not asking churches to agree a hundred percent with what we are walking for in order to extend hospitality to us. We were writing you, as a Christian leader, to ask if you would be in a position to help a small group of fellow Christians who are walking through your area in need of food and shelter. If we are not extended hospitality in your area, we can break out our tents and camp out someplace. But besides being a burden, we feel it is also a missed opportunity for fellowship with Christians in your area.
>
> We no more require people to agree with each and every one of our beliefs in order to share fellowship with them than you or the other churches in your fellowship would of their own members. And I want to underscore that we are not out to convert people to our point of view. We simply would like a roof over our heads and a meal or two and to enjoy the company of fellow Christians, even if we disagree on certain issues (chances are we agree on a lot more).
>
> If people want to hear our views, we'll be glad to share them to the extent they're interested. And just as important, we'll be glad to be quiet and listen to their views with respect and courtesy. Our core walkers are much more interested in trying to find common ground with those with whom they come into contact than to sharpen differences. We believe our country has become far too polarized already regarding matters of faith. I don't mean to suggest by this that the walk is not standing for anything or proclaiming a point of view. What I do mean to suggest is that we're not drawing lines—we're not suggesting that those who agree with us are Christian and those who disagree are un-Christian. We're quite interested in starting a respectful,

national dialogue between Christians on matters of faith, and in so doing we want to model the best of Christian behavior, not the worst of it. Do you think you or the churches in your area could help us out?

(b) As a core walker myself, I would personally like to extend an invitation to walk with me for a bit when we pass through your area. I would very much enjoy the opportunity to meet you, to hear your point of view on the various affirmations we are publicly proclaiming—both where we agree and where we disagree—and simply to enjoy your companionship for a few miles as a fellow Christian leader. I am not interested in debating points of difference. But I am interested in listening. And if you like, I'm happy to share my views, but only to the extent you are interested in hearing them. Can we walk a mile or two together? I would be honored if you would accept my invitation.

Sincerely,
Rev. Eric Elnes, Ph.D.
Co-President, CrossWalk America
www.CrossWalkAmerica.org
Senior Pastor, Scottsdale Congregational United Church of Christ
www.artinworship.com

I received no response. Seven weeks later, we were twelve days' journey from Clovis, still without any prospect of support. Concerned, Dean drove from Phoenix nearly seven hundred miles to Clovis in order to find support. He decided to start with the same minister, since he was the head of the Ministerial Alliance, figuring that some face-to-face contact might help. After locating the him and meeting with him, Dean was stonewalled again.

In the meantime, one of our core walkers, Brad Wishon, had been making calls. Brad managed to locate a teeny tiny church in Clovis named Llano Estacado Metropolitan Community Church, which serves the predominantly lesbian, gay, bisexual, and transgendered (LGBT) community. The church was ecstatic.

"We'd absolutely *love* to put you up, and you'd do us a great honor if one of the walkers could preach Sunday morning. And don't worry about food. We're going to prepare a feast you'll never forget! You'll be rolling out of Clovis, New Mexico!"

Ironically, we learned, Llano Estacado had been rejected by the same Ministerial Alliance that had rejected us! "They told us we're not Christian for affirming the very values with respect to LGBT people as you are!"

"What a turnaround," exclaimed Merrill, another of our core walkers, regarding our prospects for support in Clovis. But this was just the beginning.

While researching Clovis, our communications director, Ray Steiner, noticed a curious note from the mayor at the top of the City of Clovis Web site:

> You are welcome in Clovis!!! . . . The citizens of Clovis and Curry County are excellent examples of what being good neighbors [is] all about. As neighbors, we have always come to the aid of one another when friends are needed. . . . Please know that you will always find a friendly smile and a warm handshake that lets you know we are glad you're here. Come and see us. You will be glad you did.

Ray e-mailed the mayor, complimenting him on his warm welcoming statement and asking if it is truly representative of the town or if our experience with the Ministerial Alliance was perhaps an anomaly. Ray also sent a press release regarding our impending arrival to the *Clovis News Journal*.

When we arrived in Clovis, a number of things happened in short order, each of which delighted us and one of which utterly confounded us. First, the paper wanted to meet with Rebecca and me. As it happens, they'd heard of us well before Ray sent his press release and had been tracking our progress for weeks. The reporter was clearly enthusiastic about the walk, full of smiles and laughter from the beginning of the interview—until she heard about the Ministerial Alliance's response.

"What?" she exclaimed in disbelief. "It did *what*?" She probed for details. She wanted names, e-mail correspondence, everything. Clearly, the reporter was not amused. "We may be a conservative community overall, but we really are a welcoming place," she explained. "Clovis is a great place to live, and it boggles my mind that a group like yours, walking for the simple values of love and justice, would receive the cold shoulder. This isn't at all representative of who we are!"

In the meantime, the mayor had come across some of our walk crew at a local coffeehouse. Scott, Chris, Meighan, and Merrill were e-mailing and updating the blog. The mayor approached Scott and extended his hand, exclaiming, "How *wonderful* it is to have you folks in Clovis. If there's *anything* I can do while you're in the area, I'd be happy to help."

Not knowing about Ray's e-mail to the mayor, Scott thanked the mayor for his generous offer, concluding, "I think we're pretty well covered at this point." The mayor looked momentarily disappointed but contented himself with greeting the walkers and chatting a few moments about the walk before leaving the coffeehouse.

Overhearing the conversation was a Baptist minister and a schoolteacher. They wanted to know more. "We're walking to change the face of Christianity to a more inclusive, compassionate one," Meighan explained. "We don't believe that Christians are truly being represented by certain Christian leaders who claim to represent us in the press, drumming up fear and intolerance."

"We believe it's time for Christians who hold another point of view to stop being so silent about their faith," said Merrill.

"Rather than tearing down these leaders and proclaiming what we're not," added Meighan, "we feel we should be joyfully proclaiming a positive message about who we are."

Meighan showed the minister, Paul, a copy of the Phoenix Affirmations, expecting to find his pleasant demeanor change when he reached Affirmation 5, with its open and affirming stance toward different sexual orientations. Instead, he pointed to Affirmation 4 excitedly, with its claim that Christian worship should be as artful as it is scriptural. "This is what I'm all about!" he exclaimed, showing Meighan some brochures of religious wood carvings he'd made and inviting the walkers to stop by his workshop. Meighan and Merrill found themselves impressed once again the power of the Phoenix Affirmations to flesh out common ground between Christians even as they delineate possible points of difference.

The schoolteacher noted the commitment of the walkers to embark on a risky and difficult journey, sadly adding that many of his ninth graders often "fold up their tents and go home" at the slightest hint of a challenge. "Would you folks be willing to come and talk to my classes about the value of commitment?" he asked.

The following day, our story made the front page of the *Clovis News Journal*: "They say they are passing through the area spreading Jesus' message of love. Their self-described progressive views on Christianity, however, are not embraced by everyone."

The reporting included a photograph and an upbeat story about the walk and the Phoenix Affirmations, along with a downbeat summation of Ministerial Alliance's response. The article referenced calls made to Alliance members by the paper and its president's comment that the Alliance had chosen not to support us due to disagreement with the Phoenix Affirmations. Another Alliance minister objected to our stance on LGBT equality but acknowledged that he rarely attends meetings of the Alliance and would have welcomed us if he'd known we were coming.

Within minutes after reading the article, we received a call from our New Mexico logistics coordinator, Dean Stover. "Two local radio stations want interviews." The first, KTQM 99.9 FM (KWKA 680 AM), is a top-forty station that asked Rebecca to come on for five minutes to explain why we're walking. After giving an overview of the very Affirmations that the Ministerial Alliance found so problematic, the host's question was "How can people get involved?"

The second request came from Christian station KIJN 92.3 FM (1060 AM), otherwise known as "Jesus Radio," about twenty miles down the road in Farwell, Texas, which wanted me to come on for a fifteen-minute interview.

Recalling my experiences with Frank Pastore's and Bob Dutko's radio shows in Los Angeles and Detroit (see Chapter Three), I felt a wave of dread. My throat constricted. My mouth went dry. Even though I had actually enjoyed the interviews (it's especially amusing when the interviewer thinks he's the only one who knows the scriptures!), they were nonetheless stressful. Based on these experiences, I figured that whether the tone of the interview was combative or friendly, the host would still try to nail me one way or another. And he'd do it either while I was on the air, as Pastore did, or when I was off, like Dutko. Yet I consented to the interview—how could I not?

"You wanna trade interviews?" I joked with Rebecca.

"No," she laughed, "but I'll go with you if you want."

"Then we could deflect punches from both directions," I chuckled, thinking she was joking back at me.

"I'm *serious*," Rebecca responded.

This surprised me. I figured Rebecca would be wonderful to have on the interview, but I knew how anxious she would get about the prospect of someone's trying to argue Scripture with her. If Rebecca had found within herself the courage to speak from her joy in the face of antagonistic Scripture-quoters, I figured that anything she might lack in advanced biblical studies would be more than made up for in passion and soul.

"Sure," I said, "that would be great. But I thought you didn't want to do these kinds of interviews."

"I know," she responded, "but I've got to face them at some point. It might as well be now. Besides, *someone's* got to sound intelligent on the show!"

"Ha! If you don't mind, I'm going to take a bit of prayer time before heading out there. I'll pray for intelligence and see you in an hour."

An hour and a half later, we pulled up to "Jesus Radio" in Farwell. It was a small, blue, houselike building of perhaps a thousand or so square feet. A large antenna on the side betrayed its identity as a radio station.

"Ready?" I asked.

"Ready."

"Let's just stay on message. We'll keep offering back love and joy no matter what we get from them."

Rebecca responded, "Let's keep building on any common ground we share with other Affirmations besides the ones they object to. How can it go that far wrong if we do?"

We stepped out of the CrossWalk America van, opened the front door to "Jesus Radio," and found the station manager, Mike Rodriguez, standing there to meet us. Rodriguez is a large Hispanic gentleman, around six feet tall and weighing perhaps three hundred pounds. Mike was all smiles.

Before we could shake his hand, Mike stepped forward and gave each of us a giant bear hug, exclaiming, "I'm so glad you stopped by! This is a really great thing you're doing."

"Well, thanks," we replied, both of us wondering how much he knew about what we were doing.

Actually, Mike knew a lot. "You know, this Ministerial Alliance . . . I just can't figure that out. You're walking for Jesus, and they're *Christians*. How could they turn you down? I know we might not see eye to eye on every one of your beliefs, but I think we should be a lot more into recognizing similarity than difference. We need to support one another when brothers and sisters are standing with Jesus."

"We couldn't agree with you more."

Mike continued, "I know I'm going to get some calls this afternoon from listeners who are upset about having you guys on. But you know what I'm going to tell them? I'm just going to say, 'You worry about running your church, and I'll worry about running my radio station!'"

Mike then introduced us to our host, Kevin Gardell, a tall, thin, middle-aged man with a long ponytail and a tie-died shirt. He plays electric guitar in a rock band and would look more at home at a Grateful Dead concert than at a station called "Jesus Radio." But Kevin had "come to know Jesus," and the experience did not close him off to the world but opened him up to it. He was extremely gracious and interested in everything we were doing. On the air, he wanted to know all about the Phoenix Affirmations, the responses we'd had to them along the way, how each walker was adjusting to life on the road, and so forth. About halfway through the interview, which ran for double the scheduled time, Kevin observed, "You know, what you folks are doing—walking the land, meeting up with people face to face, treating people authentically, talking about faith, spreading the joy—this sounds just like what Jesus did with his disciples. That's cool!"

"Yeah, it's kind of like that!" we replied. The interview ended with Kevin asking me to close us in prayer on the air. Once off the air, Kevin taped a sermon to be run Sunday morning all about CrossWalk America and Jesus.

As we walked throughout the afternoon, it became obvious that the newspaper report and radio interviews had made an impression on the community. Cars and trucks honked their horns, their drivers waving and cheering us on.

That evening we arrived at a small, predominantly Hispanic Catholic church in Bovina, Texas, where the priest had invited us to attend Mass. When we'd originally contacted the priest, Father Jose Luis Chavez, he immediately offered to put us up in a local motel at the church's expense and feed us. Aware of the fact that many Catholics disagree with our stance on the full equality of LGBT people and not wanting to put the priest in an awkward situation if he should find out later, Meighan Pritchard had offered to send Father Chavez more information about CrossWalk America and the Phoenix Affirmations. Father Chavez responded without hesitation, "You're walking for Jesus. That's all I need to know."

When we arrived at Father Chavez's church, he graciously received us into his home. We learned that he's originally from Colombia, has four doctorate degrees, and is a judge on the Ecclesiastical Court of Appeals in the Roman Catholic Church. This man was obviously an expert in Catholic doctrine! We wondered how he could so warmly receive us despite the fact that the Catholic church considers homosexuality a sin. Father Chavez explained that Catholic doctrine is not properly interpreted by the letter of the law. "It is the Spirit behind the law that matters. I welcome you in the name of that Spirit."

At the Spanish Mass, Father Chavez invited us to stand up, introduce ourselves, and explain what the walk was about. After taking our seats again, a middle-aged truck driver stood up and, struggling not to choke up, told the congregation how he'd been driving his truck that afternoon and heard the interview on "Jesus Radio."

"I had tears in my eyes as I heard you folks talk about what you're doing and your message of love and compassion. I thanked God when you explained how Christians need to get back on the path of Jesus and embody his positive message. Then I came to church this evening and here you are! I can't believe it! The Lord be praised!"

After the service, we were treated to a full-blown Mexican fiesta held in our honor lasting well into the night.

"What on earth happened in Clovis, Farwell, and Bovina?" we asked ourselves. Scott suggested that God the Trickster was at work once again, scandalizing, amusing, disrupting, chastising, confounding expectations, and transforming both the area residents and us walkers. Sure enough, In Clovis we'd been rejected by the very churches we had felt so confident would support us, yet the Clovis newspaper, the mayor, a Baptist minister, a schoolteacher, a tiny church that had been ostracized by the same alliance, scores of drivers along the road, a top-forty radio station, a conservative Christian radio station in Farwell, and a Hispanic Catholic church in Bovina had stood by us, cheering us on. It felt like the entire area, upon witnessing our rejection by the Ministerial Alliance, rose up in unison, saying, "This shall not stand. This is not who we are!"

Standing with the Outcasts

Several months before leaving on the walk, Rebecca and I attended a progressive Christian leadership summit in Berkeley, California. Its purpose was to identify what justice-related issues were considered of critical importance to progressive Christian groups and to explore how we could combine our efforts to move them forward. A couple of us identified LGBT equality as being one of these issues. Much to our surprise, however, although the majority of the groups at the summit strongly affirmed that LGBT equality is one of the most important justice issues of our day, it failed to garner more than token support. The reason? "We're trying to gain support in 'Middle America,' and according to the polls, the gay issue freaks Middle America out."

Rebecca leaned over to me. "I didn't realize God read polls," she whispered.

"And even if God did," I replied, "I doubt that's what God's interpretation would be."

I thrust my hand up into the air. "I think the polls are more nuanced on this issue than most people assume. But more to the point, CrossWalk America believes that one of the reasons why Americans still waffle over LGBT equality is that people have only heard one viewpoint advertising itself as 'Christian.' In this country, nine in every ten people identify themselves as Christian, but a full six of these don't actively participate in any faith community. When these six vote—or answer surveys regarding issues concerning LGBT equality—many of them are saying to themselves, 'I'm a Christian. What's the Christian thing to believe? What's the Christian thing to do?'"

I went on to observe that when the main Christian voices they're hearing are in the media, and the media are highlighting only one particular perspective calling itself Christian, what do you suppose many of these six people do? Middle America isn't as closed-minded and bigoted as many progressives think. These people simply haven't heard a strong alternative that they consider legitimately Christian. The polls aren't going to change until either the church rises up and joyfully and unapologetically proclaims an alternative point of view or so few people care about what Christianity has to say anymore that they stop listening altogether.

During a break, someone tried to console me for the resounding lack of interest in moving LGBT equality forward. "At least on this subject, all we've got to do is wait twenty years and it will be over. For the younger generation, homosexuality is a nonissue. They're already for LGBT equality."

I replied that such things may be easy for straight people like us to say, but how do you suppose our LGBT brothers and sisters feel about waiting twenty years for the same rights and opportunities we enjoy? And how many of the younger generation can we expect to find in the church twenty years from now if we've played it safe and remained silent—or been on the wrong side of the issue—all this time?

AFFIRMATION 6

[Christian love of neighbor includes]
Standing, as Jesus does, with the outcast and oppressed,
the denigrated and afflicted, seeking peace and justice
with or without the support of others.

One of the lessons Jesus teaches his disciples is to stand with the outcast and oppressed, with or without the support of others. In his day, it was not LGBT people who were the subject of society's disdain but lepers and tax collectors, women and the poor, peacemakers and prostitutes. Not only does Jesus regularly cavort with these very people, but he lays bare the principles he follows in one of the most famous sermons of all time: the Sermon on the Mount.

> Blessed are the poor in spirit, for theirs is the kingdom of heaven.
> Blessed are those who mourn, for they will be comforted.
> Blessed are the meek, for they will inherit the earth.
> Blessed are those who hunger and thirst for righteousness,
>   for they will be filled.
> Blessed are the merciful, for they will receive mercy.
> Blessed are the pure in heart, for they will see God.
> Blessed are the peacemakers, for they will be called children
>   of God.
> Blessed are those who are persecuted for righteousness' sake,
>   for theirs is the kingdom of heaven.

Blessed are you when people revile you and persecute you and
utter all kinds of evil against you falsely on my account. Rejoice
and be glad, for your reward is great in heaven, for in the same
way they persecuted the prophets who were before you
[Matthew 5:3–12].

Apparently, Jesus wasn't paying enough attention to popular opinion,
at least if he was trying to achieve the same ends many Christians are.
Had we been Jesus' political or marketing advisers, we certainly could
have set him straight on a few things, right? We could have "improved"
his sermon to make it a bit more palatable to the masses. Then, with the
support of the masses, he could have accomplished what he really wanted
rather than being crucified. Here's how I might modify that sermon to better conform to the polls:

Blessed are the ~~poor in spirit~~ successful, for theirs is the kingdom
of heaven.
Blessed are those who ~~mourn~~ don't let anything get them down on
the road to success, for they will ~~be comforted~~ enjoy the
comforts of life.
Blessed are the ~~meek~~ proud, for they will ~~inherit~~ take over
the earth.
Blessed are those who hunger and thirst for ~~righteousness~~ more
possessions, for they ~~will be filled~~ are supporting the
economy.
Blessed are the ~~merciful~~ tough, for they will receive ~~mercy~~ respect.
Blessed are those who can pretend best to be the pure in heart, for
~~they~~ society will see ~~God~~ them as Godly.
Blessed are ~~the peacemakers~~ those who strike preemptively, for
~~they will be called children of God~~ their children will be safer
than those of their enemies.
Blessed are those who ~~are~~ persecuted for righteousness' sake,
for ~~theirs is~~ they will take over ~~the kingdom of heaven~~ the
heathen.
Blessed are you when ~~people~~ you revile ~~you~~ and persecute ~~you~~
others and utter all kinds of evil against ~~you~~ them falsely on my
account. Rejoice and be glad, for your reward is great ~~in heaven~~
on earth, for in the same way ~~they~~ you persecuted the pesky
prophets who were before you.

Now there's a sermon for Middle America, or at least for some people's *perception* of Middle America! What we found on the road was quite

different. It's not that everyone in Middle America is necessarily on board with each and every one of Jesus' teachings or our interpretation of them, but neither are people quite as closed to hearing different perspectives as many have assumed. To be sure, the blowhards are closed-minded, but such can be found on every side of the political and religious divides, and they constitute a small percentage of the population.

We learned four important lessons in the Clovis area that speak to the issue of reaching out to Middle America, contradicting the strategy employed by many Christians who seek to "reach out" to them. First, we learned that you don't have to please everybody. When you're standing with the oppressed and disfranchised, opposition is not necessarily a bad thing. As long as you stay on message, refusing to offer back the fear and negativity coming at you, standing instead for the love and joy that inspire you in the first place, you make it easy for people to support you. You call forth something deep inside that chooses love over hate and welcome over rejection, even when people may not necessarily agree with each and every one of your beliefs. People become emboldened to step forward, which emboldens you still further.

Second, we learned that some of the people who will support you the most do not come from the theological or political camps you are expecting. Many people are more loyal to Jesus than they are to their preconceived notions about Jesus. When they see passion serving the cause of compassion, and both the passion and the compassion are "on their knees" before Jesus (or "on their feet," as the case may be), they either reconsider their positions or offer support despite specific areas of disagreement. Both reactions advance the cause of Jesus.

Third, the tiny Llano Estacado reminded us of how hard-pressed certain groups are in America who have been ostracized by others and how relieved and encouraged they become when mainstream Christians stand in solidarity with them. These groups cannot afford to wait until public opinion polls shine brightly upon them. Their deep need and desire is to join hands with others who will dare to stand and shine brightly with them.

Finally, in the Clovis area we were amused by the fact that we found more support from the moderate end of the conservative theological spectrum than we did from the conservative end of the liberal one. Those who supported us most appear to have been those who value most highly their identity as welcoming, compassionate people. Based on our experiences throughout the walk, the people in Middle America who put a high value on a welcoming and compassionate identity outnumber by a long shot those who do not.

"Something's going on here that's important to remember," Scott observed. "I think the walk is telling us to be prepared to let go of our stereotypes and be surprised by God the Trickster. We need to be open to seeing God's hand at work even in the freaky stuff."

CrossWalk America volunteer Linda Prideaux Steiner shows what happens when sneakers meet hot asphalt outside Hereford, Texas.

6

ASPHALT JESUS

"DO YOU WANT TO KNOW how to get to Hereford from here?" asked a cattle hand at the Mexican fiesta held for us at Saint Ann's Catholic Church in Bovina, Texas.

"I think we know the way," I answered, but I sensed that he wanted to give me his own answer. "But why don't you tell us anyway, just in case."

He didn't miss a beat. "From Bovina you head north until you can smell it, turn right, and when you step in it, you're there!"

"There are a few cows in Hereford?"

"Three quarters of a million in a town of fifteen thousand people. And there's three million cattle within a fifty-mile radius."

"That's a lot of dung!"

"When you step in it, you're there."

We stepped in something, all right, when we arrived in Hereford, but it had only a little to do with cows and a lot to do with the soul of Christianity at the grass roots.

Before we left, CrossWalk America's logistics coordinator for Texas, a volunteer named Cati Serbiak Moreno, contacted a number of churches in Hereford, seeking support. After receiving responses ranging from "Our church doesn't have the facilities to help you" to "We *won't* help you," Cati was getting nervous about our prospects. Then, surprisingly, one church responded, "We won't help you, but we know a congregation that might." That congregation was Fellowship of Believers, a nondenominational church on the edge of town.

Cati was skeptical. In general, nondenominational churches tend to be more conservative than others. Cati was pretty sure that in the Bible Belt these churches would give us the cold shoulder. But she didn't have another option, so Cati phoned. The office administrator answered, asking Cati the reason for her call. After giving some background about CrossWalk America and our needs on the road, Cati was told, "The pastor is unavailable right now. Would you like to leave a message?"

"I'm being screened," Cati thought, but left a message that included our Web address in case the pastor got curious. There was nowhere else to turn.

That afternoon Cati was delighted to find the Reverend Tracy Dunn-Noland, of Fellowship of Believers Church, not only returning her call but expressing interest in helping out. "We don't have the facilities for you to stay in the church, but we could put you up in our homes if that would be OK."

"OK? That would be great! That's what we *prefer,*" Cati responded.

"I need to be upfront with you, though," Tracy added. "Here you'll be in the Bible Belt. We're happy to host you, and we stand strong for your right to believe and follow Christ as you wish. At the same time, from what I have gleaned from your Web site, you might consider being pleasantly surprised if you find many in my church, if any, who agree with and support all your Phoenix Affirmations. But we have a strong tradition here of genuinely valuing other points of view. I don't know how else to say this, but I've never found another church like this one—so traditional and yet brave enough to have a woman as a pastor; so conservative yet strong in affirming the freedom of others. If you all are willing to come, knowing that not everyone may agree, we'd love to host you, and we'll offer Dr. Elnes the pulpit on Sunday if he's interested."

"Absolutely," Cati replied. "We'd love to come!"

Two weeks before arriving in Hereford, I called Tracy to find out a little more about the atmosphere in her church, particularly given what I'd heard she said about the Phoenix Affirmations. After thanking her for extending hospitality, I asked, "Which of the Affirmations do you feel your congregation may have the hardest time with?"

"The hardest will be Affirmation 5," she responded without hesitation. "There's a wide range of views in our congregation over homosexuality, but most people are convinced it's a sin. You won't find people condemning you for what you believe, but they probably won't agree with you either.

"Incidentally, we all had to giggle a bit about your bios," she added, referring to bios of the core walk crew sent to host churches in advance of our arrival. "According to the bios, three of you are *vegetarian.* Bear in mind, Eric, that this is Hereford, Texas—the *beef capital of the world*! My congregation is made up of ranchers, feed lot workers, and others associated in one way or another with the meatpacking industry. My personal beef intake has doubled since I've been here!"

"Hmmmm. Tell me, what do you think your congregation has a harder time with: gays or vegetarians?"

"Frankly," Tracy chuckled, "my congregation can get along with pretty much *anybody* so long as they order *steak!*"

"That will be good news to our gay walker. Brad loves steak!"

Although we weren't aware of it at the time, Tracy maintains a personal blog on the Internet in addition to her church's blog and Web site. On it, she discusses the ins and outs of everyday life as a "woman-wife-mother-preacher-daughter-sister-friend." The weekend before our arrival, Tracy posted the following thoughts:

> CrossWalk America will be coming through our town this weekend. We're feeding and housing them, and they're worshipping with us on Sunday. We're excited about meeting them and hearing their message.
>
> I say we're excited—we're also a little apprehensive. I am comfortable with CrossWalk's agenda ("Where Christian Compassion Meets Progressive Action"), but like most pastors I know, I tend to stand a little left of my congregation. There are some things in their platform that won't fly well in our small town—wouldn't in most churches, either.
>
> I've tried to be clear to CrossWalk about who we are. ("We support your right to believe what you believe—but most of us don't believe the things you believe.") I've told the congregation, "I think you'll be interested to hear their message—you might not agree with everything they say, but it'll be good to share dialogue with them." I don't know what else to do—I'm just praying this thing doesn't come back to bite me in the butt.
>
> Funny thing: CrossWalk found us. How they found a little, unconnected congregation in the middle of nowhere—the only congregation that would even consider hosting them for miles around—well, some things are just out of our hands, aren't they?
>
> They needed beds, food, and a place to rest and do their laundry. THAT we can do.[1]

As we walked from Bovina toward Hereford along Route 60, we passed all kinds of visual and olfactory reminders of the area's commitment to cattle. Kernels of dried feed corn would appear regularly on the shoulder. We passed feedlot after feedlot in which tens of thousands of cows quietly awaited their fate after being transferred here for their last few months from ranches as far as several hundred miles away. Semis full of cows heading toward these feedlots would barrel past us, leaving the acrid smell of stale manure saturating the air. On the outskirts of town, we passed the giant Hereford cow—a larger-than-life bovine effigy standing atop a sign proclaiming Hereford's status as "Cow Capital of the World."

Several miles before the sign, our spirits were lifted as CrossWalk America volunteers arrived from Phoenix after driving nearly eight hundred miles to join us for the weekend. They included Cati Moreno as well as our communications director, Ray Steiner, and his wife, Linda.

"It's hard to believe you guys have walked this far already!" Linda exclaimed. "We thought it was a long car ride," added Cati, "but we kept thinking, 'But these guys *walked*!'"

"What's even stranger," Merrill Davison suggested, "is that it took you just two days to cover the same distance it took us five weeks to walk!"

The afternoon heat became stifling. Within a half hour after the volunteers joined us walking, we hit a patch of newly laid asphalt. The heat had liquefied the fresh tar on the highway shoulder. Suddenly, Linda stopped.

"Hey, look at this!" The bottoms of her shoes were caked with asphalt. We laughed. "That's the strangest-looking manure I've ever seen," I chided, walking past her as she searched for a stick to remove an inch-thick layer of tar and gravel. I thought I'd avoided the soft stuff, but no more than twenty yards later, my shoes were suddenly feeling heavier. Then I had to stop. Then Rebecca. Then Meighan, followed by Cati. Each of us started searching for sticks or rocks to dig out the gooey sludge and continue. For the next few miles, no matter where we walked along the road's shoulder, or even within a couple of feet in the gravel off the shoulder, there was no avoiding it. We began walking in the middle of the road where the asphalt had cured, jumping over the shoulder area into the dirt when cars approached. It was slow, hot, nerve-rattling travel.

After seven miles, the combination of blazing heat and frayed nerves took their toll on our Phoenix volunteers. Most decided to drive into town to seek shelter in air-conditioned hotel rooms before joining us at Fellowship of Believers that evening. "Are you sure you wouldn't rather drive to D.C. from here?" Ray laughed. "We could change our name to Road-Trip America or something like that!"

We arrived at Fellowship of Believers early Saturday evening, exhausted from our day of walking and a bit nervous about what was in store for us over the weekend. "Whatever happens," said Rebecca, "I'm just glad we don't have to walk tomorrow!"

We found the congregation assembled in the church parking lot, setting up serving tables, bringing out potluck dishes and coolers full of iced tea and lemonade. A number of men were hovering around the most dramatic barbeque I'd ever seen. It looked like a Formula One race car, complete with racing stripes and real racing wheels. Where one might expect to find an engine, a barrel-shaped lid was open, exposing mounds of cooking meat. The smell was intoxicating even to the hungry vegetarians in our group.

"They're here!" someone called to folks inside the church, who swiftly emerged from the kitchen. Much to our relief, the church members were all smiles and laughs. They greeted us warmly, offering cool drinks, chips, salsa, and homemade guacamole.

"Are you Pastor Elnes?" asked a woman in her mid-thirties carrying a bowl of ice and a welcoming smile. "I recognize you from the blog," she said. "I'm Tracy Dunn-Noland, the pastor of this little church. We spoke the other day on the phone. I hope you all have brought an appetite. We've got enough food here to feed the whole town!"

Tracy stands around five foot three, but her charisma and presence suggest that she's much taller. She's the kind of person who instantly makes you feel like family, and it's clear that her congregation is, indeed, like one big family to her. As we talked, she weaved through the crowd, jovially teasing church leaders and walkers alike, introducing one person to another, and making everyone feel like long-lost brothers and sisters. At one point she was called into the kitchen. "Why don't you see if those boys at the barbecue can use any help?" she said with a wink. "Betcha never saw a barbecue like that!"

I made my way over to the hovering men. Despite everyone's graciousness and high spirits, I detected a subtle hint of anxiety underneath their welcome. "Like us, they're wondering how it's going to go this weekend!" I thought to myself. Strangely, their anxiety put me more at ease. We were all feeling the same way.

I struck up a conversation with the man turning the meat. As it happened, he owned the barbecue and several more besides, each catering to Hereford's insatiable appetite for beef.

"I consider it one of my life's quests to find the perfect barbecue," I gleefully confessed, feeling hungrier by the moment.

"If that includes fajitas, you may be in luck tonight," he laughed, stirring a heaping pile of beef strips. "We've got plenty of vegetarian alternatives for you folks this evening, too," he proudly noted, pointing to warming trays piled high with roasted red, yellow, and green bell peppers, onions, corn, portobello mushrooms, and baked beans. Cheese sauce slowly bubbled in another tray. Tracy was right. No one would be walking away hungry.

When everything was ready, we all stood in a circle holding hands as Tracy led us in grace. She thanked God for the food, for the hands that prepared it, and for the opportunity to share fellowship with newfound friends. "Amen," we chimed in. "Now somebody grab these walkers some plates," Tracy directed. "They've come the farthest, so they go first."

Over the course of the evening, the subtle tension I sensed at the beginning gave way to increasing laughter and warm spirits. We traded stories and discovered places in common we'd lived before. We talked about life in Hereford, about schools and community issues. Some of us even talked about church.

"What drew you to Fellowship of Believers?" I asked a young couple with an infant.

"We love the people," the husband replied. "They're really energetic, and they care about each other."

"And they're open to new ideas," added his wife. "They don't believe in doing the same old thing just for the sake of tradition."

After chatting a few minutes about Sunday worship, I broached more difficult theological questions. "I'm looking forward to preaching here tomorrow, and I'm trying to get a sense for where the congregation stands on a couple of things. Could you give me your impression of what your congregation thinks about the Bible?"

"You mean, like is it the Word of God?" asked the husband.

"I'm interested in whatever comes to mind," I said, trying to leave the question as open-ended as possible.

"I think we read it pretty much like everyone else. We're Bible believers. We read it pretty simply," he answered.

"It's God's literal Word and all," added his wife.

"And if you were to place the congregation on a line ranging from the most conservative to the most liberal church in town, roughly where would you place it?" I asked.

"We're pretty much exactly in the middle," the husband answered, his wife nodding approvingly.

I smiled to myself. I'd asked this question in one form or another throughout the walk. No matter who I asked or what kind of church I was in, the answer was almost always the same: "We're in the middle."

I thought, "This tells me nothing." Then it dawned on me, "Perhaps this tells me more than I've realized." No matter how far apart people are theologically, most tend to distrust what they perceive as the extremes. They identify personally with what they feel is a balanced point of view. I recalled the increasing mudslinging going on between liberal and conservative Christian leaders in America and wondered what must be happening at the grassroots level. Are these leaders inspiring their flocks or alienating them? Is there a way to bring people together without watering down one's message?

"You drew the short end of the stick," Tracy told me as the evening drew to a close. "You're staying with my family tonight."

We all divided up and headed to our respective homes after dinner, stomachs bulging and, once again, stereotypes crumbling a bit more.

"God the Trickster is at work again," Scott Griessel whispered before leaving.

Tracy's home is a quaint three-bedroom ranch-style house a block from the church. She invited me into her office, adorned with handmade bookshelves built for her by a member of the congregation. As we chatted, I looked over her books. Much to my surprise, I saw a number I myself have on my bookshelves in Scottsdale. There were biblical commentaries written by scholars who do not believe that the Bible is to be taken literally. I saw books on feminist theology and environmental ethics. These aren't exactly the kinds of books one would expect to find on a conservative pastor's shelves.

"You're a Baptist minister, aren't you?" I asked.

"Yes. I was ordained by a church that's part of the Cooperative Baptist Fellowship."

"Then where did these books come from?" I asked, smiling wryly.

"When I decided to go to seminary, I sent letters to two seminaries. I received one letter back that started, "Dear applicant" and another that started, "Dear Tracy." The first letter was from a Baptist seminary; the other was from Brite Divinity School [a mainline seminary affiliated with the Disciples of Christ]. I went to the one that called me by name."

"And you remained a Baptist."

Hearing the question behind my statement, Tracy responded, "It was quite a shock attending Brite at first. I was raised Baptist. For the first time in my life, I was in an atmosphere where I wasn't surrounded by other Baptists. I was in the minority, and people were saying, 'Why are you Baptist?' That got me wondering, 'Why exactly am I Baptist?' So I started researching my heritage and learned that we have a history we can be proud of. We championed issues like the separation of church and state and the priesthood of all believers, and we have a long history of congregational autonomy [the power of churches to make decisions for themselves, free of denominational authority]. I grew to embrace my Baptist faith."

"What is it like being an ordained woman in the Baptist church," I asked. I was aware that her particular denomination ordains women, in contrast to the Southern Baptists, but I was also aware that not everyone accepts this.

"I grew up in a pretty conservative Baptist church," Tracy replied. "This church that raised me never told me I *could* be a woman in ministry, but it never told me I *couldn't*. To me, this represents the best of conservatism. Not so much that [conservatives] are preaching *against* things. They might not be *for* certain things, but not everyone's preaching against them either. So when I was exposed to it, I didn't have any negative messages to combat in my head. I could be open to what was happening."

"Are you accepted by male ministers? And what about your church?"

"My oldest brother is a Baptist minister, actually," Tracy replied. "When I was ordained, he told me, 'I never had to deal with women in ministry until my sister was one. Then I had to decide how I felt about it and think through it.' He's fine with it now. He accepts me completely and is a great colleague. I think that's how change works, one relationship at a time.

"The same goes for my church. Bear in mind that we're quite a mixed bunch. For non-Hispanic-speaking folks in Hereford, they've got only about a dozen churches to choose from. So even though we're about sixty percent Baptist, the rest come from a hodgepodge of different traditions—Catholic, Methodist, Presbyterian, and so on. Some are used to the idea of women in ministry before they get here. Most never thought they'd have to deal with women in ministry until their church hired one. And they've come to love me as much as I love them. That's just the kind of people they are. They don't want people telling them what to believe. They want to make up their own minds. They're always challenging themselves, trying to move forward step by step."

"What do you think it will be like for the congregation on Sunday?" I asked Tracy, adding, "I would imagine most of them would not have guessed they'd be hearing from a minister walking across the country bearing the Phoenix Affirmations."

"You don't strike me as the kind of person who comes out with both barrels blazing, which is good," Tracy replied, "because that would definitely turn them off. As long as you speak honestly, from the heart of what you believe, without patronizing them with lines like 'I believed as you did once, but I've grown . . . ,' they'll respect you even if they disagree with your beliefs. This congregation believes that as long as people are trying to be faithful to God and grow to the best of their ability, that's what matters. Beliefs change. They come and go. It's the heart that matters most."

The next morning, before worship, we were once again impressed by the warmth of the congregation. No one is a stranger at Fellowship of Believers or remains one long. People excitedly milled about with coffee in hand, getting caught up. Children—and a couple of adults—sneaked cookies off trays reserved for after the service. A number of people introduced themselves, saying, "I hear everyone had such a good time at the barbecue last night."

The service was simple yet full of elements I'm not used to seeing in a predominantly Baptist church. For instance, even though most members do not wish to take Communion on a weekly basis, they honor the wishes of a few who do—primarily Catholics—by setting up a Communion station at one side of the sanctuary. A prayer candle station is also set up, at the front of the sanctuary, and at a certain point those who so desire are invited forward to light candles representing their prayers for the morning.

At another point, a member stood up and announced what he had done with fifty dollars given by the congregation the week before. The idea was for that member to do some good with it in the community, to inform the congregation what was done, and then to designate another member to receive fifty dollars to do good the following week. While the amount of money is not large, we walkers were touched by how the ritual served as a gentle reminder to all of us that we've each been given gifts by God that are meant to be used for the good of the community.

When the sermon time arrived, I stood up, took in a deep breath, and turned to face the congregation. Since Tracy had been so insistent about her parishioners' commitment to stretching themselves and hearing alternative points of view, I decided to preach most of my sermon on the biblical basis of Affirmation 5 and its implications for LGBT equality.

I thanked them for inviting us and showing such extravagant hospitality. I also acknowledged what Tracy had said about their commitment to standing with people whose beliefs differ from their own, noting that CrossWalk America is similarly committed. I spoke about how my personal commitment in this regard was indelibly formed as a child when my father modeled a similar commitment (I'll tell that story later in this chapter). Then I related a story of how the apostle Peter was once challenged by God to stand with people whose beliefs and lifestyle he and his people had rejected—the Gentiles (non-Jewish Greeks and Romans). I suggested that God is challenging us in similar ways today with respect to gays, lesbians, bisexuals, and transgendered people.

While I spoke unapologetically about my beliefs with respect to LGBT equality, at no point did I ask my listeners to change their beliefs to reflect my own or those of CrossWalk America. Rather, I applauded them for their courage to hear other points of view and expressed my trust that if we will all stay committed to this discipline of crossing lines and seeing through preconceived notions, God will lead us all to higher ground.

Since I preached without a manuscript, my eyes were on the members of the congregation the whole time. I could read their faces and sense their energy. A couple of folks were clearly uncomfortable when I raised the issue of LGBT equality, but most were simply listening, concentrating deeply. To my pleasant surprise, many were nodding (not nodding off, but nodding in approval!), and some were downright joyful. The energy in the sanctuary was open and positive.

Afterward, my impressions were confirmed as a number of people went out of their way to approach me, thanking me for the sermon and for the work of CrossWalk America. Several whispered, "I have a gay son" or "I have a gay cousin." The other walkers and Phoenix volunteers were similarly engaged in upbeat conversations with parishioners all over the sanctuary. A surprising number of Phoenix Affirmations books were sold at a display table in the foyer, and a number of people made donations to help us on our journey.

Later that day, our host families reconvened with the walkers for hamburgers (and veggie burgers) at a member's home. By then we were all talking and kidding each other like longtime friends. Tracy was even teaching a few of us the correct way to pronounce and use the southern phrases "bless his heart" and "bless her heart." We laughed uproariously. Before leaving for the evening, a parishioner told Tracy, "I can't believe anyone was worried. Why would *anyone* not welcome these people? They are the kindest, most interesting group of folks."

"I think this was a success," Tracy told some of us before we left the next day.

Our filmmaker, Scott, asked, "What makes it a success to you?"

"You've got supporters in Hereford—*besides me*—because you didn't come with your guns out. You came with the desire just to make some new friends. And that's how change is going to happen in this country. Many people won't ever deal with liberalism in Christianity until their friend *is* [a liberal Christian]. And then they'll have to understand. By coming here you helped me start a silent conversation with some of my parishioners that I'm sure will continue long after you've gone."

On her personal blog site the following day, Tracy related her weekend experience this way:

> Hope you had as good a weekend as we did. We enjoyed CrossWalk America immensely. They were, above all, people—kind, loving people. We enjoyed getting to know them and felt honored to host them.
>
> I was proud all over again of my congregation. They are so very warm and loving. They put on the "whole hog" for these folks: great barbecue Saturday night, warm reception on Sunday, hamburgers Sunday night, and host homes that babied them throughout. Why, we even had a hair stylist in the church open her shop on Sunday so one of the walkers could have her highlights refreshed!
>
> Here's the thing: my congregation taught and learned again this weekend (and I think CrossWalk America pleasantly discovered) that you don't have to agree with someone to love them.
>
> Gosh—isn't that what the guy in the robe taught?

It may have been asphalt that stuck to our shoes as we entered Hereford on Saturday, but we left on Monday with something else stuck to us that we would not be able to shake for the rest of the walk: an awareness that one of the great forces of change in our country will come not through the power of rhetoric or even through the power of "superior" beliefs but through people following Jesus, crossing lines, and becoming friends.

"*Asphalt Jesus,*" I thought to myself. "He's the one who will change Christianity into a more compassionate, inclusive faith."

Ecstasy and the Golden Rule

What we discovered at Fellowship of Believers Church in Hereford was a conservative, Bible Belt congregation who, much to our surprise and delight, offered us extravagant welcome even though the parishioners' beliefs conflicted with ours. Even though they may not embrace each and every one of the Phoenix Affirmations, they've certainly made a long-term practice of Affirmation 8.

AFFIRMATION 8

[Christian love of neighbor includes]
Walking humbly with God, acknowledging our own shortcomings
while honestly seeking to understand and call forth the best
in others, including those who consider us their enemies.

To me, Affirmation 8 is about ecstasy. Ecstasy may not be the first thing that comes to mind when you consider loving others as yourself. Perhaps it should. *Ecstasy,* which comes from the Greek *ekstasis,* meaning "standing outside" (as in standing outside the self), is a form of spiritual experience often marked by intense joy or delight associated with moving beyond the individual ego to a more transcendent awareness. It lies at the foundation of all religion. The fact that each of the world's major spiritual paths—along with a host of others—advocates some form of the Golden Rule as central to the practice of its path should serve as a clue to its association with ecstasy.

Of course, just because ecstasy lies at the foundation of religion does not necessarily mean that following a religious path produces ecstasy. "Human beings by nature seek ecstasy," writes Karen Armstrong, a former nun and religious scholar. "If we do not find ecstasy in religion, we turn to art, music, dance, sex, sports, even drugs." However, Armstrong observes, "such rapture can only be temporary. Religious leaders claim that the practice of the golden rule can give us an experience of ecstasy that is deeper and more permanent."[2]

How so? The Golden Rule is rooted in Christian tradition by Jesus' command to love your neighbor as yourself. In order to love my neighbor this way, I must regularly "stand outside" myself in order to consider how I would want to be loved under constantly changing circumstances. I then make this love incarnate—put flesh and blood on it, make it "real"—by treating the other person as I myself would want to be treated. When we "step outside" our individual egos, notes the late Rabbi Abraham Heschel, we are in the place where God is.[3]

Let's consider ecstasy from a more mundane perspective. If I'm considering the purchase of an automobile, how I act toward the seller is— or is supposed to be—influenced by how I feel a loving seller should treat me as a potential buyer. Consciously or unconsciously, I must be able to "step outside" myself, imaginatively looking back at myself and asking, "How do I wish to be treated?" What I discover when I look back at myself is someone who wants to be treated honestly and with fairness above all. Stepping back into myself, I am now to act toward the seller with the same honesty and fairness I desire to receive.

Does this simple exchange produce ecstasy? At first glance, it may not seem likely. I don't mean to suggest with this example that purchasing an automobile in this way will necessary lift you into the heavens (much as the automakers might like us to think so!). Yet have you ever purchased an automobile from a seller who truly treated you as you wished to be treated, listening to whatever hopes, questions, and concerns you expressed and answering them honestly and fairly? I've had this experience a couple of times. Even after many years, I still remember the exhilaration of driving off with an automobile I felt good about owning because the seller and I had both received a fair deal.

Now imagine extending these moments into every possible interaction you have with others. How would you feel if literally *everyone* treated you as you'd want a sincerely loving person to treat you? Would not life become a series of ecstatic moments? As Armstrong notes, "Living in this way, day by day, hour by hour, moment by moment, we would enjoy a constant, slow-burning ecstasy."[4]

Of course, not everyone treats us this way. People may in fact treat us shabbily. Here we run into the deep wisdom of Jesus and others who regularly experience life as ecstasy. Recall that Jesus himself was frequently treated shabbily by others. Yet Jesus commands us not only to love our friends and neighbors as ourselves but also to love our enemies this way. In other words, Jesus asks us to be consistent in our practice, applying it regardless of how others treat us in return. Jesus doesn't ask this in order to make us more pious or righteous. He insists on it because, if practiced regularly, it really does lead to an experience of ecstasy that is deep and permanent. Jesus recognized that when we "step outside" ourselves in order to look back and behold someone we dearly love (us), and when we put flesh and blood on this love by accepting it into ourselves and acting on it, we reap a benefit of that love and transcendence of self even if no one reciprocates.

It is therefore in our *self*-interest to love others as we ourselves wish to be loved. If you have doubts, consider the people you know who embody this approach to life, who consistently treat others with the same love and respect they wish to receive. Every single person I know who makes this a practice regularly experiences deep joy and delight—deep ecstasy.

Bear in mind, though, that I'm not talking about people who let others walk all over them. I'm not pointing to "selfless" people who are so busy working for the benefit of others that they never take time to care for themselves. Such people experience precious little ecstasy in the service of others. Rather than "stepping outside" themselves, they let others step on them. Rather than asking, "How would I wish to be loved in this particular situation?" and reflecting that love toward others, they ask, "How would someone else wish to be served?" and do their best to provide service without ever considering their own needs. Do you see the difference? The love of neighbor that produces ecstasy is intimately connected with the love of self, even as one steps outside oneself.

It is this principle that I believe motivated the Fellowship of Believers Church to show extravagant hospitality to CrossWalk America. The parishioners could not have predicted exactly how we would treat them, knowing upfront that some of our beliefs conflicted with some of theirs. For all they knew, we might have preached at them all weekend, belittling their faith and pumping up our own. What motivated Fellowship of Believers members to act as they did was not so much their love for us as the love they had for themselves, which was then given concrete expression in love for us. They were able to "step outside" themselves and consider how they would wish to be treated if they were out on the road walking for beliefs that they knew could be controversial in the Bible Belt. Had we walkers failed to love them back, they still would have benefited from "stepping outside" themselves and embodying their love in concrete action. They still would have experienced ecstasy.

A First Lesson in Ecstasy

The Sunday I preached at Fellowship of Believers, I related the story of my very first experience of this kind of ecstasy, an experience so profound it still sends chills up my spine to recall it thirty-six years later.

It was July 3. I was six years old. My father and I had just shared lunch at the Guadalajara Mexican Restaurant. The Guadalajara, ensconced in the basement of the building where my dad worked at the corner of Fourth and Pike Streets in Seattle, was my favorite. The cheese enchiladas there were better than candy, and my dad used to pay me a full dollar anytime I could eat a whole jalapeno pepper (this probably explains why I love to sweat when I eat Mexican food!).

After lunch, Dad and I walked down to the Pike Place Market, a popular gathering place even now, where fishmongers, farmers, and artisans sell their wares. I loved the market for all its frenetic activity and the street performers who were almost always there to entertain.

On this particular day, however, as we approached the square, there was a different kind of entertainment on the street. A man was standing behind a booth, shouting through a megaphone and inviting everyone to join a party!

I read the sign in front of his booth over and over but couldn't figure out what kind of party he wanted us to join. I'd never heard of the S-O-C-I-A-L-I-S-T party.

I also couldn't figure out why the party guy seemed so serious. He was shouting into his megaphone, and his tone of voice didn't exactly seem festive. Perhaps this was why no one seemed to be signing up. I felt sorry for him.

"Why, we'll sign up!" I thought. But when we got to the edge of the square, we observed a short, rotund man moving toward the S-O-C-I-A-L-I-S-T party guy. He was carrying a little American flag in one hand and a shopping bag in the other. At first I thought he was heading over to sign the invitation list, but then I noticed his angry expression. He was muttering something that sounded hostile.

As he drew near the guy at the table, the flag-carrying guy's muttering turned to shouting. He used words I'd never heard before as he demanded that the party guy leave the square. The party guy kept shouting into his megaphone, trying to ignore the flag guy. Then the flag guy ripped the S-O-C-I-A-L-I-S-T party sign off the man's table, crumpled it up, and tossed it onto the street!

"That's not nice!" I declared under my breath. The party guy seemed a bit nervous now but continued shouting into his megaphone. I had no idea what he was saying; I was too shocked by the behavior of the flag guy, who, not content with tearing down the man's sign, proceeded to knock over his table.

When not even this stopped the party guy from speaking into his megaphone, the flag guy set his shopping bag down and threatened to punch the party guy. At this point, the party guy stopped shouting into the megaphone and thrust out his hands in a vain effort to prevent the flag guy's assault.

At this point, my dad stepped in. He jumped between the flag guy and the party guy. At six foot five, Dad created an imposing presence. The flag guy only became more enraged, shouting now at my dad to get out of the way. Dad coolly held out his hand in a "Stop!" gesture, asserting that the party guy had as much right to be out on the street speaking his mind as the flag-carrying guy and that the flag-carrying guy had best accept this fact and move on. The flag guy only got angrier.

He tried to punch my father.

From this point on, my memory is something of a blur. I became hysterical. In my world—the world of Batman television shows and Spider-Man comics—when adults fought one another, it was to the death. I literally believed that one of these men—my dad or the flag guy—was going to die. I screamed.

Through my tears, I saw my dad deflect the first punch and the second. Then he held out his arm full length against the flag guy's chest, shouting, "Back off, sir!" Given the size difference between the two men, the flag guy couldn't hit my dad as long as he extended his arm.

The flag guy backed off, muttering something to my dad I couldn't hear. He picked up his shopping bag and stomped away. The S-O-C-I-A-L-I-S-T party guy gave my dad a sheepish but grateful smile, and my dad hastened over to me. I was still crying and trembling uncontrollably. In my world, Dad had just put his life on the line for a perfect stranger.

My dad suggested we go get a Coke, and I readily agreed. Anything to leave the square.

Over Cokes at a nearby restaurant, my dad tried to explain what transpired in the square. He grabbed a napkin, took out a pen, drew a line down the middle, and gave me my first lesson in politics. He explained the differences between Socialists and Democrats, which he put left of the line, and Republicans on the right.

From my dad's explanation, I could tell that there was probably nothing the Socialist guy stood for that my dad agreed with. He was definitely a Republican and thought everyone capable of rational thought should be one too.

I was astonished. Here my dad had just risked his life on behalf of someone's right to say things he entirely disagreed with. In this moment, from my child's-eye perspective, I perceived little difference between Dad and Jesus.

What motivated my dad to step into harm's way to protect a stranger on the square? Surely it was not his love for the Socialist party or anything the man was saying. My dad was able to act so quickly and decisively because he had a clear and certain love for *his own* right to free speech, and he was so used to treating others as he himself would want to be treated that he didn't have to think about it. He simply went into action, putting flesh and blood on his love. In that moment, like Jesus, he became love incarnate.

This same love extended also to the flag-carrying man. Rather than returning the man's blows with his own or deriding him when he had the chance, my dad simply treated the man as he would have wanted to be treated if he were acting belligerently and wrongly. He would want to be treated peacefully, and he'd want someone to tell him why he was in the wrong ("He has as much right to speak his mind as you do").

I would like to believe that something in my father's actions spoke deeply to the assailant. Rather than backing off simply because he'd made a simple (and accurate) calculation of relative force, perhaps something of the justice and grace behind my father's response called to the man's own inner sensibilities, inspiring him to change his intended course of action. Whether or not anything remotely like this actually happened, what I do know is that my father's action called out to *my* inner sensibilities. Although I was too young and hysterical to perceive what was going on at the time, once I grasped it, it produced such a strong sense of ecstasy within me that I've never gotten over the high.

CROSSWALK AMERICA

Photographs by Scott Griessel

PBS television covered the Easter Sunday walk kickoff along with local stations and publications.

Dr. James Forbes preaching at a walk support event at Church of the Beatitudes, Phoenix, Arizona.

Joining hands with fundamentalist Christians at Jesus First Baptist Church.

Mark Creek-Water, Pie Town, New Mexico.

Ray "The Beast Master" Gentry, our RV support driver inside the Pie-O-Neer Restaurant, Pie Town, New Mexico.

Rev. Tracy Dunn-Noland, Fellowship of Believers Church, Hereford, Texas.

Prayer circle before walking in Albuquerque, New Mexico.

Walkers along Highway 60 in New Mexico.

Meighan Pritchard calling
ahead to our next destination.
With ten cell phones and eight
laptops with wireless Internet
cards between us, we were
wired to the world!

Walkers outside Jesus Radio, Farwell, Texas, where Eric and Rebecca were
interviewed.

Walkers pose with members of Saint Ann's Catholic Church, Bovina, Texas.

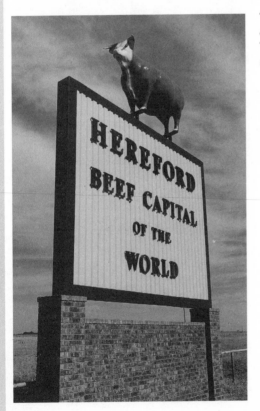

Three quarters of a million cattle inhabit Hereford. Three million live within a fifty-mile radius.

Meighan and Eric take a cool break on a hot day at the Canadian River, Canadian, Texas.

Eric Elnes holding up a steel object found on Highway 50 entering Missouri. The inscription reads, "What moves you?"

Rebecca Glenn walking with Jay Price, event organizer, at a walk support rally in Wichita, Kansas.

Candlelight walk in support of CrossWalk America in Columbia, Missouri.

Child "protestor" behind antiabortion sign in Saint Louis. We were amused to be protested by antiabortion folks, even as we were saddened by their use of children. CrossWalk America takes no specific stand on abortion. It does stand, however, for people's right and responsibility to make decisions about what happens to their own bodies.

Metropolitan Community Church member giving water to antigay protester in Saint Louis.

Rebecca Glenn and Brad Wishon carrying frozen bottles of Gatorade outside Franklin, Illinois.

Art and Soul Café Artistic Director, Lydia Ruffin.

Most Sundays, walkers preached and taught in a variety of churches wherever they were. Here, Eric Elnes preaches at First Presbyterian Church, Springfield, Illinois—the church of Abraham and Mary Todd Lincoln.

Drummers at a walk support rally at First United Methodist Church in downtown Pittsburgh.

Walkers along one of West Virginia's many winding roads.

Merrill Davison (right) and Brad Wishon (left) jubilantly kiss the Washington, D.C., welcome sign, followed by Katrina Glenn close on their heels.

Merrill Davison walking in the
rain in Washington, D.C.,
followed by Eric Elnes.

Bishop John Shelby and Christine Spong join the walk for the last two days.
Bishop Spong published three articles about the walk and spoke at the final
rally in Washington, D.C.

Walking the final mile in Washington, D.C., joined by approximately three hundred friends and supporters. Eric's daughters, Maren and Arianna, are to his right.

Surani Joshua, from the Center for Progressive Christianity, joins us for a day of walking.

Chris Brown filming part of the 300 hours of footage taken of the walk for the film, *The Asphalt Gospel*.

Back end of "The Beast," our 38-foot RV used as a support vehicle.

Each walker wore out three pairs of shoes on average from Phoenix to D.C.

Pentecostal-Turned-Progressive-Christian Bishop Carlton Pearson speaking at the ending rally in Washington, D.C.

Susan Jacobs meets walkers in Podunk Corner with goodies.

7

FAITH IN PODUNK

"WHY ARE YOU FOLKS *walking* across the country?" asked a television news reporter in Amarillo, Texas, fifty miles east of Hereford. "Why not fly or drive or at least bicycle?" People asked us similar questions constantly as we made our way across the country at three miles an hour.

"Sometimes actions speak louder than anything we can say," Rebecca answered the reporter. "For people who believe that the true face of Christianity is compassionate and inclusive, it's time to embody what we believe by 'walking our talk.' Of course, we have to do more than just walking, but it's a start. By walking, we slow down our sixty-five-mile-an-hour lifestyle to walking speed. We get connected to the earth. We have time to think more deeply about issues and have meaningful, unrushed conversations with people we meet. If we as a nation want to overcome the increasing polarization between religious and political liberals, moderates, and conservatives, we need to get to know each other better, have extended conversations, and really listen. Otherwise, we'll end up living from sound bite to sound bite, never understanding the real issues that confront us or how we can move beyond our differences."

As Rebecca answered the reporter, I realized that one of the most surprising and gratifying aspects of our journey to that point was taking exorbitant amounts of time to travel through areas that I normally would have blown through in the blink of an eye driving on a freeway—or missed altogether on the interstates. Small, rural towns seemingly in the middle of nowhere, where people had advised us we'd find nothing interesting and certainly no support, proved instead to be surprising oases of hope and opportunity.

We'd been told that even if we could find support in rural America, traveling there would be an inefficient investment of resources. One urbanite's comment summed up the issues: "Why waste time in towns of a few hundred when you could focus on cities of several hundred *thousand* or more? You're not going to influence the national landscape walking through Podunk, USA."

As the reporter continued to interview Rebecca, I thought back to a number of metaphorical Podunks we'd been through to get to Amarillo. There was Mountainair, New Mexico, for instance, forty-five miles southeast of Albuquerque. With a tiny population and no church interested in providing us hospitality, we had visited a local RV park on the east side of town seeking to rent a campsite and a slot for the thirty-eight-foot RV we used as a support vehicle. When the RV park owner heard about the principles we were walking for, he wouldn't take our money. He insisted that we stay for free.

The next evening, we went out for pizza in Mountainair. Before being seated, we struck up a conversation with a party of eight who were finishing up their dinner. They became quite animated when they found out what we were doing, particularly over our being Christians proclaiming a message that included openness to other faiths, respect for the environment, promotion of the arts, and full equality of LGBT people. After being seated and enjoying some of the best pizza some of us had eaten in years, we went to pay our bill. The waitress told us, "Those folks you were talking to on your way in paid it. They really love your message."

After dinner, a couple of us walked down the street to a "redneck" watering hole. When we tried to pay our bar tab, the bartender said, "The gentleman at the end of the bar paid it already." It was someone we'd conversed with at a state park earlier that day. We talked with him and his friend long into the night about the history of Mountainair, Native American peoples, Spanish conquistadores, faith, and automotive repair.

Our experiences in Mountainair were repeated over and over as we made our way to Amarillo and would continue in various ways all the way to Washington, D.C. Even in places where churches outright refused to support us, people kept appearing who would offer aid and appreciation when they heard about our mission. With few exceptions, no one told us to get out of town. Indeed, the most frequent comment we heard was "Thank you—you're walking for me."

Ironically, a little over a hundred miles beyond Amarillo, we found support in a real Podunk: Podunk Corner, Oklahoma. Combined with all the other experiences, what happened in and around Podunk Corner convinced us that we had made the right choice to spend so much time in rural America. What's going on in Podunk has a lot more to do with the emerging Christian faith in America than most people realize.

Podunk Corner sits at the intersection of U.S. 60 and State Highway 283, between Higgins, Texas, and Arnett, Oklahoma. Higgins and Arnett are "big cities" compared to Podunk, each with around four hundred inhabitants. Podunk's sign, now gone, had officially boasted "Population 4."

Long before walking through the area, our logistics volunteer for Texas, Cati Moreno Serbiak, contacted churches in Higgins, five miles west of Podunk Corner, seeking support. None were willing to offer it. Then, several weeks before we passed through, an inquiry was received at our CrossWalk America Web site from a ranching couple living nearby. They were excited to find that we would be walking just a few miles from their ranch. The couple offered to lodge and feed our entire ten-person crew. "Will they need tents?" Cati inquired. "No, all of them can have their own bed in our ranch house if they don't mind sharing rooms" was the reply.

Cati gladly accepted the offer even as she wondered why ranchers from rural Texas would be so excited about CrossWalk America's presence when the churches clearly were not.

When we arrived, Doris and Robert Akers greeted us warmly in the front yard of their ranch house. By outward appearances, they looked no different than any other ranching couple one would find in rural Texas. Robert was dressed in a denim shirt and blue jeans held up by a large Texas Star belt buckle. Doris was wearing shorts and a white T-shirt with American flags on the front. Though their home is not far from the Texas-Oklahoma border, the Akers leave no doubt which state you are in. The red, white, and blue Texas state flag and Texas star are everywhere—emblazoned on everything from the cow skull hanging outside their front door to the towels hanging in the bathroom.

"We've lived in this same house, ranching this same section of land, for forty-six years," Doris told us. "My grandfather purchased this section in 1906," Robert added. "Next spring it will be recognized by the state of Texas as a Centennial Heritage Ranch."

"Your family's been here a long time!" Meighan replied. "Do you have children?"

"We have four children and eight grandchildren. While our kids were growing up, we also took in thirteen exchange students from eight different countries," Doris answered proudly.

"Looks like you also take in kittens," Meighan added, glancing down at a black-and-white furball tugging at her shoelaces.

"Yes, we adopted a whole litter of strays the other day. They'll be good mousers," Robert observed with a grin.

"I assume you raise cattle too?" I asked.

"I've cut the herd down to just a few hundred head since I semiretired. I also raise a little wheat and milo. Just enough to feed them."

Entering the Akers's home, it quickly became evident that they are not what one might expect in typical Texas ranchers. The bookshelves were full of titles by progressive Christian theologians, biblical scholars, environmentalists, and religious leaders. Their video library contained titles produced by the Southern Poverty Law Center and by environmental and peacemaking groups. "Here's one about the White Train protests," Doris pointed out as a couple of us glanced over their videos.

"What were they?" Merrill asked.

"When you guys walked past Amarillo toward Panhandle, did you see the Pantex Corporation east of town?"

"Yes," Merrill answered, "that's where they used to assemble nuclear warheads."

"Some of us were stopped and questioned by Homeland Security when we walked past Pantex on the highway," Rebecca added.

"Yes, it's a pretty high-security place. But now they're *disassembling* warheads. Before, they were assembling them in secret, hauling the raw materials in and finished products out on white trains that passed right through this area. I helped organize protests as they came through. I'll show you the film later if you like. I'm in it! But for now, why don't you just relax and make yourselves comfortable until dinner.

"I hope you all brought an appetite with you," said Robert. "Doris has been cooking for two days in anticipation of your arrival."

Robert wasn't joking. As we settled in, Doris put the final preparations on a Texas country dinner fit for twice our number. Over dinner the couple told us that they first heard of CrossWalk America through a weekly e-newsletter published by Bishop John Shelby Spong, the author of such books as *Rescuing the Bible from Fundamentalism,* and *Why Christianity Must Change or Die.*

"Are you folks representative of others in the area?" I asked, a bit bewildered.

"Not exactly," Doris sighed. "Most people are pretty conservative. They're not bad people, but I think many regard me as 'that crazy liberal lady.' I just have a hard time keeping my mouth shut when there's so much that needs to be changed in our country."

"Do you attend a church?" asked Meighan.

"Yes, but we're not that happy," Doris responded matter-of-factly. "We love the people but not the preaching. It's like you've got to check your mind at the door and turn the clock back a few hundred years to listen. So we scratch our intellectual and spiritual itch in other ways," she added with a smile.

"Through your books and videos?" I suggested.

"Yes, they help," responded Doris, "but there's this group we're a part of that really keeps us sane." She explained, "A couple of years ago we formed a group that gathers at our home each month to explore progressive faith and values. There's nearly twenty of us now. We read books together or watch videos and discuss them. In this group you can ask the kinds of questions and explore the kinds of issues that people are uncomfortable addressing in church. We've become like family. It helps us feel connected and not so alone."

"These people are from around here?" Rebecca asked.

"Not everyone," Doris responded. "In fact, some drive fifty to seventy miles to get here.

"That reminds me, I know tomorrow is a day of rest for you all, but I'm wondering if you'd be open to a couple of visitors' stopping by. Some people from our monthly group are dying to meet you. Also, two women from Oklahoma City are interested in driving up, if it wouldn't inconvenience you."

"Isn't Oklahoma City several hours away?" Meighan asked.

"Four and a half hours, actually."

"I'm sure we'd all love to visit with these folks," Rebecca responded, "but that seems like a long way to drive just to meet the likes of us! Do they have another reason for being in the area?"

"No, you're the reason," Doris answered. "One of the women has a son who died of AIDS sixteen years ago. Tomorrow would have been his birthday. She told me she couldn't think of a better way to honor her son on his birthday than to meet with Christians walking across the country to promote the values you do."

During our stay at the Akers's home, we enjoyed their gracious hospitality and met the visitors, one of whom bore homemade cookies and all of whom brought bundles of excitement. We talked about faith, ranching, rural Texas, and the environment until all of us were nearing exhaustion. When the visitors left, Doris asked what time we'd be passing through Podunk Corner the next day.

"Around elevenish," Meighan said.

"Perfect," replied Doris. "There's some local folk who have been preparing for a week for your passing by. They've got some refreshments for you."

Sure enough, the next day as we rounded the bend approaching Podunk Corner, we encountered a Subaru Outback parked off to the side of the road. Its owner was Susan Jacobs, a sixty-something woman with long silver hair that's quite dramatic against her black jeans and T-shirt. Her paternal grandparents homesteaded near here.

"Welcome to Podunk Corner!" Susan exclaimed with a bright smile. "We thought you might like something to keep your energy up."

Opening the back of her Outback, Susan announced, "We've got granola bars, homemade cookies, homemade beef jerky, homemade chocolate brownies that are vegan-friendly, and some homemade pumpkin bread that's really good with these jars of homemade apple butter. We've got fresh ice-water and lemonade in these jugs, too. You can take all the leftovers with you in your RV."

We looked over the spread in awe. If we ate nothing but what was in the back of her car for three days, we wouldn't be able to finish it all!

"This is fantastic," exclaimed Katrina, a core walker from Chapman University in Orange County, California. Katrina flew to Amarillo the day after school finished to continue with us to D.C. "Thank you *so much*."

"Hey, we're just delighted that a group like yours would pass our way. It's a real honor."

We had a lot of miles to walk to get to our finishing point for the day, but none of us wanted to leave Podunk anytime soon. We dived into the food and leisurely conversation. Soon a local reporter showed up for an interview. "I'm going to send out a story about you too," Susan noted after the reporter left. "I used to be a journalist, and I'll send an article to all my contacts within a hundred miles of here. We need to get the word out about Christians walking for such positive values. Most people don't know people like you exist, and there's such a hunger out here."

After eating and drinking far more than we could walk off, Scott lined the walkers up for a photo that he later posted on the CrossWalk America blog to announce our entrance into Oklahoma. "Who would have imagined that we'd find all this in Podunk?" he exclaimed.

Little did we know, but this would not be the end of our surprises in the area. More were waiting for us a few miles down the road in Arnett.

Arnett

We stopped for the day a few miles outside of Arnett, carefully marking our end point as usual before driving into town. With a population the size of Higgins, Arnett is no metropolis. Economically, it appears a bit better off, however, with a developed town square in which shops, offices, and a couple of restaurants surround a historic red-brick courthouse.

When we pulled up to the United Methodist Church of Arnett, our host church, we immediately had the impression that the church and its pastor were a bit different from most. The sign out front read, "Laugh a lot. It's like mental jogging!"

This is advice that pastor Jene Miller not only preaches but also practices. He takes people seriously, but not too seriously. With a wry smile and an enthusiastic demeanor, Jene greeted us wearing a Kiwanis hat with a one-dollar bill folded and glued to one side. When asked about the purpose of the dollar, Jene replied, "I've never met a Kiwanian who doesn't get all excited about dollars. I wear this so they'll like me."

When complimented on the ornate cross hanging from his neck, Jene exclaimed, "I wear this to scare off Christians who want to convert me. It's kind of like warding off vampires with garlic. They think I'm Catholic or Madonna [the pop singer] and run away." No one was immune from Jene's jesting. When I told Jene I'm a United Church of Christ minister, he responded, "God don't care about denominational or faith boundaries. She's Jewish."

We were hooked. After yet another enormous dinner prepared lovingly by church members, several of us talked with Jene and a couple parishioners well into the night. Although Jene represents an older generation of Christians, getting to know him is like peering into the future of Christian faith at the grass roots. It's earthy, welcoming, intellectually honest, open-ended, and compassionate.

"Christianity's not about getting into heaven," he observed. "It's about getting heaven into you. People tell me they're waiting for Jesus to return. I tell them, 'If you're looking for Jesus, come to my church. He's right here!'"

"Who is Jesus, for you?" asked Scott.

"People ask me, 'Do you believe Jesus is God?'" Jene responded. "The real question that interests me isn't 'Was Jesus like God?' but 'Is God like Jesus?' I think God's a lot like Jesus. At least, I keep finding God the more I get to know Jesus.

"We need to get away from printing passports to heaven," Jene continued. "In the first place, nobody will accept them if we print them. And I think I already got one on my baptismal certificate. Anyway, God was never baptized, so I don't think God's terribly interested in that either. What God's interested in is *compassion*. God challenges us to grow by caring, not by owning or even by doing. Caring will lead us to do what will fulfill us and enable our lives. That's the paradigm shift that's happening in Christianity right now—moving from passion to compassion and through compassion discovering what kind of person we were created to be."

"Do you think this paradigm shift is enough to save the mainline church from further decline?" Scott asked.

"The way I see it," Jene observed, "the institution of the church may be dying, but the church is more alive now than ever. The true church is made up of people led by the Spirit. The church is being brought to life in our time. Collapse is actually waking the church up. We're no longer an institution but a *mission,* which means we've got to ask, 'What are we here for?' To me, we're here to help people become what God created them to be. This is the great gift of this day. Yes, the church is going to go through some agony, but while the institutional church is dying, it's spreading seeds. These seeds will grow up into a whole different church—no, a whole different *system* but the *same* church. The symbols won't get in the way because we'll be busy making a new system, a system that will eventually solidify into a whole rigid system that will need to die and become new again."

Jene's observations reminded me of the difference between tradition and traditionalism. A *tradition* is a living thing whose essence remains the same over time even as its outer forms—its rituals, symbols, language, aesthetics, and so forth—constantly change. *Traditionalism* arises from a confusion of outer form with inner essence. Traditionalism locks tradition into one particular, rigid manifestation associated more strongly with social custom than living spirit. When time and spirit move on, anything tied too strongly to one particular manifestation of spirit breaks apart like a boat tied to its moorings in a hurricane.

"I had this big-city church once," Jene reminisced. "It was high-steeple and high-pressure but not necessarily high-faith. One of my parishioners had a friend for whom morality was tied to modesty. If you are immodest, you are immoral, even if the immodesty is accidental. One day, my parishioner's daughter was walking home from school with his friend's daughter. They both got flashed by some man in a trench coat. My parishioner's daughter went home laughing and joking. His friend's daughter was so distraught she had to go into therapy. These were two kids the same age, growing up in the same town, yet they had a totally different reaction. Like anything so rigid, when it gets hit, it collapses."

Turning to Jene's parishioners, Scott asked, "Why do you folks come here?"

"It's because of Jene," one responded immediately. Another added, "We feel like we can ask any question, express any doubt, explore any aspect of faith or life, and Jene will take us seriously. We're not condemned for having doubts. We're set on a journey."

"A journey," the first added, "that values both the heart and the mind."

As we continued talking into the night, I noticed a sign posted on a wall of the sanctuary listing the previous Sunday's worship attendance: forty people. That translates into perhaps eighty active members. I thought to myself, "What a shame that just eighty souls regularly experience the kind of faith embodied by this church." Then I realized that it's twenty percent of the whole town of Arnett! This little church had a bigger witness in the community than it seemed.

Arnett United Methodist Church became part of the great untold story we kept discovering all the way across America. Many Christians who yearn for a more inclusive, compassionate, and intellectually honest form of faith feel so alone, like they're the only ones who feel the way they do, but they're not. Even in the smallest towns in the most conservative areas, many people are not only sympathetic to these same desires but also actively gathering in house fellowships, book groups, and unsung churches around the country—or are yearning mightily to do so. I wondered how such a phenomenon could be so vast and yet so hidden. These are certainly not the Christians who get noticed by the media! "Funny," I thought to myself, "fifty years from now we're likely to look back and see that the angry, intolerant Christians who get most of the publicity ultimately represent a dying tradition while those who are on the forefront of something wonderful are the last ones the media are interested in. The media are so busy covering the funeral that they're missing the resurrection!"

Noticing the World

One of the reasons we discovered so much interest in the kind of inclusive, compassionate faith embodied by the Phoenix Affirmations in the literal and metaphorical Podunks of America is that we took the time to look. Ignoring the skeptics who insisted that we would be "wasting time" in areas that were small and "hopelessly conservative," our gut instincts told us otherwise, and we're glad we followed them. We wondered how our detractors could be so confident in their opinions, given that they were apparently so busy being "efficient" in metropolitan areas that they never even talked to anyone in the countryside.

AFFIRMATION 11

[Christian love of self includes]
Caring for our bodies and insisting on taking time
to enjoy the benefits of prayer, reflection, worship,
and recreation in addition to work.

Affirmation 11 has to do with how we spend our time. To many people, taking time out of their busy lives to pray and play, to reflect and worship, is a "waste" and "inefficient." What many contemporary Americans have yet to discover is what the Christian mystics as well as contemporary people from other cultures have always known. One rarely discovers what really matters in life without "wasting" a lot of time in pursuits that have little directly to do with getting ahead in life. In a sense, we must spend time in our spiritual Podunks if we are ever to comprehend what on earth we're doing in Pittsburgh.

In his book *Sabbath: Restoring the Sacred Rhythm of Rest,* Wayne Muller tells of a South American tribe that took a long walk. Day after day the people would march along "when all of a sudden they would stop walking, sit down to rest for a while, and then make camp for a couple of days before going any farther. They explained that they needed the time of rest *so that their souls could catch up with them.*"[1]

Can you relate? If you Google this story on the Internet, you'll find it cited in scores of sermons and lectures encouraging busy people to slow their lives down and take time for rest and relaxation—essentially, encouraging people to take Affirmation 11 seriously.

Yet there's a curious dynamic in the story that most people miss. That South American tribe wasn't living life in the fast lane. When its members needed to travel a long distance, walking was likely the only option they had. Their universe turned at three miles per hour, not sixty-five. So why did their souls have a hard time keeping up with them? Isn't that *our* problem, not theirs?

Having now participated on a "long walk" like the South American tribe, I hear this story quite differently than I did before. It now seems quite obvious why the tribe would have to slow down and even stop for a couple of days moving so slowly. It has nothing to do with physical exhaustion or depletion of any kind. It has to do with fullness. Soul-fullness.

When you slow your life down from breakneck speed to walking speed, something strange happens that is both wonderful and terrifying. You notice things. You notice the temperature of the air, the direction of the breeze, the subtle changes of flora and fauna as you move along. You experience nearly everything in the natural world around you—the one you *thought* was so familiar—as if for the first time. You discover layer after layer of life humming, plodding, and buzzing around you, both human and nonhuman, that had previously gone unnoticed.

Not only this, but when you're walking with others, you begin to converse with them about more than simple trivialities. Gradually, you begin to talk about what matters most in life. You share your hopes and dreams, your trials and tribulations. You reveal your growing edges—and sometimes they are revealed for you!

As you begin to interact on this level, some of the things you thought were important start seeming trivial—particularly things related to material or social success—while things you thought were trivial move center stage—particularly things having to do with relationships and one's spiritual quest.

In addition, almost everyone you meet along the way is new to you. And because you're moving slowly, you actually have time—and want to take time—to talk with these people. You hear about their hopes and dreams and discover in some cases how strikingly similar they are to your own and in other cases how amusingly different they are. Either way, you begin to realize that each and every person you meet is tremendously *interesting*. Every one has stories to tell that may rock your world and others that may help you locate missing pieces of it.

As you move along meeting people, experiencing the natural world, building experiences with your fellow walkers, and actually taking the time to process your interactions, all these experiences begin coalescing inside you. What happened in Albuquerque bounces off what happened in Chanute, Kansas, which bounces off what happened in Kansas City. Life moves onto a deeper plane as more of your experiences, like synapses in the brain, fire and become connected to one another.

Patterns emerge that both confirm and challenge your perceptions of reality. Why haven't you noticed them before? Are you going crazy? Or has the world gone crazy? Has the world spent too much time in the fast lane to notice what's going on?

I am not in the least bit surprised that the South American tribe should need to stop and rest every few days while moving so slowly. Without question, their souls became too full to keep up with them! They needed time to readjust their paradigms—just like we did. They needed to face the stereotypes they'd held about others, as we did, and to reconsider what's important in life. Based on our experience, I suspect as well that they needed time to celebrate. They needed to celebrate the fact that some of their deepest intuitions that started them walking in the first place held firm while everything else shifted around them. When so many things get turned topsy-turvy, the ideas, understandings, and perceptions that *don't* get overturned become all the more noticeable and wondrous.

For us, the intuition that remained rock solid throughout twenty-five hundred miles of walking, never shifting whether we were in rural or urban areas, red states or blue states, religiously "conservative" areas or "liberal" ones, was this: that there are more than enough people in this country who resonate with the kind of faith represented in the Phoenix Affirmations to shift the course of Christianity for the next five hundred years in a more inclusive, compassionate direction. You just have to take the time to notice them and then give them a reason to come out.

Affirmation 11 is about slowing life down enough to actually live it. It's about opening our eyes to the amazing things God is doing right in front of us that we've rushed past too fast to see. It's about taking time to open our ears to hearing our neighbors' hopes and dreams and our hearts to the hopes and dreams of God. Affirmation 11 is ultimately about changing the world by noticing it.

University of Missouri student Jason Ksepka takes walker Meighan Pritchard
on a campus tour.

8

SILENCE OF THE
(CHRISTIAN) LAMBS

IF YOU WERE TO ASK ten people in America what faith they identify with, if any, how many say they are Christian? Four? Six? Three? It may seem hard to believe, but nearly nine call themselves Christian.[1] Of course, if nine in every ten Americans were active participants in a faith community, people would be spilling out of the churches into the streets.

Given that this is far from the case in most churches, a second question is suggested: How many of the ten would say they've been to church lately, if asked? The answer is four.

Still, if four truly attended church regularly, people might not be spilling into the streets, but nearly every church in America would be packed. Thus, a third question is suggested: Of the four who claim they go to church, how many actually do so? The answer is between two and three.

Let's be optimistic and take the higher number, three. This means that of the nine in every ten Americans who say they are Christian, no more than a third actually participate in a faith community with any regularity. Apparently two-thirds of all Christians in America feel so alienated or so indifferent or see church as so irrelevant that they aren't showing up. I call these Christians the "spiritually homeless." Many of those we met on our walk across America told us they have faith but had found no spiritual community in which they felt at home practicing it. They felt spiritually disconnected and alone.

When you spend mile after mile on the road walking, as we did, far away from home, eating every meal in a different location and sleeping every night in a different bed, you can't help but identify with homelessness of all kinds, physical and spiritual. Physically, you yearn to sleep in your own bed. You hunger for certain foods you haven't had in a while. You look forward to places you can rest and put your feet up for more than a day at a time. You look forward eagerly to showering off the sweat and grime built up from the day and putting on freshly laundered clothes.

We felt the same way spiritually at times. Even though we were hosted by a hundred and fifty different churches and seminaries between Phoenix and Washington, D.C., we all yearned to be back among the people we knew and loved in our home churches. No matter how engaging the worship was or how interesting the people or how enthusiastically we were welcomed, we continually sensed a void we knew could only be filled by returning not just to our biological families but also to our faith family. Our experience tapped us into the basic feeling of loneliness and alienation that many Christians experience all year long, not simply on a 141-day walk.

The experience sometimes gave rise to a sense of anger and despair over the ways churches frequently contribute to the problem of spiritual homelessness. Many churches display great interest in reaching out to the physically homeless, hosting food pantries, operating soup kitchens, and raising quite a bit of "mission money" to end or soften their plight. But many of these same churches show comparatively little interest in reaching out to those who have no spiritual home.

Of course, some churches attend only to spiritual homelessness and never to homelessness of the physical sort. They seek to "save the lost for Jesus," delivering them passports to heaven with every new confession of faith. Yet this kind of outreach actually creates more spiritual homelessness than it resolves. For each "born-again" convert, it seems, there are ten who have left the faith community, turned off by a God who would torture people for eternity for not believing or acting in a certain way.

In light of the current state of affairs in many churches, it is no wonder that two-thirds of American Christians are adrift. As we inched our way across the country, many people spoke to us of their hopes and dreams for the Christian faith and also their deep concerns. The more we listened, the more we came to understand spiritual homelessness as stemming less from a lack of faith as from a lack of exposure to the kind of faith for which people yearn.

At Home with the Spiritually Homeless

We stayed in the home of three spiritually homeless people in Columbia, Missouri. As gay men, all of whom grew up Christian but no longer associate with organized religion of any sort, they are part of a population that experiences a high degree of "spiritual homelessness." Whatever one's feelings about homosexuality, their story teaches us much about both the plight of the spiritually homeless and the complicity of both liberal and conservative Christians in making them so.

Dean is a tall, strikingly handsome individual with a gracious demeanor, a sharp wit, and a passion for environmental conservation. For the past year, he has rented out a room in his home to Jason, a gay college student double-majoring in forestry and in fisheries and wildlife management at the University of Missouri. Jason's boyfriend, Eric, also a college student, is a frequent visitor.

Before we arrived in Columbia, there was a buzz in the community about CrossWalk America's coming to town, particularly on certain e-mail lists. Although Columbia was not directly on our walk route, we stayed there for three nights as we passed south of town, holding a special candlelight walk hosted by the Columbia Christian Church (Disciples of Christ) on one of those evenings. Seeing one of the e-mails in his inbox, Dean became intrigued. He didn't go to church himself, but he was eager to help any group calling itself Christian that is openly inclusive of gays, lesbians, bisexuals, and transgendered people. He made two of the rooms in his home available, and Rebecca and I went to stay with him.

Before we arrived, Dean was nervous, especially since he'd learned we were CrossWalk America's presidents. We learned later that he was expecting us to look and act more like a priest and a nun than like everyday people. He wasn't sure how he would be expected to act around us.

Shortly after we got settled in Dean's home, Jason arrived from a long day at school. Standing at least a foot shorter than Dean and slighter of build, Jason nevertheless conveys a strong sense of presence. With short, jet-back hair, mustache and beard, and dark brown eyes that could best be described as fiery despite their color, Jason comes across with a prophetic air. He is at once sincere and yet a bit stand-offish, like he's deeply interested in you yet skeptical as well. He could be a clean-cut version of John the Baptist.

As soon as we were introduced to Jason, he surprised us by stating upfront, "Please don't take this personally, but I hate Christians. I mean, I respect your right to believe what you do, and I'm really impressed by your commitment to walking across the country for what you believe in, but my experience of Christianity hasn't been a good one. It hasn't been good for the people I hang out with, either."

Being a gracious and good-natured host, Dean's eyes widened as he tried to make light of Jason's remark, fearing that Rebecca and I would take offense. It wasn't necessary. What both of us sensed from Jason more than anything was his sincere desire for all of us to be real with each other. He didn't want to play games all weekend, pretending to appreciate a faith he wanted no part of.

"No offense taken," Rebecca readily responded with a chuckle.

"If we weren't angry over certain things Christians are standing for these days, we would never have taken a step out of Phoenix," I added.

Jason immediately lightened up. "Do you like tea?" he offered. "I'm not going to be home tonight, but I've got all kinds of teas in my room—you can help yourself to them if you're interested."

"I love tea," I said, as much for the sake of affirming any common ground we might share as personal interest in tea.

Jason took us into his room and showed us his stash, which could rival the offerings of any teahouse: jasmine, chamomile, yerba mate, and even more exotic kinds. More striking than his tea collection, however, were all the creatures that keep him company. In various cages, terrariums, and aquariums, Jason had a veritable zoo of reptiles, rodents, and bugs. As he introduced us to each one, his passion for the natural world in all its beautiful and ugly manifestations became clear.

Over the years, I have heard many people claim that they value every creature's life as highly as their own. Most of them have struck me as being little more than romantic or sentimental idealists. With Jason, though, you know you're in the presence of a true believer in the glory exhibited by all living things. His world revolves around the creatures inside and outside his home.

As we were being introduced to the creeping and slithering creatures inhabiting Jason's room, Eric showed up. In contrast to Jason, Eric is quiet and unassuming. He is friendly but shy. Soon they were gone for the evening.

The next day, Rebecca and I walked together on the morning crew, reflecting on our evening at Dean's.

"I wonder what makes Jason so angry," Rebecca pondered. "I'd imagine that as a gay man, he's got plenty of reason, but there's a sense of rage I haven't seen very often."

"I agree," I answered.

"I wonder if those guys would go out for coffee or a beer tonight. It would be interesting to hear more from all of them."

"I vote for beer," I replied. "I heard there's a good brew pub in town, and Jason's so high-strung, I'd hate to see him on caffeine!"

Much to our delight—and a bit to our relief—the guys readily agreed to join us for a drink that evening at the Flat Branch Pub and Brewing

Company. Over creamy stouts and hoppy pale ales—and soda for Eric—we talked about family histories, religion, and life in Columbia.

"I grew up Catholic," Jason volunteered. "I participated in church up through confirmation, but I've never really considered myself a Christian. I found my sense of spirituality in the environment and in science. I think scientific truth and spiritual truth are basically the same. I started drifting away from the church when I'd had enough of Christians claiming to have dominion over the earth. They treat creation without reverence. They think that only human beings really matter to God. So by the time I was eighteen and finally admitted to myself that I was gay, I was already pretty far from Christianity. The gay thing was simply the last straw."

"What was it like to 'come out' as a gay man to Catholic parents?" I asked.

"That wasn't really a big issue. My parents love people unconditionally and without judgment. Religion works for them. But they're pretty silent about their beliefs. They get what they need from their faith and don't try to change others. This wasn't the case for Eric, though."

"What was *your* experience?" Rebecca asked Eric.

"Well, my parents are pretty conservative Christians, and my dad's Mexican. There's a lot of machismo in Mexican culture. When I came home for Easter last year with Jason, I told them I was gay. My dad and I nearly had a fistfight. It was pretty ugly. We had to leave. Things have been pretty strained ever since. My mom and I still talk, though," Eric added.

"The thing is," Jason continued, "neither of us has an issue with people who believe differently than we do about homosexuality. If they believe it's a sin, fine. If they thank God every day for not making them gay, that's their concern, not ours. But when Christians start insisting that *we* have to believe like they do, and then do everything in their power to take away our rights and make our lives miserable, *that's* where the problem lies."

"Tell them about Jed," Dean chuckled, attempting to lighten Jason up without changing Jason's train of thought.

"Ahhhh, Jed." Jason exclaimed, his eyes flashing with white heat tempered by the slightest suggestion of sympathy and perhaps a touch of amusement.

"Jed is our campus evangelist. He takes over the speaker's circle near the center of campus and roars at us. I don't think there's a thing any student is doing that he approves of."

Now Jason was smiling fiercely. "He'll point his finger at women who walk by, screaming, 'You college women are worse than whores! Whores at least *sell* their goods. You *give* them away!'"

"Quite a guy," Rebecca commented. "I take it he's not too keen on gays, either."

"Jason stops and argues with him," said Dean. "Jason asks question after question, running circles around Jed's logic. He draws Jed into all kinds of contradictions, but I think Jed enjoys the challenge."

"Jed thinks Jason's straight," Eric added with a wry smile. "He thinks Jason's just an interested straight guy who likes a good debate."

"And he's right about half of that statement," Jason grinned.

"I think Jason gets some sort of perverse joy out of debating Jed," Dean winked.

"I'll admit, I respect Jed's passion. He has the courage to speak even though he's Loony Tunes. The thing is, Jed will yell at you and tell you you're going to hell day after day, but at least you know he's personally committed to saving you from something he considers horrible. I don't mind Jed because Jed doesn't use his beliefs to try to take away our rights. He doesn't go to the school administration to try to have your enrollment revoked, even if he thinks you're 'worse than a whore.' He doesn't stand there with petitions to amend the constitution to prevent people in love from marrying. He doesn't show up at the state legislature arguing that you shouldn't be able to visit your partner if he's in the hospital or that your health care benefits should be taken away."

"And he doesn't picket funerals," added Eric, quietly.

"Don't get me started," Jason glared.

"Started?" prodded Rebecca.

"Listen," Jason responded, "I'm really worried I'm going to offend you or get too upset for my own good. I work on that—my anger. I find myself getting so angry and rigid in my beliefs that if I'm not careful, I become little different than they are. If I become as angry and full of rage as those other guys, I'm just as much a part of the problem. I don't think Christianity is a bigoted religion. But sometimes Christianity and bigotry become so entangled that it's hard to tell them apart."

Jason was getting wound up. "What really gets me is not the funeral protesters but all the other Christians who stand silently by and let them do it. The protesters hold up signs like 'GOD HATES FAGS' and 'MATTHEW SHEPHERD IS BURNING IN HELL,' all in the name of Jesus, and other Christians don't utter a word of protest."

Of course, Rebecca and I were both aware of Christians who actively seek to counter such voices, but we were also keenly aware of how little enthusiasm there is to offer a countervoice even among progressive Christian groups who believe in LGBT equality. Many of these groups say they don't want to alienate so-called Middle America by taking a vocal stand, preferring to retain influence in other areas. Other groups feel they'd lose some of their core constituency if they aired their views. We continued to listen.

"I just don't get it," Jason continued. "For years, Christians have remained silent over gay-bashing funeral protesters, but now that these same people have started protesting *military* funerals, suddenly everyone's up in arms calling for constitutional amendments and the like.

"And when protesters have held up signs outside the legislature claiming 'AIDS IS GOD'S ANSWER TO HOMOSEXUALITY,' people were silent then, too. What's with that? You know that if these protesters were holding up signs proclaiming 'CANCER IS GOD'S ANSWER TO SMOKING' or 'DIABETES IS GOD'S ANSWER TO OBESITY,' Christians would be coming out of the woodwork to stop them."

"No one ever stands up to offer a positive alternative?" I asked, wondering if he was aware of any of the countervoices within Christianity.

"If they do, their voice is so small that we never hear of it, at least publicly," Jason responded. "Again, I'm not saying that all Christians are bigoted. I know a number of Christians who are privately open and accepting of homosexuals. They just never speak up. We even know pastors in this town who are accepting of us, but they never preach their belief in the pulpit. Not one word."

"How do you know?" I asked.

"A couple of them have told me so," Jason replied. "And we've got friends in their churches who tell us the subject never comes up. The pastors are too afraid of people in their congregations who would get upset.

"So I ask you," Jason continued, "how can you Christians expect me to give my life to a faith that won't give its life to me?"

My stomach sank. I took a sip of beer, and as the conversation continued, my thoughts went back to an incident in Kansas a week earlier. I was visiting with a pastor over lunch at a CrossWalk America event. He was telling me that he had recently retired from full-time ministry and was currently serving as a part-time interim minister for a small, progressive congregation. "I'm having the time of my life," he told me. "I'm preaching better than I ever have and enjoying my ministry more than ever. I'm just having a ball."

"That's great," I affirmed. "Why is it so much better? Is it because you're only working part time?"

"No," he responded. "In fact, in this church, I kind of wish I was working full time. The difference is that in this church I can say what I really believe. I don't have to step around touchy subjects. I don't have to pull my punches. The congregants embrace it all. I feel like I can finally be me."

"This is different from your last church experience?" I asked, remembering that he'd served his last church for twenty years.

"Oh, you bet," he replied with a sigh. "There are people in that congregation that would have had my hide if I preached like I'm doing now. I could never be myself."

As lunch was ending, a parishioner from his former church walked in and spotted him. Grinning from ear to ear, she strode up to us. "Pastor!" she exclaimed.

He introduced her to me, adding that "she's one of my former parishioners."

Turning to me, the woman beamed, "But he'll *always* be *my* pastor."

I wanted to respond, "No ma'am. He's *never* been your pastor. In twenty years he's never told you what he really thinks is important. He's never stretched your thinking. He's never moved you to look beyond yourself to really embrace your neighbor. He's never offered you the ecstasy of discovering a God who is so much bigger and more gracious and loving than you ever imagined. He's never *trusted* you enough to have an authentic relationship with you or your congregation."

Instead I replied, "How nice."

I knew that it would have been inappropriate of me to have spoken my mind to this pastor's former parishioner. It wasn't my place, and in any case, my point would have gotten lost in my rudeness. (For all I knew, she could have been one of those who would have "had his hide.") Besides, who was I to judge this pastor? I have been in his shoes before in my own ministry at times.

Sitting in the Flat Branch Pub and Brewing Company that night with Dean, Jason, and Eric, hearing their stories of Christian silence in the face of bigotry practiced in the name of Christ, and experiencing viscerally their pain and sense of betrayal particularly from that silence, I felt an inexplicable sense of relief simply to say, "I'm sorry."

The next morning, we were surprised to find Dean, Jason, and Eric in the church where I was preaching. They came to the evening event there as well. At their home later that evening, we all hung out, laughing and joking together until after midnight. Before retiring for the evening, Jason asked what time we'd be leaving the next morning. He wanted to make breakfast for us.

"Oh, don't bother," Rebecca groaned. "We have to be out of here by seven."

"That's fine," Jason replied. "If I get up at five, I can have my special homemade biscuits and gravy on the table by six-thirty."

"Really, you don't have to do that," I said. "We've got granola bars and fruit to tide us over until lunch. You should all sleep in. We'll let ourselves out without waking you up."

"It's really not a problem," Jason insisted. "I'd like to do it."

"His biscuits and gravy are the best," Dean added with a smile.

The next morning we discovered that they really were the best. How could anything made with so much care and enthusiasm not be?

We've stayed in contact with this household since the walk ended. We've learned that as a result of CrossWalk America's time there, Dean has become active in the Christian faith community, not as "a believer" but as a supporter of progressive Christians who might try to raise an alternative vision to the bigotry they've seen against the LGBT community. Jason still wrestles with anger but says he will never forget our visit to Columbia. "I don't share your faith," he has told us, "but I think we may share the same God."

AFFIRMATION 5

[Christian love of neighbor includes]

Engaging people authentically, as Jesus did, treating all as creations made in God's very image, regardless of race, gender, sexual orientation, age, physical or mental ability, nationality, or economic class.

Silence, Reconciliation, and the Three Mothers

If more pastors and laypeople took Affirmation 5 seriously, I have little doubt that many of the spiritually homeless would find a home in faith communities across America. I am not referring only to spiritually homeless homosexuals. I have in mind anyone whose beliefs and practices do not reflect those of an often small but vocal group within many churches.

I'm thinking, for instance, of an attorney we met at a coffee shop in Canadian, Texas. He quietly left church after twenty years of faithful service because every time he questioned the historicity of certain events in the Bible—the same ones most mainstream biblical scholars also question—he was made to feel like an unfaithful heathen by certain members. Many of his peers who silently harbored the same doubts advised him not to "rock the boat." They insisted, "The church can't afford division." So he left as silently as his friends had been in the face of conflict.

I'm thinking, too, of the countless women who have been denied leadership roles in the faith community, ethnic minorities who have been treated as "tokens" or ignored altogether by racial majorities in churches, and youth who are rarely given the opportunity to do more than carry on what an older generation has established. Frequently on the walk we encountered people who were hurt as much or more by the *silence* of churches and church members as they were the by what some were actively proclaiming.

While some of the spiritually homeless, like Jason, do not shrink from telling people why they've left the church, most quietly fade away, like the attorney, without so much as a whisper. Why should they speak out when everyone is demanding their silence? Usually, it seems that those who are most stridently intolerant are the ones whom people bend over backward to please. They're the ones who get noticed. While church members strive so hard to hang on to these folks, they overlook the many others who slip quietly out the back door when they get no support or feel like they're the ones with the problem. Given the silence of the Christian lambs in the face of vocal opposition, do we honestly wonder why six in every ten Americans have fallen away from faith communities?

Almost to a one, churches we encountered on our journey that were growing in both numbers and spirit were ones that had finally decided to let go of their fears. They were not intolerant toward the vocally intolerant in their midst. They had simply lost their *fear* of them.

Just outside Kansas City, for instance, we encountered three mothers who attended a church that had lost its fear of intolerance—even the types of intolerant people they themselves had been. These three women had attended a Bible study on homosexuality as part of the church's consideration of seeking "Reconciling" status (the United Methodist term for a congregation declaring itself open and affirming of LGBT people). Each woman felt strongly that homosexuality was a sin and attended the study feeling that she would come away confirmed in her views. All three were surprised to learn that there are only six passages in the entire Bible that could be construed as having anything directly to say about homosexuality. At the end of the study, in which each passage was studied in depth, one mother exclaimed to the group, "I guess I owe my son an apology."

"Why?" everyone responded.

"Because he's gay," she confessed. "For years we've been estranged over the issue, and now I'm convinced that *I've* been in the wrong, not him."

The group was shocked. No one knew she had a gay son.

Emboldened by this woman's confession, a second mother spoke up. "My son is gay too!"

"What?" people exclaimed. No one had a clue about her son, either.

"OK, since everyone is confessing," added the third mother, "I must tell you that I have a gay son too."

That day no one was more in shock than these three mothers. They had all been friends for many years, often serving on the same church boards and committees together. All that time, they never knew about each other's gay children. Each woman was too embarrassed to talk about what she had considered her son's "sin."

Now these three mothers visit other churches telling their story. They assert that it's just as important for heterosexual people who are open and affirming of gay people to "come out of the closet" about their beliefs as it is for gay people themselves to do so.

Their story reminds me of something William Sloane Coffin once observed in an open letter to the Conference of Catholic Bishops several years before he died. Coffin asserted, "For Christians, the problem is not how to reconcile homosexuality with scriptural passages that condemn it, but how to reconcile the rejection and punishment of homosexuals with the love of Christ."[2] To the end of Coffin's statement I would add, "or the church's silence in the face of intimidation by those who most stridently reject any of God's children."

Members of the "First Amendment Players" inside the Saint Alban's Episcopal Church sanctuary.

A LITTLE LIGHT THAT SHINED

FULTON, MISSOURI, a tidy, serene city of just over twelve thousand people located thirty miles east of Columbia, is also the county seat of Calloway County, otherwise known as the Kingdom of Calloway. The county received this latter designation after it pulled a remarkable feat of deception in 1861. When Union troops attacked a neighboring county, residents of Confederate-aligned Calloway County hastily assembled what troops weren't off fighting in other areas of the country to defend themselves. They were far outnumbered. Rather than accept what appeared to be inevitable defeat, residents erected rows of logs to resemble cannons when backlit by campfires. Intimidated by the sight, Union forces hastily consented to a cease-fire agreement and left. From that point on, residents buoyantly proclaimed themselves the Kingdom of Calloway!

Happily, the area later became known for more than Confederate optical illusions. In the mid-nineteenth century, Fulton saw the establishment of a school for the deaf; a women's seminary; a school for orphans, which later became William Woods School for Women; and Westminster College, which later served as the site of Winston Churchill's famous "iron curtain" speech of 1946. Given Fulton's history of educational diversity, it is perhaps ironic that the story we stumbled into starts as a story of educational censorship.

The day after Independence Day, we were walking along the Katy Trail south of Fulton. The Katy Trail is a beautiful "rails to trails" project extending more than two hundred miles through central Missouri. Although most of our walk across the country took place beside highways (which offered great visibility but little shelter from traffic), the Katy Trail afforded us a welcome stretch of isolation from traffic. Even though it was often just a hundred feet from Route 50, its grand trees and dense foliage provided a sanctuary from noise and speeding cars. At the end of the day we drove to Fulton to have dinner at our new host church and split up into home stays.

Little Church in a Big Spotlight

We arrived at Saint Alban's Episcopal Church as dinner preparations were under way. A couple of the men stood outside grilling pork chops and veggie burgers on a gas barbecue. Other members were inside Fellowship Hall brewing coffee, setting out covered dishes, and arranging desserts.

Saint Alban's is a small church. With an average worship attendance of twenty souls, it is not large enough to support a priest. Instead, worship is led by laypeople on all but the first Sunday of each month, when a local priest comes to a number of small parishes to administer the Eucharist.

Over dinner, I casually asked my tablemates, "What are some of the challenges facing Fulton right now?"

The forty-something woman across from me perked up. "There was a big brouhaha this past year at the high school. It blew up so big that the *New York Times* came in to cover it. And after the *New York Times* came, the story went around the world. Talk show hosts from Sweden even flew in to cover it!"

"Oh, really?" I responded. "What happened?"

"Last fall the high school drama department put on a production of the musical *Grease.*"

"That's a fun one," I interjected. "I heard somewhere that it's one of the most popular musicals performed by high schools in America."

"That's right," she said, "and the kids worked superhard. Each night, the auditorium was packed. The night I attended, they received a standing ovation. But last spring, when the drama department was gearing up for a performance of *The Crucible,* the school superintendent yanked the production."

"Yanked *The Crucible* by Arthur Miller?" I asked. "I've heard that that's one of the most popular dramatic productions in high schools right now."

"Yes, it is," she confirmed. "But three people from a fundamentalist church didn't like *Grease,* so the school pulled *The Crucible.* The administrators were afraid of more complaints."

"So the school, in response to religious intimidation by three fundamentalist Christians, censored a play that was written to protest religious intimidation and censorship?" I asked, astonished.

"Exactly. And that's when everything erupted. People couldn't believe that in a town of twelve thousand people, three Christians' complaints could change the curriculum at a public high school. The drama teacher eventually resigned over the whole mess and moved to Saint Louis."

"How sad," I responded.

"Yes it is," she answered with a sigh. Suddenly brightening, she added, "But our church took a stand in the midst of all this. I'm so proud . . ."

"What did you do?"

"We hosted a public reading of *The Crucible*. The woman who's hosting tonight's dinner, Nancy Gilbert, helped organize the whole thing. You should ask her more about it."

I did. What I learned was so interesting that I asked to meet with her and some of the students involved with both *Grease* and *The Crucible* before heading back to the Katy Trail the next day. She readily consented.

The next morning, Scott, Chris, and I gathered in the sanctuary of Saint Alban's with Nancy Gilbert and two students, Torii Davis and Rob Erikson.[1] Torii served on the tech crew for *Grease,* and Rob was an actor. Both participated in *The Crucible* reading hosted by Saint Alban's.

"I think the superintendent didn't want to make people angry," said Rob, regarding the superintendent's decision to pull *The Crucible* from production, "but in the end he made a whole lot of people angry."

"What can you tell us about the complaints about *Grease* that he thought he was responding to?" Scott asked.

"One of the three who originally complained hadn't even seen the play," Nancy noted. "He'd only heard about it secondhand and thought it was inappropriate."

"One of the letter writers complained that Rizzo [a character in the play] wasn't wearing shorts underneath her slip outfit, but she was," insisted Torii.

"The thing is," Rob interjected, "we cut a lot of material out of *Grease,* like all references to marijuana, and still we clearly advertised the play as PG-13. You had to show ID to get in, and you had to have a parent with you if you were under thirteen. The play was very well received every night."

"*Grease* may deal with issues involving drinking, smoking, and sex," said Nancy, "but these issues are all part of our kids' everyday struggles. And it's tame enough that you can watch it on the ABC Family Channel," Nancy added, referring to the network home of Pat Robertson's *700 Club*.

According to the *New York Times,* Fulton High School's superintendent justified his decision to pull *The Crucible* to Wendy DeVore, the drama teacher, by explaining that high school actors "shouldn't do anything on stage that would get a kid in trouble if he did it in a classroom," apparently referring to an adulterous relationship in *The Crucible*. Ironically, one of the things that can get a student in trouble in the classroom is refusing to read *The Crucible*.

"*The Crucible* is required reading for juniors," Torii explained. "We couldn't figure out why we couldn't hold a dramatic production of something that's required reading in English class."

"The set [for *The Crucible*] was already beginning to be built, and the lights had already been angled for the show. All that was left was to assign parts when he pulled it," said Rob.

"We were all so excited to do *The Crucible*," Torii added. "We had read through it in class, and pretty much everyone who had read through it had already been memorizing the parts they wanted."

"Incidentally," Nancy interjected, holding back laughter, "the superintendent said they could do *A Midsummer Night's Dream* instead," referring to Shakespeare's play involving pagan magic and bestiality. "That play is exactly the racy kind of context he thought he was avoiding!"

"That was *soooo* much worse!" Rob added, referring to the content.

"We just kind of giggled," said Torii.

"And you held a reading of *The Crucible* anyway, at the church?" asked Scott.

"Yes, a group of people from Westminster College and William Woods University got together and decided that we should form the First Amendment Players and give a dramatic reading from *The Crucible* to let the public see and decide for themselves what's right. They asked the public library if they could hold the reading there, but that fell through."

"You couldn't hold it at the *library*?" I asked.

"It turned out that the sons of the woman who reserved the room were friends with the school superintendent's sons, so she had second thoughts about the reading," Nancy shrugged.

"A lot of people in school and the community, and a few of the drama students themselves, didn't want to make an issue over it. They said we should just keep quiet and let the whole thing blow over," Rob observed.

"After the library fell through, one of the ladies from our congregation called me and asked if we could have it here. I said, 'Yes, of course.' We read through part of the play and held a public discussion about it afterward."

"Did anyone in your congregation object to Saint Alban's taking a stand like this amid all the controversy?" I asked.

"Some people were nervous," Nancy replied. "They agreed that there was an issue of separation of church and state involved here, and censorship, but they were afraid of making waves. We're such a small church that waves can topple us! But in the end everyone decided it was the right thing to do, and the community response was fantastic. The church was packed. *Nobody* regrets it."

"Interesting," I thought to myself. "Just as Calloway County was declared the Kingdom of Calloway after a few Confederates created an illusion of power that caused the U.S. government to buckle and retreat, so it continued this year with a few letters causing public institutions to cower in fear. But this little church represented a different Kingdom. Their little light exposed the cannons to be logs."

Torii reflected, "Schools and, I guess, libraries now, they're pretty political, so they say, 'Well, we can't do this because such-and-such might happen.' Saint Alban's . . . is a more acceptable place to have a public reading for the community."

"How did you feel when you heard you could read *The Crucible* at Saint Alban's?" Scott probed.

"When I heard the offer to host the production," Torii smiled, "I said, 'I can't believe we're actually going to be able to do this. This is *amazing*. We're finally going to be able to do this after all this trouble and hassle.'"

"It was really weird to have people call you and say you're going to come to a church and read something that just got thrown out from our school," Rob grinned. "It was really awkward at first, but we got used to it real fast. Just knowing that a church just five miles away from here wrote three letters and changed a play in our school . . . and now a church ten minutes from school is inviting us to read *The Crucible*. It was pretty cool."

"I think it was good to hold the reading at Saint Alban's," Torii added, "because the people who complained were Christians and since we performed *The Crucible* in a church, some of them might have thought, 'Well, I guess it can't be that bad.'"

Shortly after visiting Saint Alban's, I wrote on our blog about the church's courage to take a public stand against censorship when public institutions buckled in the face of religious intimidation. "How interesting," wrote someone from Saint Louis, a hundred miles to the east. "We in Saint Louis never heard about the Saint Alban's production in the media, just the initial ban and the teacher's resignation over it."

"Yes," I thought. "The media rarely seem to report the stories where people shine a light in the darkness. When it comes to religion, they are far more interested in reporting on the darkness, which gives the darkness more power when it's the exclusive focus."

In hindsight, the story of Saint Alban's reminds me that while the rest of the world may have only heard of the darkness, what is most important is that the people of Fulton knew that a light shined there and the people of Saint Alban's were a part of it. In the opening words of the Gospel of John, the writer observes regarding Christ, "The light shines in the darkness and the darkness did not overcome it" (John 1:5). To my knowledge, the media weren't much interested in that story either, but that didn't stop it from changing the world.

The Wall That Unites

To some, what the members and friends of tiny Saint Alban's Episcopal Church did by holding a public reading of *The Crucible* may be a courageous but not particularly noteworthy way of shedding the light of Christ in a darkened world. They may consider freedom of speech to be a high ideal, but not as high as preaching the Gospel of Jesus Christ. Still others may wonder what stake Christianity has in maintaining the wall of separation between church and state in the first place, which is ultimately what was affirmed by the church's action. After all, it is neither a law nor a commandment in the Bible.

Yet if these concerns are reflective of yours, I invite you to consider what the stakes would be if a religion other than Christianity were exercising influence on our public life, particularly in the schools. Would that wall of separation be more welcome then?

AFFIRMATION 7

[Christian love of neighbor includes]
Preserving religious freedom and the church's ability
to speak prophetically to government by resisting
the commingling of church and state.

As I was writing the first few chapters of this book in Sedona, Arizona, I tuned in to a nationally syndicated Christian radio show on which commentators were expressing incensed opinions about what they felt to be the lack of Christian influence on public schools. They decried instances in which teachers had been reprimanded for praying in Jesus' name in their classrooms and in which schools had been forbidden from teaching what they felt to be the Christian doctrine of Creation. Yet when the subject turned to a school curriculum that covers world religions, in which Islam is covered along with Christianity, they accused schools of proselytizing on behalf of Islam. One participant claimed that the Islamic faith is run by demons. Another claimed that covering the central tenets of Islam, however briefly, was enough to turn young children into junior members of the Islamic jihad who would one day kill Americans.

I thought to myself, "Wow, these folks must think Islam is pretty powerful compared to their own faith if the mere mention of it could turn their children into Muslim fanatics who kill in the name of Allah." I wondered what their response would be to a schoolteacher being reprimanded for praying in Allah's name in class. Would they rush to defend the teacher, as they did the Christian one, or would they lead the charge against her?

Given the diversity of religious beliefs in America, maintaining a wall of separation between church and state is part of following Christ's command to love our neighbors as ourselves and to do nothing to our neighbor that we would not have done to us. It's that basic. As the Christian evangelical Tony Campolo has observed regarding American democracy, "A democracy is not where the majority rules. A democracy is where it's safe to be in the minority."[2] Is this not a political articulation of Jesus' command to love our neighbor?

To be fair, it must be acknowledged that many Christians who argue for tearing down the wall of separation between church and state are doing so not out of spite for the principle of loving one's neighbor as oneself but out of their perceived respect for it. They believe that God will torture their non-Christian neighbors in a lake of fire for eternity if they do not convert to Christianity before they die. In many a debate over the separation of church and state this unacknowledged elephant stands in the middle of the room. The elephant has little to do with differing views of political governance. It has to do with differing understandings of salvation. The wall of separation is understood by many Christians as an impediment to saving souls for eternity. It is seen as an impediment to Jesus' command to love one's neighbor as oneself, not an aid. Many Christians thus conclude with the Christian dominionist D. James Kennedy that

> as the vice-regents of [the only true] God, we are to bring his truth and
> his will to bear on every sphere of our world and our society. We are
> to exercise godly dominion and influence over our neighborhoods, our
> schools, our government, our literature and arts, our sports arenas,

our entertainment media, our news media, our scientific endeavors—
in short, over every aspect and institution of human society.[3]

If Christian debate over the separation of church and state is to move
forward, the elephant in the room must be acknowledged. Kennedy and
others believe that Christians should control all aspects of public life because it will result in more Christian conversions. If we are to engage in
meaningful dialogue with those who hold this belief, we must address our
varying understandings of salvation as much as issues of governance. This
is not to imply that everyone must be convinced that God may provide
other paths to humanity besides the Christian one (Affirmation 1). If we
wait for all Christians to agree with Affirmation 1, it may be a long time
before Christians generally agree on Affirmation 7! Rather, we may move
discussion forward by asking how people's understandings of salvation
are most effectively lived out in public life. Non-Christians are not likely
to convert to Christianity simply because Congress says they should. As
the Christian minister Bruce Van Blair asks:

> Do I think that Christians in our time should be working to turn the
> United States into a Christian country? I think it would be a lot better
> if we concentrated on turning the churches into Christian churches. If
> the country protects our rights to worship as we please, why do we
> need more than that? Why is that not enough to be grateful for? We
> need the government to make us be religious? Don't we know yet
> where that leads?[4]

Indeed, even if one believes that all non-Christians will suffer in hell
for eternity, it does not logically follow that laws favoring Christian belief
will result in Christian conversions. One need look no further than Christian history for this to become abundantly clear. During the first four centuries after Christ walked the earth, Christianity witnessed the most
spectacular surge of conversions it has ever seen. This happened during a
time when Christianity was officially illegal and Christians were, in fact,
actively persecuted. It could be argued that one of the surest ways to grow
the Christian faith in our time would not be through turning America into
a Christian nation but by making Christianity illegal!

The bottom line is that people do not convert authentically to any faith
simply because the state tells them to or because they've been pushed into
it. They do so because they meet people who, in their mind, have found
a more compelling path than the one they're on. The best way for mem-

bers of any faith to convert others, therefore, is to practice a truly compelling path—by living more graciously; by embodying a more expansive love of God, neighbor, and self; and by exuding a greater sense of the sacred in everyday life. These things don't happen in Congress. They happen in living, breathing communities of faith.

This is why many Christians who believe there is no salvation outside of Christian faith affirm the separation of church and state alongside those who hold different understandings. They believe that this wall of separation protects their ability to practice (and teach) their faith fully without intrusion by others. While this wall may also protect other faith communities' right to believe and teach something quite different (Christian or non-Christian), they understand that political forces change with the wind. Politics that favor one system of belief one day quite easily favor another system the next. Thus the best chance that the members of any faith community have of truly loving their neighbor as themselves is to ensure that all faith communities have the freedom to practice love of neighbor to the very best of their understanding.

Walkers crossing a bridge on a hot Saint Louis day.

10

ART AND SOUL

"THERE ARE PROTESTERS outside the church!" exclaimed a gray-shirted usher just before the 8:00 A.M. service commenced at Christ Church Cathedral in downtown Saint Louis. "Just what exactly are you preaching on this morning?" the man asked with a wink.

"Religious self-righteousness and intolerance," I laughed. My subject was the years leading up to Israel's exile to Babylon in the sixth century B.C.E., when the religious and political authorities placed increasing restrictions on Israelite worship and practice. The more they tried to force everyone to believe and worship the same way, the more they thought they were pleasing God, yet according to the prophet Jeremiah, God's reaction was just the opposite. Through the prophet, God excoriated the Israelites for being so quick to assume that God was on their side when they were only interested in the *appearance* of faith, not faith itself. What God really wanted, according to Jeremiah, was for Israel to care for the poor, the widows, and the orphans. In Jeremiah's view, the Israelites might just as well have been worshiping the Canaanite god Baal because they worshiped their God, Yahweh, in name only.

"You might find some good sermon illustrations standing outside if you'd care to meet the protesters," someone remarked.

I did. Leaving the entrance of the grand Gothic cathedral, I stepped into the street in my gray preaching robe. Immediately, I caught the eye of ten or twelve protesters. Some were holding up signs protesting same-sex marriage, while others were waving gruesome posters of dead fetuses with antiabortion slogans. One protester wore a black T-shirt proclaiming (affirmatively) that Jesus was "intolerant" and that "homosexuality is a sin, Islam is a lie, and abortion is murder." He called out, "Hey, pastor, are you going to preach lies to the congregation this morning?"

"Why don't you come inside and find out?" I responded. "You're more than welcome to worship with us."

"I only go into churches that preach the gospel," he shouted back, proceeding to ask me how I could "condone the murder of innocent children."

I found his statement puzzling. I had not preached one sermon on the walk about abortion, and CrossWalk America takes no stance as an organization on any specific political issue, including those involving abortion. Through the Phoenix Affirmations, however, we do take a theological stand on the sacredness of the human body and each person's responsibility to make decisions about what happens to his or her body (Affirmation 11).[1] Apparently, Affirmation 11 was close enough for them to figure that we actively condone abortions.

Despite the protesters' hostility, I made my way down the line, shaking hands with those who would accept the offer. One woman, who refused to take my hand, simply shouted Scripture verses to me when I affirmed her right to her beliefs. Later that day, this same woman, in response to Merrill's telling her, "I love you, sister," responded, "I hate you real good."[2]

A child cowered behind a sign proclaiming "In God's court abortion is murder" as I approached with a simple smile and a "Hello, my name's Eric." As I made my way back toward the church, the man in the black T-shirt continued to accost me. "Can you tell us why you encourage women to murder their babies?"

Welcoming Difference

Back inside, I found the congregation more amused than upset by the protesters. Whereas the protesters seemed to need an outlet for their rage, no matter how inappropriate the fit, Christ Church Cathedral, an Episcopal church founded in 1819, has a long history of seeking an outlet for their *joy*. Their numerous social justice and caregiving ministries reflect a core belief that all people are created in God's image. Their buoyant faith drives them to take an inclusive stance toward the poor, the LGBT community, and others who don't fit in well within established religion.

In the mid-1960s, for instance, members recognized that the cathedral's formal Gothic architecture could seem cold and distant to individuals not steeped in their tradition. They removed the cathedral's hard wooden pews, replacing them with padded chairs that could be rearranged to create an open, airy space. They set movable platforms up front that could be cleared out to create space for dance and for musical ensembles. To this day, the platforms are often rearranged for different

Sunday services to create a different atmosphere in each one, ranging from "high church" formal to "low church" casual. Witnessing how much trouble the cathedral goes through to rearrange these giant wooden platforms to accommodate a diverse membership was inspiring. I thought to myself, "If Christians in our country were better known for taking pains to welcome difference rather than protest it, we wouldn't be walking across the country right now."

Christ Cathedral's effort to welcome diverse understandings of worship does not end with modifying pews and platforms. For the past couple of years, the cathedral has made a distinct effort to create sacred space for non-Christians and Christians who have ceased participating actively in any faith community. This effort is embodied in a ministry the church calls Art and Soul Café, which meets on the first Friday evening of each month.

We had heard of the unique ministry of Art and Soul Café long before coming to Saint Louis, so we were delighted when Art and Soul's primary facilitator, Lydia Ruffin, spent the better part of an afternoon with a few of us. Lydia is a fifty-something laywoman with sandy-brown shoulder-length hair and a piercing gaze that reflects sincerity and commitment. As a singer-songwriter and visual artist, Lydia's passion for integrating worship and the arts is fueled by the conviction that people of highly diverse backgrounds may discover common ground and experience the Divine through mutual creative pursuit.

As we conversed together at Eden Seminary, where we were staying for several days while walking through the Saint Louis area, we were impressed by Lydia's sense of awe and wonder over how Art and Soul is changing lives. Her infectious enthusiasm and the success of her ministry are two reasons why the national Episcopal church regularly calls on her to lead workshops around the country for groups seeking to start new churches or revitalize old ones. Their purpose is not necessarily to create copies of Art and Soul but to lift people's vision of worship as a creative pursuit, showing them something "outside the box" in order to pass on insights that can transform the box itself.

"I grew up Southern Baptist," Lydia told us. "I later became a Presbyterian and then an Episcopalian. In between times I wasn't part of any church. I'm a nontraditionalist at heart. I don't mean to say anything pejorative about church or liturgy. I love the Episcopal liturgy, but I often feel like I come into traditional worship, sit down, and tap into only a part of myself. I leave a lot of who I am at the door. Through Art and Soul Café, I feel like I'm honoring all of who I am, in a complete way. I know a lot of people who feel the same."

"What *is* Art and Soul Café," asked Scott. "Is it worship or a café?"

"We call it an interspiritual, interactive evening."

"Interspiritual?" I asked.

"We use the term *interspiritual* because the people who attend come from a wide variety of backgrounds and faiths. We want to signal to people that whether you're Christian or Buddhist or Muslim or just see yourself as a seeker with no particular label, you're welcome. It's not that we're trying to disguise the fact that we're Christian or that we're in an Episcopal Christian church, but we're not trying to get you to become Episcopalian either. We're not even trying to get you to say you're a Christian. We just invite people to come and join with others who are searching for the sacred. In a way, we see Art and Soul Café as a doorway—as a way in for those who have either been hurt by the church or disfranchised in some way. The exit door of Art and Soul may be into our formal Eucharistic service on Sunday mornings, or it may not be. Either way, we're happy to be of help on the spiritual journey."

"So what happens at one of these 'interspiritual' experiences?" Scott asked.

"Each Art and Soul is based on a theme that's both spiritual and concrete, such as finding water in the desert. It lasts around two hours. We set up a casual, cafélike setting for around a hundred and fifty people right in the middle of the sanctuary. We serve dessert and feature different music each time. Sometimes we'll also bring in a speaker who can talk about the theme and lead us in conversation. But we never sit in one place for very long. Each Art and Soul gets people involved in the creative process. We use multimedia, hands-on artistic exercises, movement, and so on, to get people interacting with the theme in creative, multisensory ways.

"For our 'water in the desert' night, for instance, we set up large canvases in four different corners and invited people to paint scenes depicting where they find spiritual water when they thirst. At different points in the evening you'd find ten to fifteen people standing around the canvases discussing the paintings and where they find the sacred in their everyday lives."

"What if you're no good at painting?" I asked, realizing that sixth graders paint better than I do.

Lydia smiled. "People tell us all the time that they're 'not creative' or have 'no artistic ability.' But we've found that everyone can be creative. They just don't realize it and may be scared to try."

"How do you help them discover their creative side?" Scott asked.

"One of the most intimidating things we do regularly is use movement or dance," Lydia acknowledged. "People who aren't used to dancing in worship sometimes freak out when we say we're going to move around a little. So we brought in the Liz Lerman Dance Exchange, a dance company from the D.C. area. Liz's specialty is bringing disparate groups together through dance. We started with people sitting in their seats and asked them to perform a simple movement they may do in their everyday life, like brushing their hair or stretching. Liz was watching while we were doing it. She then chose five of those motions and strung them together. Then she helped us learn the routine. After that, she had us stand up and do it. Finally, she said, 'Now come out, come out into the room, and let's do it together.' I could see the fear in some people's eyes when they were asked to come forward, but for the rest of the evening, people were out there in the middle of the sanctuary in motion. Nearly everyone said they'd had a transformative experience of some sort—even those who had told me, 'I don't dance.' It was wonderful!"

As Lydia was speaking, I thought back to our experience in Arnett, Oklahoma, with Jene Miller, and how he had spoken of the "old guard" in his church. He said you can't just rush past them on the way to a new tomorrow. "You have to dribble," I remembered him saying, using a metaphor from basketball. "You can't let them stop you from moving forward, but you can dribble. Many will come along with you if you move them forward one step at a time." Art and Soul was dribbling!

"Why do you find it so important for people to engage artistically?" I asked.

"We find that it helps people step around their inner censors," Lydia answered without hesitation. "Through the act of creation, they discover surprising insights that would have been closed to them if they had simply sat there and thought about something. People are so used to being observers in church, not participators. When they participate, they tell us, 'I didn't know I felt this way about such-and-such,' or 'I didn't know this emotion was going to come forward,' or 'This got me in touch with something that was kind of out of reach for a while.'"

"Do you consider these Art and Soul Café experiences worship?" I asked.

"Not in the Eucharistic sense," Lydia replied, referring to the practice of holding Communion. "But Communion takes place at Art and Soul in a very tangible and spiritual way. It just comes through different means. We also integrate a fair amount of contemplative prayer. We like to use walking meditation, for instance, and guided meditation. At each Art and Soul we also do something we call Meditations of the People. Throughout the evening, participants are invited to jot down things they would like us to pray for in a special book. At the end of the evening, I integrate their requests in a multimedia piece. It really anchors our time together.

"Of course, what *really* anchors the evening is the Electric Slide," Lydia added with a grin.

"The *what?*" Meighan asked incredulously.

"The Electric Slide," Lydia chuckled. "You know, the line dance people do at wedding receptions and parties."

"For real?" I asked.

"Yes, we all gather up in the chancel," Lydia answered, referring to the formal area where the clergy and choir normally sit at the front of the church. "We get up there and do the Electric Slide. You wouldn't believe how freeing it is to be doing the Electric Slide in this Gothic cathedral right in the chancel. It's a hoot! At the end of the evening, people leave saying, 'I can't believe we did that in church!' And they're not just talking about the Electric Slide. They mean everything that's happened from start to finish—cutting out colored figures for a collage or painting a canvas or dancing. Behind what they're telling us, what they're really saying is, 'I had no idea church could be so much fun. I didn't realize it could touch me in this way.' One thing we hear a lot from newcomers is 'I never thought I'd go back to church again. I didn't even want to come tonight, but I'll be back.' And they do come back."

"Why wouldn't they?" I thought to myself. Art and Soul Café may not be everyone's ideal for a worship experience, but for many of Saint Louis's spiritually homeless, it offers a way of connecting to the sacred that they have not been able to find in more traditional settings. Through Art and Soul Café, they discover they can bring their whole selves into worship, not just the parts they haven't left at the door.

Curiously, through the cathedral's efforts to reach out to those who worship differently than the majority of the congregation, its congregants are discovering ways to reach themselves as well. Through Art and Soul Café's use of the arts, the cathedral is discovering avenues to the sacred that resonate with even the most traditional folks. On a recent Sunday, for instance, the cathedral brought a video projector into the "moderately formal" 9:00 A.M. worship service. In place of the usual Prayers of the People, which includes a long list of names of people for whom the congregation is seeking prayers, the officiants played a multimedia piece made up of photographs the congregation had submitted of these same people. One of the photographs was of a woman for whom the congregation had prayed regularly for nearly ten years but whom few people recognized by name.

"When her face went up on the screen and people finally made the connection with her name," Lydia said, "there was an audible gasp. You would have thought Jesus had just walked into the room!"

Who would protest that?

AFFIRMATION 4

[Christian love of God includes]
*Expressing our love in worship that is as sincere,
vibrant, and artful as it is scriptural.*

The Excesses of Orthodoxy

As noted at the beginning of this chapter, one of the greatest disasters ever to befall ancient Israel, the Babylonian Exile, followed on the heels of one of the most zealous religious reform movements in Israelite history. Ironically, this reform movement, which sought to tightly regulate Israelite worship and spiritual practices, likely contributed to the disaster, albeit indirectly. I was preaching about this reform movement, known as Josiah's Reform, the morning the protesters showed up outside Christ Church Cathedral. In this strange episode of Israelite history one finds both a profound warning and a reason for hope in the future of Christian faith in America, provided we heed history's lesson.

So that we do not lose the forest for the trees, I will do little more than sketch the historical and biblical details that form the basis of this story. Many books have been written about Josiah's Reform and the Babylonian Exile, filled with countless footnotes, historical arguments, and counterarguments proving and disproving various theories about what happened, when, and why. Suffice it to say that not everyone will agree with my assessment of the historical situation. Yet were I to justify each and every detail of my interpretation of this period, it would turn a lively, deeply interesting story into a dull one that gets lost in the details. If you wish to pursue this story from a scholarly standpoint, I refer you to scholarly histories of Israel in the endnotes.[3]

What happened was this. In the late seventh century B.C.E., a king arose in Israel named Josiah. By all estimations, King Josiah was a pious man with an authentic faith in Yahweh, the God of Israel. In the eighteenth year of his thirty-one-year reign, Josiah embarked on a grand project to restore the Jerusalem Temple, which had fallen from its former glory into neglect. To this end, he hired carpenters, construction workers, and masons to make long-overdue repairs and renovations.

Much to everyone's surprise, at some point during this restoration, a long-forgotten book was discovered in the Temple that many biblical scholars (myself included) believe to be the core of the Book of Deuteronomy, the fifth book of the Christian Old Testament and Jewish Torah. Hearing the content of this lost book read for the first time in anyone's memory, the religious and political leadership of Israel became terrified. While the book promised rich blessings for Israel for following a strict set of rules regarding worship and spiritual practice, it also promised that severe curses would befall Israel for failing to live up to the rules. When the leadership assessed how well the Israelites were following these rules, their conclusions were sobering, particularly with respect to their tolerance of other gods, which some had incorporated into Israelite worship and piety and which the book specifically forbade. Josiah himself tore his clothes in an act of despair and contrition, seeing that Israel had drifted substantially from "true" worship of Yahweh according to the book. Thus Josiah initiated a reform of Israelite worship and spiritual practices, much of which is outlined in 2 Kings 22–23.

Acting in concert with leadership from the Jerusalem Temple, Josiah apparently vowed not to rest until all of Israel was worshiping in the exact manner prescribed in the lost book. He had figures of foreign gods removed from the Jerusalem Temple and destroyed. He tore down altars dedicated to any god but Yahweh and desecrated their sanctuaries. As a result, certain religious practices that were clearly abhorrent, such as the burning of children as sacrifices to the god Molech, ceased.

As Josiah's Reform grew in size and scope, the Israelite leadership noticed something happening that encouraged still more zealous reform: Israel's political and military power in the international arena seemed to increase, particularly with respect to the Babylonians, to whom Israel had been paying tribute as a vassal state—a practice that Israel had long despised.

To make a long story short, the more Israel clamped down on the worship and spiritual practices of its citizens, the more powerful it seemed to become with respect to other nations. The blessings promised in the long-lost book appeared to be coming to pass! This encouraged Josiah all the more. Not only did he continue to tear down and desecrate sanctuaries dedicated to other gods, but he also closed down sanctuaries dedicated to Yahweh outside Jerusalem that the Jerusalemite religious establishment judged as not conforming to the officially prescribed rules and beliefs.

Eventually, believing Israel's worship and spiritual practices were finally orthodox enough to please Yahweh, Josiah boldly decided to throw off the yoke of Babylon for good and to stop paying tribute. Apparently, Josiah and his fellow leaders assumed that God was pleased enough with their devotion that God would come to their rescue should the Babylonians attack.

If one were to read only the book of Second Kings, one might assume that the ensuing disaster happened *despite* Josiah's Reforms rather than *under the influence* of them. Second Kings claims, for instance, with respect to Josiah, that "there was no king like him, who turned to the LORD with all his heart, with all his soul, and with all his might, according to all the law of Moses; nor did any like him arise after him" (2 Kings 23:25).

The book further claims that "the LORD did not turn from the fierceness of his great wrath, by which his anger was kindled against Judah [the nation of Israel] because of all the provocations with which Manasseh had provoked him" (2 Kings 23:26). Manasseh was one of Josiah's predecessors. According to Second Kings, Manasseh was so bad that not even a great king like Josiah could avert the curses set in motion against Israel.

Other interpretations are possible, however. The prophet Jeremiah, for instance, saw things quite differently. As one who lived in Jerusalem during Josiah's reign and was there to witness the results of Josiah's Reform, one might think Jeremiah would be pretty impressed. Yet he clearly was not. Jeremiah railed against the Israelites for missing the whole point of their faith and actively encouraged them to accept the yoke of vassalage to Babylon rather than throwing it off under the pretense that God would side with them. Jeremiah warned that Israel was acting too confidently, too self-righteously for its own good. He predicted that disaster would surely result if the Israelites continued on their present course. Jeremiah was right.

Jeremiah's words in chapter 7 are haunting. Though Jeremiah is speaking to good, back-to-basics Yahweh followers, he claims that they are presently worshiping Baal, as if their fervent Yahweh worship was really serving a very different god. Is it any wonder that people tried to kill him? Says Jeremiah:

> Do not trust in these deceptive words: "This is the temple of the LORD, the temple of the LORD, the temple of the LORD." For if you truly amend your ways and your doings, if you truly act justly one with another, if you do not oppress the alien, the orphan, and the widow, or shed innocent blood in this place, and if you do not go after other gods to your own hurt, then I will dwell with you in this place, in the land that I gave of old to your ancestors forever and ever [Jeremiah 7:4–7].

Jeremiah continues:

> Here you are, trusting in deceptive words to no avail. Will you steal, murder, commit adultery, swear falsely, make offerings to Baal, and go after other gods that you have not known, and then come and stand

before me in this house, which is called by my name, and say, "We are safe!"—only to go on doing all these abominations? Has this house, which is called by my name, become a den of robbers in your sight? You know, I too am watching, says the LORD [Jeremiah 7:8–11].[4]

What was Israel's big mistake? As noted earlier, according to Jeremiah, Israel was more interested with the *appearance* of faith than the faith itself. The people were more zealous about making sure everyone was following a set of rules than living with compassion toward the poor and the marginalized. They might as well have been worshipers of Baal as far as Jeremiah was concerned.

Think of it this way. When modern-day schoolteachers are required to shift their focus from teaching children how to think to instructing them how to pass standardized tests, what happens to real education? To be sure, standardized tests may ensure that a certain basic level of knowledge is achieved throughout the student population, but at what cost? How much good does it do if children no longer learn how to think for themselves or think creatively? Over time, a certain kind of rote knowledge at best or ignorance at worst is what results, which is exactly what "teaching to the test" was meant to combat in the first place.

Similarly, when the focus of religion shifts from empowering people to freely discover and live out their spiritual path to indoctrinating them into a certain set of beliefs and practices, does true faith result? To be sure, a marginal level of orthodoxy (or "right belief") may result, but it often comes at a high cost. When orthodoxy is more highly prized than compassion (or "right faith"), orthodoxy itself has little value.

By systematically destroying every sanctuary that the Jerusalem authorities viewed as potentially unorthodox—even many dedicated to the worship of Yahweh—what Israel gained in "right belief" may very well have been offset by what it lost in "right faith." The Israelites' beliefs became a source of pride, the number one killer of faith according to fifteen hundred years of Christian tradition that has identified pride as chief among the deadly sins. Pride led Israel to assume that God was on its side and against all others who did not hold the same beliefs. And that led Israel to thumb its nose at a superpower capable of squashing it like a fly if angered. The rest is history. Babylon attacked. Israel was exiled.

Why drudge up this sad history in relation to Affirmation 4 and worship that is "as sincere, vibrant, and artful as it is scriptural"? If we are to worship in a truly "scriptural" way, Israel's story suggests that we must ensure that our worship is also sincere. We must worship with our whole selves, not just our orthodox parts. We must worship with heart and soul, not just the mind. This means that our worship must be creative if it is to achieve the kind of orthodoxy that gives life rather than kills it.

I cannot help but wonder what would have happened if Josiah's Reform had been undertaken a bit differently. What if, for instance, Israel had removed the obvious heresies to any true faith, such as sacrificing children to Molech, but had been more generous in the assessment of other practices, such as the free worship of Yahweh in sanctuaries not under the direct control of the Jerusalem establishment? Had Josiah allowed people to freely throw heart and soul into worship—even at the risk of making mistakes—would the people have stayed connected to their compassion and humility? Would they perhaps even have remained humble enough to recognize that they could not simply do what they pleased in the international political arena under the assumption that God loved them better than others? Could Israel have averted disaster?

Answers to such questions can only be speculative, but they are important. What is not speculative is that it is not mistakes that kill worship or faith. God is gracious. What kills worship is lack of authenticity. Our heart and soul must be in it. And as the experience of those who attend Art and Soul Café attests, for many people the best way to ensure that heart and soul show up for worship is to engage in worship that is as sincere, vibrant, and artful as it is scriptural.

Mark "Perfesser Creek-Water" Dorazio.

11

"PERFESSER CREEK-WATER"

WHAT DO YOU DO if you're walking across the country proclaiming God's love for all people, including the poor and the marginalized, and a homeless person shows up who wants to walk with you the whole way? That's the question we faced on Easter Sunday when Mark Creek-Water arrived at our kickoff sunrise service.

I never would have guessed that the answer might include, "You bask naked under an Illinois sun while a gentle creek courses over you, and you walk barefoot in the Pennsylvania grass for miles."

For the record, that's part of my *personal* answer, not CrossWalk America's answer, and I was alone and secluded for the creek part! Also for the record, Mark Dorazio, who prefers to go by the name, Mark Creek-Water or "Perfesser" Creek-Water, does not accept the title of "homeless." He describes himself, rather, as "voluntarily houseless, *not* homeless." According to Mark, the world is his home. He would not live in a house if one were given to him.

Welcoming the Stranger

As I mentioned in Chapter Two, we had heard that Mark might be coming long before Easter. In January, the CrossWalk America Web site received an e-mail in which Mark stated his intention to set off walking from Oakland, California, on March 1 to make a nine hundred–mile journey by foot to Phoenix in time to join us on Easter Sunday, April 16, and continue across the country. We thought he was just one of several mentally unstable people who send mail to our Web site. After all, not only did the mileage seem unreasonable, but his intended route would take him across the Mohave Desert. "There's no way this guy's going to do that," we concluded, and promptly forgot about him. Then, eight days before Easter, I received a call from Wickenburg, Arizona. It was Mark.

"I'm almost there. Is the walk still on?"

Sure enough, Mark showed up on Easter Sunday in tattered blue jeans and shoes two sizes too big and falling apart at the seams that he had stuffed with newspaper for arch support. Despite his lanky frame and fifty-nine-year-old body, Mark had managed to make the journey carrying a heavy backpack with a broken strap, a plastic bag containing food and personal items, and a bag of plastic bottles and aluminum cans he had recently found by the side of the road and was seeking to recycle.

A group of CrossWalk America supporters hastily took up a collection and presented him with over a hundred dollars to purchase some new shoes and clothing.

"I really thank you, folks, but I'm doing fine with what I have," said Mark. "I'm just so grateful for what CrossWalk America is doing that I'd like to donate this money to you. Besides, I've got some book income that keeps me supplied with what I need."

Later, I asked Mark what book he had written, figuring he was receiving publishing royalties. I had Googled him on the Internet and found a couple of poems posted that he had read at a Berkeley coffeehouse. When I asked him if it was a book of poetry, he showed me some papers he had written by hand and photocopied.

"I write down my thoughts occasionally and sell them for two dollars." This was the extent of Mark's "book income."

CrossWalk America's leaders quickly put our heads together once it became clear that Mark really planned to walk with us. Apparently he had participated on several cross-country walks in the past twenty years, in addition to taking long personal journeys on foot. If he had already walked nine hundred miles to Phoenix, we had every reason to expect he'd be with us for the long haul.

Since we had put out an open invitation to the nation to join us on the walk for as long as the participants liked (provided they furnish their own food and housing), we did not want to turn him away. Yet he was, in essence, a perfect stranger, and it seemed logical to expect that at some point Mark would not be able to support himself.

"What will happen then?" a board member asked.

We decided to walk with Mark for the next several days to assess his situation and mental stability before making any firm decisions. Until then, we would provide him with food. Our RV support driver, Ray, offered to let him sleep on the sofa bed in the RV if he wanted. If Mark proved reasonably sane—and he had given us no indication to think otherwise aside from his unusually long walk from Oakland—we would start calling ahead to our host churches, explaining the situation and inquiring if they would consider accommodating another walker at our home stays. To the extent possible, we would also share whatever food came in.

Over the next several days, Mark proved to be a delightful conversation partner, full of stories of his previous cross-country walks. Originally from Delaware, Mark had moved to the Oakland area several years ago, where he spent much of his time volunteering for an organization called Food Not Bombs that feeds the homeless. He slept outdoors mostly, under bridges and in parks. Despite his eccentricities, Mark struck us as a reasonable, intelligent person. Through Mark we were receiving an intimate glimpse of a world we did not inhabit. Over the next several days, we decided we were glad to have him along. I was pleased that he wanted to continue with us to Washington, D.C., and he did.

This is not to say that everything went smoothly with Mark or that he did not challenge us—mightily—at times. The first time I realized we might be in for a bit more than we bargained for was a week into the journey. I asked him why he went by the name Creek-Water when his real one was Dorazio. I knew he wasn't running from the law because we had quietly checked into his background, but I was curious.

For the next hour, the walk team heard about his love of drinking creek water and his vision that everyone in America would one day renounce drinking any form of purified water—especially reverse-osmosis filtered water—in favor of what Mother Earth freely offered up in creeks, streams, and rivers.

Merrill piped up: "Don't you worry about parasites?"

"That's what everyone says," Mark responded. "People just don't know what they're talking about. Creek water is perfectly safe. Your system can live peacefully with whatever creatures may be there. Sometimes the water may be polluted with pesticides or other chemicals, but you can taste that right away and spit it out."

"What's wrong with filtering the stuff?" Merrill asked.

"It takes away all the vitality!" Mark shot back. "Most people think purified water is good, but the more you filter it, the more you take away its essence. If you would try creek water, you'd see why I think it's so important that people drink it. It'll give you energy you never thought you had. Look at me! I walked nine hundred miles before the walk started, and I feel great. I'm bursting with energy!"

In addition to walking the nine hundred miles, Mark was actually walking double shifts. Whereas our team was split into morning and afternoon groups, each walking an average of 13.5 miles a day, Mark took both shifts—a practice he continued for much of our journey. Still, none of us were ever persuaded to drink unfiltered creek water, much to Mark's chagrin. After bringing the subject up almost daily for the first three months, he finally gave up and decided to focus his energies on getting us to at least agree to stop purchasing bottled water purified using reverse-osmosis filtration. To Mark, reverse osmosis, which filters out pretty much every mineral or impurity in water, is about as close as you can get to the devil's creation.

"You should *at least* purchase mountain spring water. That's still got a little of the vitality in it. Or better yet, use tap water. The source is a lot closer and a lot of the minerals are still there."

The Creek-Water Gospel

As we moved across the country, Mark practiced the creek-water gospel he preached. While we purchased very little bottled water compared to our overall consumption, Mark would have none of it, preferring instead to take our empties and fill them in creeks and streams.

Nearly every creek we passed provided Mark not only with drinking water but also an opportunity for bathing and washing clothes. "We're going to be passing over some great creeks and rivers as we move along," he'd tell us. "I hope you're not in such a hurry to get to D.C. that you won't take time to stop." We proved to be a disappointment to Mark in this area, too, for most of the journey.

"No one ever listens to me," he'd say, "not on this walk or any of the other walks I've been on. They just don't believe how healthful it is to drink and bathe in creeks. It's like being baptized by Mother Earth. It's a *sacred* experience."

"When the weather gets hot," I vowed early on, "and the streams aren't muddy, I promise to get in a creek."

After a week or so on the road, Mark began to accept the offers we made of food and shelter. Apparently, he was checking *us* out, too, and took longer to make up his mind. Nevertheless, he was impeccably careful never to be a burden. Any food he found or was given, he would offer to share with others or outright give them before taking any himself.

Once he began accepting food, we learned that Mark would sooner go without eating than accept food containing meat or dairy products. Mark is not just a vegetarian but nearly a vegan. This surprised us considerably, given that Mark normally forages for food when he's on his own. When his meager cash supply runs out, he eats what he finds beside the road or goes "Dumpster diving," foraging through the trash outside restaurants and convenience stores. Given the slim pickings one might expect to find in these places, I was amazed that he would voluntarily forgo certain foods in order to remain true to his ideal of not participating in the harming of animals. "You'd be surprised at all the food people throw out," he told me. "I don't starve. People waste *a lot* of perfectly good food."

Over the course of our journey, we were taught several lessons about other practices Mark considers wasteful. He never ate rotten food but would gladly and thankfully consume any non-meat-or-dairy-containing leftovers long after others had turned up their noses at it. It made little sense to him that we would not do the same.

More than once, we were overloaded with peanut-butter-and-jelly sandwiches people had donated for our journey. This situation arose because before the walk started, our logistics team had instructed host churches to have our home-stay families send us off with three sandwiches "such as peanut butter and jelly" in the morning. The idea was that we would eat one for breakfast, one as a midmorning snack, and one for lunch. (We didn't want to inconvenience families by asking them to prepare us breakfast early in the morning.) As it happened, most families fed us breakfast *and* provided the sandwiches. For the first half of the trip, we did our best to keep up with all the sandwiches piling up in our refrigerator and even tried sending word ahead that we didn't need so many. People did not always get the word or heed it, and eventually the core walkers never wanted to see another peanut-butter-and-jelly sandwich again!

On more than one occasion, a home-stay family or church would say something like "You probably get a lot of peanut-butter-and-jelly sandwiches on your trip, so we've arranged for [something really, really good] to send with you."

"Oh, no," Mark would reply. "You don't need to send *any* food with us. We've got more food than we need already in the RV."

Needless to say, Mark wasn't exactly Mr. Popularity when he did this. Nor was he particularly popular when people would ask if we needed money to help fund our trip. Even though we had raised only half of the total we needed when we left Phoenix, Mark would tell people who asked, "We're fine. We have everything we need."

"Mark, you don't understand," Rebecca once gently reminded him. "It takes a lot of money to do what we're doing and broadcast it to the world through the Internet and the media. And I know your lifestyle works for you, but it's not for everyone. You can see that we're not exactly living extravagantly on this walk. We're not staying in hotels, and we barely ever eat in restaurants, but what we're doing still costs money."

Of course, how we lived *was* extravagant in Mark's eyes. Some of us wore prescription sunglasses, for instance, where Mark chose to do without any eyewear even though he could not see clearly past fifty feet. We made personal purchases of toothbrushes, sunscreen, and deodorant, all of which he did without. We wore new, specialized walking clothing and shoes, whereas he wore only the clothes he found along the road or purchased secondhand. We walked the country with an RV support vehicle and a fifteen-passenger van to shuttle guest walkers. Although he readily made use of these, he would have been content without them.

As days turned into weeks and weeks into months, we found that Mark could push nearly every emotional button that could be pushed. Normally those buttons were related to his attempts to conserve resources and reduce consumption. With Ray, our RV driver, and Meighan, our walker logistician, for instance, Mark would go over their carefully prepared itineraries in detail, questioning route decisions. Sometimes he would prevent us from taking a wrong turn, but mostly he would try to save the RV a cup or two of gas.

If Merrill wanted to spend some of his own money to purchase a couple of plastic boxes to hold supplies for our presentations, Mark would admonish him for wastefulness and offer to search dumpsters for cardboard ones. If any of us threw a plastic bottle in the trash, he would excitedly remind us of a recycling bag he had placed in the RV. Even long after we had been trained to recycle everything that could possibly be recycled, if someone momentarily got careless, we would hear, "No one ever listens to me! Not on this walk or any other. These things can be recycled! The earth's buried in trash!"

A Spirit of Abundance

Despite Mark's idiosyncrasies, we learned to appreciate deeply the pleasure he derives from the simplest of things. A crusty piece of two-day-old bread here, a gurgling creek there; a change in wind direction, an old wrench by the side of the road, a new moon, a few pieces of discarded paper with nothing written on the back that he could use for a new pamphlet, the kindness of someone who made him photocopies of his pamphlet free of charge.

Even though Mark walked a double shift for much of the journey, he was never in a hurry to finish walking for the day. The rest of us walked at 3 to 3.5 mph, thinking we were doing pretty well to slow down from our 65-mph lifestyles. Mark preferred to walk at 2 to 2.5 mph, and not because he was out of shape. "You miss too many things if you rush like that," he'd say. "Slow down! What's your hurry? Look, there's a creek up ahead. I'm going to check it out." He would stop for fifteen or twenty minutes, jogging afterward to catch up with us (his thin legs are amazingly strong!), or occasionally he would accept a ride from Ray as he passed by in the RV.

One day when we were walking through Wheeling, West Virginia, Mark suddenly became giddy with delight when he realized that we would be passing by a trio of sycamore trees growing from the same root standing behind a Hardee's restaurant he had visited years ago. "They're my sacred sycamores," he exclaimed excitedly. On our next day off, we were staying a few miles from those "sacred sycamores." Mark walked back and spent the day luxuriating in their shade. Had he not pointed out the sycamores in the first place, I doubt that we would have noticed anything more than the burger joint when we originally passed by.

So much pleasure did Mark derive from the little he had and the much he noticed that he was instinctively generous. Not only did he donate the money he had received from CrossWalk America supporters on Easter Sunday, but anytime Mark found himself with some spare cash, he reacted with the kind of generosity that only comes from an unwavering sense of abundance. Unbeknown to Mark, I once saw one of his homestay hosts slip him twenty dollars on the way out to our van. Once inside, Mark asked me if I needed any money. When Mark learned from a relative that he would be receiving an inheritance check for a thousand dollars, he tried to give it all to CrossWalk America. We thanked him but turned it down. When he became distressed at our refusal to let him share his windfall with us, we finally settled on receiving no more than a tithe (ten percent).

While I cannot imagine myself ever going "voluntarily houseless" like Mark, I find it quite easy to imagine slowing down my life and simplifying my lifestyle to become more mindful of the abundance that surrounds me. And while I have been sensitive to environmental concerns ever since serving as president of an environmental club in high school called the Committee to Save the Earth, I find it easy to imagine ways to adjust my lifestyle to leave a smaller footprint upon the earth. Under Mark's influence, I have traded in my station wagon for a smaller, more environmentally friendly car. I am more vigilant than ever about recycling. I purchase less to begin with. I turn off lights more readily. I fix leaks more quickly. I've put more insulation in my home.

I can even imagine once again sunbathing naked in a clear, Illinois creek and walking for miles barefoot in the grass behind Mark along a Pennsylvania roadway.

Creation, Worship, and the Environment

In a high school textbook for home-schooled Christian youth, *America's Providential History,* the authors contrast the "secular or socialist limited resource mentality" with a supposedly Christian one regarding stewardship of the earth. According to the textbook, "The Christian knows that the potential in God is unlimited and that there is no shortage of resources in God's Earth. The resources are waiting to be tapped."[1] While the authors may correctly assume that "the potential in God is unlimited," does this necessarily imply that the potential of Christians to exploit the earth is unlimited as well?

Reflecting a similar ideology, former secretary of the interior James Watt, a Christian, was reputed to have told Congress that it is not ultimately important to protect our country's natural resources because "God gave us these things to use. After the last tree is felled, Christ will come back."[2]

AFFIRMATION 3

[Christian love of God includes]
*Celebrating the God whose Spirit pervades and whose glory
is reflected in all of God's Creation, including the earth
and its ecosystems, the sacred and secular, the Christian
and non-Christian, the human and non-human.*

For years, environmentalists have assumed that statements like those made by the authors of the Christian textbook and by James Watt reflect an orthodox understanding of Christian faith. "After all," many say, "does not God command humanity in Genesis 1 to "have dominion" over the earth and "subdue it"?

Much to my chagrin over the years, many environmentally sensitive Christians assume that the Creation account in Genesis 1 does in fact support a theology of environmental exploitation. They argue that we must move beyond Genesis into a new environmental ethic. In so doing, however, these Christians actually move away from one of the most powerful allies of environmental stewardship in the entire Bible.

If we were truly to understand what the ancient Hebrew author of the Creation account in Genesis 1 is trying to tell us,[3] not only would our commitment to environmental stewardship be radically deepened, but our conception of worship and relationships would be transformed along with our understanding of Jesus.

These are tall claims, to be sure, but they are supported by the Bible. Much of what I am about to convey may be new information to the modern reader, but it would have seemed obvious to many ancient Jews and Christians. Taking a brief walk in their sandals, with the aid of a few insights from modern biblical scholarship, opens our eyes to a side of the Jewish and Christian faiths that is as majestic to behold as it is potentially redemptive.

According to Genesis 1, God created the cosmos out of nothing, right? *Creatio ex nihilo* is the classic technical term. God commands, "Let there be light," and *voilà!* Light appears. Very impressive. God commands, "Let there be a dome in the midst of the waters, and let it separate the waters from the waters" and again, it is so. Again, very impressive, if a little odd. That reference to separating "the waters from the waters" comes from the writer's assumption, shared by many in the ancient world, that the earth was flat and that there was water both above and below the earth. Why else would the sky be blue and water fall from the sky? And why else would there be deep oceans where there is no land?

Some Christians, focusing on these displays of God's authority and absolute power of command, take this to signal the way that we too are to "have dominion" over the earth. "Did God consult with anybody before giving orders?" they ask. "Of course not. Whatever God wants, God gets. God's creations have no say in the matter. No need to consult the birds or the trees for their opinions."

In their better moments, these Christians may speak in terms of "stewardship" of the earth. However, their version of stewardship is still based on the assumption of a completely passive natural order that is entirely dependent on God—and now on us as God's vice-regents—for protection, and care.

Yet when one digs a little deeper into Genesis 1, one soon finds that not even God acts consistently with this kind of direct, absolute authority. God acts not simply as a commander in chief but also as an empowerer, a relationship builder, an artist, an organizer, and a loving parent.

The Meaning of Dominion

Take the very first verses of Genesis, for instance. Immediately we find that God is actually *not* thought to be the Creator of everything. Some things (water and undefined solid matter) were around *before God spoke a word*. According to the opening verses of Genesis, "When God first created the heavens and the earth—the earth being a formless void and darkness covered the face of the deep while the Spirit of God hovered over the face of the waters—God said, "Let there be light," and there was light" (Genesis 1:1–2).[4]

While God is said to have created certain things out of thin air, like light (and air!), a lot of God's creative activity actually takes place not through *creatio ex nihilo* but through God acting as an *organizer* of that which already existed before Creation—the watery chaos. Hence, for instance, the "dome in the midst of the waters" separates the watery chaos above and below, providing a space in between for air. Then God gathers together the watery chaos that is below the dome, which allows the solid materials that have been a part of the waters since before Creation to become solid ground (Genesis 1:9–10).

Even more intriguing, a significant part of God's activity in Creation takes place through acting as an *empowerer*. In several places, God freely gives up direct control over what God has created in order to allow the creations themselves to become cocreators with God. God commands, "Let *the earth* put forth vegetation: plants yielding seed, and fruit trees of every kind on earth that bear fruit with the seed in it" (Genesis 1:11). Similarly, God commands, "Let *the waters* bring forth swarms of living creatures (sea life)" (Genesis 1:20), and "Let *the earth* bring forth living creatures of every kind: cattle and creeping things and wild animals of the earth of every kind" (Genesis 1:24).

Why would God give up direct control in favor of investing others with the power to accomplish God's objectives? Why not simply say, "Let there be vegetation," and "Let there be land and sea animals," and call it good? We're not told. But a good guess is that according to the author of Genesis 1, God does not conceive of God's own role in Creation primarily to be that of commander in chief. While it is clear that God exercises sovereignty over Creation, the kind of sovereignty God exercises is far more nuanced than is commonly supposed.

Another way by which God exercises sovereignty in Creation is by acting as a *relationship builder*. After God empowers the earth and the waters to become cocreators, these very creations are given power to create. For instance, God commands the swarms of living creatures created by the waters to "be fruitful and multiply and fill the waters in the seas, and let birds multiply on the earth" (Genesis 1:22). Thus a relationship is established between God's direct creations and the creations of these creations. God also establishes relationships between the sun, moon, and stars, differentiating their roles and prescribing their domains of activity in relation to one another (Genesis 1:14–18). God establishes the food chain as well, creating a survival system based on herbaceous rather than carnivorous consumption (Genesis 1:29–30). The eventual result of God's relationship building is a vast web of interdependent, mutually beneficial relationships that promote life. These relationships exist between and among God's direct creations, the creations of these creations, and the creations of these creations' creations.[5]

Like an *artist,* God steps back and evaluates the masterwork regularly. At the end of each of the first five days of Creation, God pronounces the work "good." On the sixth day, God surveys the whole canvas, with its symmetry and balance, its playful and sometimes even humorous flares (such as the platypus, as the opening of the film *Dogma* notes), its light and dark tones, and its unity, pronouncing it not just "good" but "very good."

It is perhaps the Sabbath rest that most dramatically brings this all together. Accustomed as many are to understanding the Sabbath in light of the later commandment to the people to abstain from work, it is easy to overlook the fact that in Genesis 1, it is only God who ceases activity on the seventh day. God's creations, meanwhile, function of their own accord, without direct intervention. On the seventh day God's creations are clearly not dependent on God barking commands but rather on the fruitful *relationships* God has nurtured between and among them that allow the ecosystem to function without God's direct intervention. Like a *loving parent,* God watches the children grow and play.

If human beings are to "subdue" the earth and "have dominion" over it in ways reflective of God's having dominion, this command must be interpreted within the whole context of God's Creation in Genesis 1. If we are to act as God acts, we are hardly given license simply to do what we please as assistant commanders in chief. And the rest of Creation is far from a rag doll, utterly dependent on or responsive to our actions.

In certain cases, in fact, trying to act as assistant commanders in chief or even as righteous stewards who fail to understand the nature of true stewardship of the earth can end in disaster. Twenty-five hundred years ago, before there were such things as smoke-spewing factories or automobiles or genetically engineered plants and animals, people were aware of this danger. The author of Genesis 1 knew it perhaps better than anyone else.

An Overlooked Relationship

Why? Was the author a scientist or an ecologist? No, the author was a *priest*—likely a group of priests, actually. The specialty of priests is *worship,* not science. Modern scholars refer to this person or group simply as the Priestly Writer, which is the term I'll use for simplicity. It was out of the Priestly Writer's deep understanding of worship that his environmental ethic was likely formed. Thus the next step along our journey in the ancients' sandals is to a text penned by this same Priestly Writer in the book of Exodus concerning what the Writer deemed to be the ultimate worship space: the Tabernacle—the movable tent-shrine used by Israel for worship during its wilderness journey between Egypt and the Promised Land.

In the opening chapter of Genesis, the Priestly Writer sows seeds that for the most part lie dormant until suddenly sprouting and bearing fruit in the later chapters of the book of Exodus, where the creation of the Tabernacle is described. Curiously, this particular creation account concerning a simple tent and its furnishings extends for thirteen chapters (Exodus 25–31 and 35–40), which is far longer than the Priestly Writer takes to describe the creation of the entire cosmos!

One of the reasons why the creation of the Tabernacle is so important to the Priestly Writer is that priests spend a lot of time thinking about, creating, and leading worship. It's only natural that the Priestly Writer would want to describe what is really going on in his primary domain. More important, however, the Writer considers what happens in the Tabernacle to be directly connected to what happens in the cosmos and takes extra pains to get the point across. If the Creation account in Genesis 1 could be described as painting a picture of God's perfect ecosystem, the creation account in Exodus portrays the creation of God's perfect social system.[6] What happens in one system is thought very much to affect the other, in ways many modern Christians fail to realize.

The account takes place within the context of Israel's wilderness wanderings on the Sinai peninsula following their miraculous exodus from Egypt. Israel is encamped at Mount Sinai, which is frequently covered in thick clouds due to the presence of God's "glory" descending to meet with Moses. The cloud protects Moses from beholding God directly, which is about the only thing considered more dangerous than touching the Ark of the Covenant in which the tablets of the law are kept.

In Chapters 25–31 and 35–40, God gives Moses instructions for the creation of the Tabernacle, which will house the Ark of the Covenant in its innermost sanctum, known as the Holy of Holies. From here on, the Tabernacle will serve as a designated meeting spot between God and God's people. Meeting with God, of course, has its upsides and its downsides. On the upside, the Tabernacle allows God and the people to dwell together as they move across the great wilderness. God will no longer be confined to mountaintops surrounded by billowy clouds of smoke but will dwell in the center of the Hebrew camp.

On the down side, living with God can be dangerous. According to the Priestly Writer, God's holiness was considered a good thing, but just as it is possible to have too much of a good thing, so it is with holiness. The Israelites, in fact, took great precautions *not* to become too holy. Objects thought to be extremely holy were cordoned off from people for their protection lest they contract too much holiness simply by touching them. In this sense, holiness was thought to be contagious.

A clue to why holiness was considered dangerous is given in the literal meaning of the word *holy*, which in Hebrew is *qadosh*. *Qadosh* means two things primarily: "separated from" and "consecrated to," in the sense of "devoted to," "given over to" so as to be "united with." If you were to touch something of supreme holiness—like the Ark of the Covenant— you would be entirely "separated from" one thing and entirely "consecrated to" another, according to Israelite belief. Given that the Ark was supremely holy *to God*, and God is Spirit, this means that one touching the Ark would become "separated from" his mortal flesh and wholly united with or "consecrated to" God. In essence, the soul would be united with God, leaving its mortal shell of a body behind. One would die. Thus, according to the Priestly Writer, God wants people to be careful. God therefore gives extremely detailed instructions concerning the Tabernacle's creation.

Significantly, these elaborate instructions bear a great deal of resemblance structurally and thematically to the Creation account in Genesis 1.[7] They are divided into seven segments as in Genesis.[8] In each segment God acts in much the same way God acts in the Creation account. For instance, God acts not simply as commander in chief but as an *empowerer*, investing Moses with the authority to oversee the Tabernacle's creation rather than making it appear out of thin air. God further empowers an assistant named Bezalel to direct the construction, going so far as to invest Bezalel with the same Spirit that was said to have hovered over the watery chaos before Creation in Genesis 1. The effect on Bezalel is that he becomes supercreative in a manner suggestive of God's own creativity.[9]

Similarly, we find God acting as *relationship builder* in the Tabernacle account, establishing a web of interdependent associations between and among the people who create and maintain the Tabernacle. Artisans, craftspeople, foremen, and priests all are depicted as working together fruitfully and enthusiastically to create the Tabernacle. So enthusiastic are they that when Moses asks for contributions of raw materials from the Israelites' personal possessions, they give so much that Moses actually has to restrain the people from giving more (Exodus 36:1–7)![10]

If you read through the entire narrative of Exodus 25–31 and 35–40, you will find that God is shown to be the consummate *artist* as well. God gives extremely detailed instructions to the artisans regarding how to fashion each and every object and with what materials. The whole Tabernacle, complete with its finely crafted furnishings and multicolored tent cloths, is a magnificent artistic creation to behold. It is also something magnificent to smell, with all kinds of aromatic oils, perfumes, and incense in use regularly once the Tabernacle is in operation.

God also acts as the consummate *organizer*. This is a critical function for God in the Tabernacle account. Because the Ark of the Covenant was housed in the inner sanctum (Holy of Holies) of the Tabernacle, above which God's holy presence was thought to be invisibly enthroned, the Tabernacle was considered potentially a very dangerous place to spend time if not properly prepared. As one walked through the entrance of the Tabernacle toward the Holy of Holies, the danger level—and consequently the amount of protection one needed to have in terms of priestly training, ritual anointings and cleansings, and personal righteousness—increased gradually. Remember that even touching a supremely holy object, such as the Ark, was thought to deliver a fatal dose of holiness. The increasing holiness of sacred objects was signaled visually by the gradually more precious materials used with finer workmanship. Considering the implicit threat thought to be posed by holiness, one might naturally wonder why it would be considered such a good thing to have all this dangerous holy stuff sitting in the midst of the people. The answer is given in the very last verses of the book of Exodus, which describes what happens when the Tabernacle is finally completed:

> Then the cloud covered the tent of meeting, and the glory of the Yahweh filled the Tabernacle. Moses was not able to enter the tent of meeting because the cloud settled upon it, and the glory of Yahweh filled the Tabernacle. Whenever the cloud was taken up from the Tabernacle, the Israelites would set out on each stage of their journey; but if the cloud was not taken up, then they did not set out until the day that it was taken up. For the cloud of Yahweh was on the Tabernacle by day, and fire was in the cloud by night, before the eyes of all the house of Israel at each stage of their journey [Exodus 40:34–38].

In other words, the payoff is that Israel's God moves off the mountaintop of Sinai to actually dwell in the midst of the people as a loving parent. According to the Priestly Writer, before there was a Tabernacle, this was impossible—not because Yahweh was too impotent to dwell with the people but because Yahweh was considered too powerful. Safeguards were necessary to contain God's holiness (as much as God could be said to be contained, anyway). Once the safeguards were in place, the people could benefit from God's presence without getting killed.[11] In fact, they could flourish, and flourish so abundantly that now not only God but they themselves would need to rest on the Sabbath day. The seventh segment of the Tabernacle account is devoted to the people honoring the Sabbath by resting just as God rested in the seventh segment of the Creation account. The Sabbath is said to serve as "a sign forever between me and the people of Israel that in six days Yahweh made heaven and earth, and on the seventh day [Yahweh] rested and was refreshed."

Creation in Worship

Stepping back a moment to glimpse the big picture, one reason why the Priestly Writer appears to place so much energy and emphasis on connecting the creation of the cosmos with the creation of the Tabernacle is that the Priestly Writer believes that worship itself is an act of creation. If you worship in God's presence, stuff happens. Stuff happens that may never have happened before in a person's life, in the life of the community, or even in the world itself (*creation ex nihilo* revisited!). In worship, this wild, uncontrollable, unimaginably deep and expansive love of God moves from the realm of pure spirit to the world of spirit and flesh in which we dwell. The result is not necessarily safe, at least in terms of preserving our lives the way they were before.

You never quite forget times when worship works this way. You walk into the sanctuary, perhaps not expecting anything much to happen at all, perhaps so caught up with something going on in your life at the moment that you're hardly aware of stepping into the sanctuary to begin with. Then, for reasons that may not be entirely explainable, something hits you right where you live. It may come through the preaching, a piece of music, a prayer, a community ritual, or a smile from someone sitting next to you. When it hits, it goes straight to the heart of whatever issues you brought in with you. Tears flow—tears of sadness, of joy, of wonder. You leave a different person than you walked in. You are never the same again. This is exactly what the Priestly Writer is trying to convey in the metaphorical language of the Tabernacle creation account. It is as fresh, vital, and relevant today as it was then.

More closely related to our topic of care for the environment, the Priestly Writer connects the creation of the cosmos and the creation of the Tabernacle because the Writer believes that all of God's creations are actively worshiping God. The cosmos, in effect, is a grand Tabernacle. Just as the Israelite Tabernacle serves as a vessel through which God may dwell in the midst of God's people without overpowering them, so the cosmos serves as a vessel of God's indwelling presence. Worship is what maintains the integrity (and protection) of the vessel.

I am not claiming here that the nonhuman elements of God's Creation are necessarily aware of the fact that they are worshiping God. They are probably no more aware of what they do than the furnishings of the Tabernacle would be aware. Worship is more than conscious praise of and submission to the Creator. What the Genesis 1 Creation account teaches us and the Exodus creation account confirms is that worship occurs at the heart of a life-promoting relationship between an *empowerer* and the empowered, between an *organizer* and that which is set in order, between a *relationship builder* and that which is set in relationship, between an *artist* and the product of artistry, between the *loving parent* and the child. In other words, worship is not just a conscious act of praise and surrender. It also happens through the conscious or unconscious exercise of fruitful, interdependent relationships that promote life.

We human beings remain blissfully unaware of all this at our peril. For, if we run roughshod over all these relationships God has so carefully established, according to the Priestly Writer we are in grave danger of crossing lines that are not meant to be crossed. It would be as if you and I were to wander into the Tabernacle lighting cigars on the candelabras, drinking from the libation cups, wiping our faces on the priestly garments, and resting our feet on the Ark of the Covenant. Not a smart idea! Why? God may love us dearly, but the interrelationships between and among God's holy creations are not supposed to be destroyed. These relationships are there for our *protection*. Remove them, and everything reverts to chaos.

Pitching Tent

Jesus not only confirms what we have been discovering thus far about the ancient Israelites but also radicalizes it. In the opening lines of John's Gospel, we read the following lines about Jesus, who is identified as "the Word" (Greek, *logos*):

In the beginning was the Word, and the Word was with God, and the Word was God. He was in the beginning with God. All things came into being through him, and without him not one thing came into being. . . . And the Word became flesh and dwelt among us, and we have seen his glory, the glory as of a father's only son, full of grace and truth" [John 1:1–3, 14].

What escapes the attention of many not familiar with the Greek text of this passage is the intriguing use of the word translated as *dwelt,* as in "the Word became flesh and dwelt among us." The Greek word is derived from a verb that literally means "to pitch tent." Does the connection between the creation of the cosmos and pitching a tent seem too much of a coincidence in light of our exploration of cosmos and Tabernacle (tent-shrine)? In fact, it is no coincidence at all. The noun form of that Greek verb, *skana,* "tent," is the very word used in the Greek translation of the Hebrew scriptures (Septuagint) to translate the word *Tabernacle* in our Exodus story.

The implication is clear. Where the Priestly Writer saw a critical unity between cosmos and Tabernacle, so did the early church. Early Christians perceived God's cosmos and God's Tabernacle coming together physically in the one in whose path they walked: Jesus Christ. It is no wonder, since Christ represented for them the God who came down from on high and dwelt in their midst, as God had done in the wilderness Tabernacle. Christ also acted a lot like God acts "in the beginning" of Creation: not simply as commander in chief but even more so as an empowerer, relationship builder, artist, organizer, and loving parent.

This same Jesus is the one who bears witness to God's intimate interest in the natural world when he notes that not one sparrow falls to the ground outside of God's knowledge (Matthew 10:29; cf. Luke 12:6) or when he notes that not even Solomon in all his splendor could match the beauty of a field of flowers (Matthew 6:28–29).

Perhaps most intriguing of all the New Testament writings linking Christ with the Tabernacle are the Synoptic Gospels' accounts of Christ's crucifixion.[12] At the moment Christ breathes his last, these accounts claim that "the curtain of the temple was torn in two, from top to bottom" (Matthew 27:51; Mark 15:38; Luke 23:45). This is the curtain of the Holy of Holies (the Holy of Holies being transferred from the Tabernacle after the Temple was built). The implication is that God is no longer confined to a little space behind a curtain in the Temple. God is on the loose! And with God on the loose, the whole world has become infected with

God's holiness. Rather than dying as a result of contracting God's holiness, we may now "touch God" and live. This is because with the whole world permeated by God, the separation that holiness entails is rendered inoperable. Now one may be fully "consecrated to" God without "separation from" the world—because the whole world is holy! Do you think this lowers or raises the need to care for God's holy Creation?

For those who wonder how a Christian can be concerned with the care and protection of the environment, we may rightly respond, "How can a Christian *not* be concerned with these things?" Our relationship with the environment is intimately connected to our relationship with Christ. They are woven from whole cloth into the very tapestry of our faith. A Christian can no sooner be disinterested in Creation than be disinterested in worshiping God or serving as Christ's disciple.

This lesson, which comes straight from the heart of our tradition, is one to which I believe "Perfesser Creek-Water" would give an enthusiastic "Amen!"

Sharing faith stories at Cross Creek Community Church, Dayton, Ohio.

12

FAITHFUL DOUBTING

"O GOD, COULD WE BE more miserable?" I exclaimed in exasperation as we walked across the border of Indiana into Ohio in blazing heat and suffocating humidity. The few drops remaining in my two-liter water bottle were as tepid as bathwater. Unusually hot temperatures in the Northern Plains and Upper Midwest had already made July one the hottest for the United States since the data were first recorded in 1895. Already a hundred and fifty people had died around the country of heat-related causes.[1]

"You asked God if we could be more miserable *yesterday*," Rebecca replied, "and today is your answer. You need to start asking if we could be *less* miserable!" Just two days into August, we had no reason to expect a reprieve anytime soon. "I think our stopping point is less than a mile from here."

Much to my relief, the CrossWalk America van was parked on the edge of a cornfield just a couple of turns in the road ahead. Meighan was standing outside the van looking unusually chipper. "You look like you could use some ice water," she said, grinning.

"You have no idea," I sighed.

"It's waiting for us in the driveway of that house," Meighan replied, pointing across the freeway.

"You're kidding, right?" Rebecca ventured, thinking Meighan sounded a little too confident to be joking.

She was not. As Meighan explained, she had been catnapping in the van as she waited for us, awakening with a start when a bright red pickup pulled up next to the van and stopped. A fifty-something man climbed out and started placing a note underneath our windshield wiper.

Figuring the man was a farmer angry that we had parked on his property, Meighan sat up, opened the door, and said, "Hi. Is there a problem?"

"No," replied the man, suddenly aware that the van was occupied. "I was just offering you some water." The man's name was Joe. Joe lived on the farm across the freeway and had noticed our van with the giant yellow, red, and green CrossWalk America logo emblazoned on the side. Joe said he wanted to do something nice for us on such a hot, humid day. Outside his home, Joe had set out a pitcher of ice water and a few Styrofoam cups.

As Joe explained, he had become a Christian not long ago while on vacation. Walking along a jetty on Lake Michigan, someone had handed him a "letter from God" made up of simple Bible verses strung together. He choked up as he recounted the overwhelming feeling of joy that overcame him when he read it. He wanted to return something of the kindness he felt he had received.

"Thank you so much!" Meighan said. "You know, one of our walk leaders just posted a 'letter from God' on the Internet," referring to a letter I had published on our blog three days earlier based on the Phoenix Affirmations. It wasn't the same letter Joe had received, but it, too, had quickly been picked up and distributed by others on the Internet. (My letter is reprinted in Chapter Thirteen.) Joe wished Meighan well and headed for town with a couple of CrossWalk America brochures in his hand.

After hearing Meighan's story, we eagerly made our way across the freeway to the house where we found the ice water and cups just as Joe had indicated. I don't know if I have ever tasted water so refreshing. We sat in Joe's front yard for a while soaking in his generosity as much as anything else. We wondered what kind of church Joe attended. Was it conservative? Moderate? Liberal? It really didn't matter. All we knew was that we were thirsty and he had provided us with something cold to drink.

"Isn't there a Bible passage about that?" Mark asked, referring to a passage in Matthew 25 where Jesus talks about whom he considers to be his true followers. Notably, Jesus doesn't say "They're liberals" or "They're conservatives." Rather, he says things like "I was thirsty and you gave me something to drink" (Matthew 25:35).

"That's enough in my book," Rebecca said.

"Mine, too," I replied.

Later that afternoon, we made our way into a suburb of Dayton, where Cross Creek Community Church was hosting an event for us. An excited crowd of a hundred or so gathered, buzzing with energy and setting out the most extravagant potluck we had encountered on the walk. I had heard of Cross Creek and its pastor, Reverend Mike Castle, long before our arrival. Their outreach to the community is well known in its parent denomination, the United Church of Christ. Like Joe, Cross Creek is remarkably focused on providing hospitality to the stranger.

Over dinner, we conversed with a number of people who had come to Cross Creek because of its hospitality—and not just to meet their physical needs. They came to Cross Creek feeling a profound spiritual void for various reasons and spoke excitedly about the nourishment they received here.

I spoke with Debbie, for instance, a thirty-something mother of two who came to Cross Creek a year ago after a long period of absence from church. The church of her childhood had taught her that the Bible could not be taken seriously if it was not understood literally, without error.

"That just didn't work for me," she said. "I couldn't accept that the cosmos was created in only six days, as Genesis claims, or that the earth was just a few thousand years old. When I was in high school I would argue that fossils are millions of years old. I'd talk about carbon-14 dating. The youth leaders just glared at me. They said, 'God put fossils on the earth to test our faith.' They claimed that God is challenging us to either accept science's answers or the Bible's. I chose science. And I chose to stop attending church."

"What brought you back?" I asked.

"I went through a divorce," she grimaced. "The divorce was pretty hard on my kids. I realized they were going through a crisis I just couldn't meet on my own. I thought maybe we should try going to church. So I brought them to Cross Creek thinking I'd have to shut up and swallow my doubts for the sake of my children. Instead I found that people *value* doubts here. They even held a class recently called 'Living the Questions'![2] I thought you had to step outside the Christian faith to ask questions and take science seriously, but here people believe that scientific inquiry is connected to the truth that sets you free."

"How does all this feel to you?" I asked.

"For the first time in my life," she confided, "I'm *happy* to be a Christian. I don't have to shove my questions into a dark closet, hoping they'll stay in there until I leave the church parking lot. I have a faith I can share with my children without feeling embarrassed or guilty about teaching them things I don't believe myself."

Next to Debbie sat Don, a man in his seventies who was quietly nodding his head and smiling as Debbie spoke of finding faith through doubting. When we asked what brought him to Cross Creek, Don did not hesitate.

"Ditto to what Debbie said. Only at my age, it wasn't a child crisis that got me here. It was my own!"

"What happened, if I may ask?" I probed.

"Well, I'm a fairly conservative guy when it comes to faith," Don explained. "I won't say I was a literalist, but I was pretty close to it, and I'm still more conservative in general than many people at this church. But it has never made sense to me that a God who loves everybody would one day throw people into hell if they're not followers of Jesus. I'm a committed Christian, and I love Jesus, but the Jesus I've always known and loved just wouldn't do that. I spent forty years in the aviation industry and traveled all over the world. In my time I've had quite a number of colleagues who were Muslim, Jewish, and Buddhist. You can't convince me that these people who practice their faith with deep humility and commitment are enemies of Jesus. Heck, in my time I've encountered more *Christians* who seem to be against Jesus than I have Buddhists! In any case, I don't think God throws people into burning lakes of fire even if they're against Jesus."

"Did you leave your old church because of your feelings about non-Christians?" asked Debbie.

"That was a large part of it," Don replied. "I still love those people. I was a member there for twenty-five years, and I'm friends with many of them. I think they're trying to follow Jesus as much as I am. But when 9/11 hit, the anti-Islamic rhetoric went into high gear. We were hearing that the Muslim religion is evil and that the only way there can be peace in the Middle East is if everyone converts to Christianity. Yet my brothers and sisters in Christ were actively banging the drums of war! It was too much for me to stomach. About that time, a friend invited me to a class called 'Introduction to Progressive Christianity.' Ordinarily, I would have turned him down flat. I'd already rejected a number of invitations he'd made over the years to visit Fireside Chat, which is a progressive Christian house-gathering sponsored by Cross Creek. That word *progressive* made me nervous. I thought *progressive* was just another word for *liberal* or *secular humanist*. But when he said Cross Creek was joining with an American Baptist and Episcopal church to offer the class, I guess my frustration with what was going on at my church made me interested in exploring other ways of being Christian."

Don was not alone in this desire. One hundred people from the Dayton area and as far away as Cincinnati fifty miles to the south attended. Like Don, many were members of churches whose beliefs were quite different from those discussed in the class. Although each participant's understanding of what the term *progressive* meant was a little different, what most people had in common was a desire to explore faith "outside the box," asking deep questions without feeling constrained by any expectation to arrive at a "standard" or traditional answer. Because the group did not meet on Sunday mornings, people could attend their home churches and come to the group as well. When the class ended, many participants, like Don, wanted to go deeper. Don started attending Cross Creek's Fireside Chat on Friday evenings at a member's home. Eventually, he found the disconnect between what he experienced on Friday evenings at Fireside Chat and on Sunday mornings at his church too great to bear. Don left his faith community of twenty-five years and joined Cross Creek.

"Through the intro class and Fireside Chat, I found myself discarding a number of beliefs I'd held since childhood," said Don.

"Was that difficult?" I asked.

"More like *freeing*," Don smiled. "I mean, hallelujah, I'm no longer burdened by the belief that Christianity is about doing this and doing that and not doing this and not doing that. It's not even about believing one thing or another. It's not about creeds or catechisms or believing that Jesus was born of a virgin or that the Bible is without error. It's about *love*. Loving God and loving your neighbor as yourself. And it's about *grace*. Trusting that God loves us because of who God is, not because of anything we do or fail to do. For me, this journey has been revolutionary. You really *can* teach an old dog new tricks!"

AFFIRMATION 10

[Christian love of self includes]
*Claiming the sacredness of both our minds and
our hearts and recognizing that faith and science,
doubt and belief serve the purpose of truth.*

As I continued to listen to other Cross Creek members' stories, I was struck by how similar their stories were to others we'd been hearing regularly since we left Phoenix on Easter Sunday. Despite the wide variety of Christians we encountered from across the political and theological spectrum, many were experiencing a similar reawakening of their faith. Almost to a one, these people spoke to us of deep questioning they had undergone—and were still undergoing in many cases. For many, this questioning had driven them into dark nights of the soul where some had even felt they had lost their faith. Yet they discovered that the faith they thought they had lost was more powerful than their deepest doubts and many times more resilient. They had learned to trust in their doubts.

As one Cross Creek member put it, "I prefer the doubt to the knowing. Knowing that I knew God is what messed it all up for me in the first place! It was doubt that made God possible again for me. If I know exactly who God is or what God's about, it's almost as if I don't need God anymore. I don't need a relationship. All I need is a rule book or a book of doctrine. I think many of the scariest things that have happened in the name of faith have happened out of certainty, not doubt. To have doubts means that one is open to new revelation. I don't want to be certain about anything because I believe that God is still speaking."

I believe that what Cross Creek, Fireside Chat, and other like-spirited churches and gatherings are doing right now is adding a new twist to Jesus' words about disciples offering water in Matthew 25. In place of water (or in addition to it), they are offering doubt. Whether extended by liberals, moderates, or conservatives—intentionally or unintentionally—doubt has become a source of living water for many Christians. I believe that's enough for Jesus.

Walking Toward Easter

As we made our way farther into Ohio, the impact of our many and varied encounters with Christians at the grass roots began to hit us like a sonic boom that trails a jet flying faster than the speed of sound. At first you see the jet soaring by and wonder why it's so quiet. Then the concussion comes crashing at you, and you stop wondering! This concussion caught up with me at First Congregational Church in Columbus.

First Congregational's senior pastor, Reverend Tim Ahrens, invited our walk team to stay in his church while in the area, extending an invitation to me to preach the Sunday before we walked through Columbus. I knew of Reverend Ahrens through his leadership of We Believe Ohio, a loose confederation of liberal, moderate, and conservative Christian and Jewish leaders serving houses of worship in urban, suburban, and rural areas who have accomplished something that seemed impossible to many: they have raised a unified voice of inclusion and compassion on behalf of the poor, children, and others who are voiceless or otherwise unrepresented in public life.

On Saturday evening I found myself in the darkened sanctuary of First Congregational struggling to find words to adequately articulate what we had discovered in our journey along the highways of America. In my mind's eye, I was replaying our experiences with Christian fundamentalists, such as those at Jesus First Baptist Church, who supported us in surprising ways. I recalled groups of evangelical Christians, such as those at Fellowship of Believers in Hereford, Texas, who had welcomed us heartily even as they disagreed with some of our beliefs. I thought of the Hispanic Catholics of Bovina, Texas; the folks at Jesus Radio in Farwell, Texas; and the LGBT Christians in Clovis, New Mexico, all of whom had welcomed us warmly. I recalled our numerous encounters with the spiritually home-less, such as those in Mountainair, New Mexico, who came forward to lend us a hand when they heard what we were doing. I recalled our dis-covery of progressive Christian house-gatherings and "alternative" church groups, such as those meeting in Higgins, Texas; Saint Louis, Missouri; and Dayton, Ohio, all of which have become places where the spiritually homeless are finding fellowship with others for whom faith is reawaken-ing in new and creative ways. I thought also of the faith communities we encountered who are boldly articulating a vision of inclusive faith despite opposition in their communities, such as little Saint Albans Episcopal Church in Fulton, Missouri. I could sense a common thread running through our experiences of these and other groups, but was at pains to de-scribe what it was as I prepared my sermon.

Certainly, the embrace of doubt is a critical part of the common thread. Each individual and community has had to let go of certain no-tions of faith or about practitioners of faith who are different from them when faced with fresh awareness or insight. Yet even as doubt has proved to be a linchpin, it struck me as being connected to a much larger story. A new form of Christianity seemed to be emerging at the grass roots that is as vibrant, inclusive, and compassionate as it is label-defying.

I prayed in that darkened Columbus sanctuary, "God, we have ex-perienced time and again something new and wonderful you are doing across the country even as we have encountered indifference, opposition, and protest. During this walk you have caused us to let go of each and every stereotype and preconceived idea of what Christians are like. We no longer know what a 'liberal' Christian is or a 'conservative' or 'moder-ate.' We have discovered the fallacy of categorizing people into red state and blue state, Republican and Democrat. We have seen that labels like 'urban,' 'suburban,' and 'rural' break down as quickly as they are applied. Yet amid all this, there clearly are differences between Christians. Your followers are certainly not all the same. Please, God, give me some way of understanding and describing what we are experiencing!"

In less than a minute after praying, three images appeared in my mind's eye that I couldn't quite shake: a cross, a locked room, and an empty tomb. I let these images dance around inside my head, gently swirling in and around my memories of the walk. The more I pondered this dance of images, the more powerful and confident the dance became. Gradually, I could see in my mind's eye three distinct, interlocking circles of energy or influence. Each circle developed a distinct timbre and tone and then finally a name: Good Friday, Holy Saturday, and Easter Sunday—the last three days of the Christian Holy Week. Associating our experiences with these three ancient holy days hit me like a sonic boom, breaking open my thoughts and reconfiguring them in such a manner that my whole being seemed to shout, "Aha!" at the insight.

Before characterizing each of these influences, let me note at the outset that Good Friday, Holy Saturday, and Easter Sunday do not serve simply as new labels to affix to people. They serve as metaphors. As metaphors, they do not *define* grassroots Christianity so much as *describe* certain tendencies within it. And just as any metaphor or analogy breaks down if applied too rigidly to specific situations, so these metaphors are only helpful for seeing the big picture—the forest rather than the trees. Examining specific situations requires more nuance than these metaphors can sustain. There are probably more than three circles of energy, too, even as these three appear to be dominant at present.[3] Finally, I note that each person and community of faith draws from all three of these circles of influence at once. While one tends to serve as "home base," dominating actions and reactions at least for a time, all three influence each other.

Good Friday

Christians whose "home base" is Good Friday draw primarily from the energy of *anger.* These Christians are not hard to spot these days. Whether labeled by others as "conservative" or "liberal," Good Friday–oriented Christians are loudly decrying the loss of something they hold sacred or sacrosanct. Someone has crucified their Jesus. They are pretty certain they know who is responsible. In righteous rage, they spend most of their time and energy trying to crucify those they deem to be crucifiers. In so doing, they generate far more heat than light.

On the more conservative end of the theological spectrum, some Christians blame society's ills on "secular humanists" and "liberals" whom they claim have stripped America of its core Christian values. As we walked through Ohio, these Good Friday voices received ample representation by Christian leaders such as Reverend Rod Parsley, who called for a spiritual army to "track down our adversary, defeat him valiantly, [and] then stand upon his carcass." They characterized their mission as "a battle between the forces of righteousness and the hordes of hell."[4] Based on their rhetoric, one wonders what happened to the Jesus who proclaimed, "Blessed are the peacemakers," and "Love your enemies," "Do good to those who hate you," and "Judge not lest you be so judged."

Yet we found plenty of Christians at the opposite end of the theological spectrum orbiting under the influence of Good Friday. These Christians often focus their anger on Christian fundamentalists who have, in their view, "hijacked Jesus" in an attempt to replace Christian tolerance with Christian Taliban. We ran into such Christians, for instance, while walking through Illinois, where an invitation to preach at a mainline church was rescinded by church leaders who felt that CrossWalk America was being too nice to Christians who oppose us. They were quick to remind us that the last Great Reformation in Christianity sparked the Thirty Years' War. Apparently they were disappointed that we were unwilling to help start another and so withdrew their invitation.

Despite the fact that the Good Friday energy radiates more heat than light, it should be noted that its basic energy is sacred. No doubt Jesus' disciples felt deep anger and rage over his crucifixion on that original Good Friday. To witness such a tragedy and not be enraged would be a sign of spiritual deadness, not life. As the saying goes, "If you're not angry right now, you're not paying attention."

In essence, Good Friday anger is like salt in a stewpot. When used in appropriate quantities, it focuses and enhances the flavor of all the ingredients. If you keep pouring the salt, however, the dish quickly becomes inedible. Pouring still more turns the dish from food to poison.

Holy Saturday

Although Christians drawing from the influence of Good Friday tend to receive the lion's share of media attention, creating an impression that nearly all Christians are oriented this way, we encountered far more Christians orbiting around the influence of Holy Saturday than Good Friday. The primary energy of Holy Saturday is not anger but *angst*. On the original Holy Saturday, Jesus' disciples locked themselves away in upper rooms, afraid to come out in public lest they be associated with their crucified Savior. They were in shock over what had happened to Jesus and likely wondered about the future of their faith. Just as likely, they wondered if perhaps they had been misled into giving their hearts to Jesus in the first place. They certainly were not about to venture into the public square proclaiming how wonderful it is to be a lover of Jesus! They were plunged into a dark night of the soul—or at least significant doubt—wondering if they would ever see the light of day again.

Today, many Christians who resonate with the energy of Holy Saturday come from traditional mainline churches—Presbyterian, Methodist, Lutheran, Episcopalian, Disciples of Christ, and United Church of Christ. Having experienced a dramatic loss in numbers and social status since the mid-1960s, these believers express strong concern regarding the future of their churches and denominations and even the Christian faith itself. Among the most persistent comments we heard from these mainline Christians are that they feel alone in their beliefs and that their values of inclusiveness and compassion for others are out of sync with both society and organized religion. Three of the most persistent comments we heard from these Christians were, "So I'm *not* crazy!" "I don't feel so alone anymore," and, "You're walking *for me.*"

Significantly, the influence of angst is not limited to Christians from mainline traditions. Many evangelical and fundamentalist Christians are hiding away in locked upper rooms as well. Many of these quietly support the full equality of gay, lesbian, bisexual, and transgendered persons. Others affirm the separation of church and state, lamenting the growing association of Christianity with certain political parties or issues. Many do not read the Bible literally, as the inerrant Word of God. Rather than face what they perceive to be overwhelming opposition in their faith communities, these Christians resolutely bite their tongues or quietly slip out, joining the vast ranks of spiritually homeless in America.[5]

Again, it is important to note that the basic energy of Holy Saturday is sacred. One can no more blame Christians today for fearing to speak out in the face of opposition or for doubting the future of their faith than one could blame Jesus' first disciples two thousand years ago. Holy Saturday is a time for silence, for quiet contemplation, for doubt, and for experiencing the soul's dark night. Without regularly experiencing the draw of Holy Saturday, it is unlikely that any of us would come to know a God whom the author of Psalm 139 describes as the one for whom "even the darkness is not dark to you; the night is as bright as the day, for darkness is as light to you." Still, Holy Saturday does not have to be, nor is it meant to be, a Christian's final resting place.

Easter Sunday

Perhaps the most remarkable discovery in our journey is the presence of so many Christians who appear increasingly to be less influenced by anger or angst than by *awe.*

While these Christians are less numerous than those orbiting around the influence of Good Friday or Holy Saturday, their energy often surpasses those of both groups combined. Regularly we found Christians who are discovering a faith that is more vital and fresh than they have ever known before. Time and again we heard comments like "Something's in the air. I can feel it. There's a growing movement coming together. God's on the move." Not all of these Christians were able to describe fully what they are seeing and experiencing, but they are convinced that something great and wonderful is emerging and beginning to take shape.

Significantly, the most common characteristic we discovered in these Christians is the embrace of doubt as an ally of faith. Most of them have experienced marked challenges to their beliefs, and many report having lost their faith for a period of time. They found themselves spiritually homeless or at very least "spiritually uncomfortable" and discovered in their alienation and despair something drawing them forward, calling them to walk step by step in the dark until they began to see glimmers of the twilight of a new day. These Christians now act very much like one would imagine the women and men outside the empty tomb acted as they excitedly milled about in the twilight hours of Easter. Some are jubilantly proclaiming, "I have seen Jesus!" Others are whispering, "I haven't seen Jesus yet, but I see this stone that's been rolled away. I know God is up to something new!"

Many of these Christians are actively involved in difficult struggles for justice and issues of Christian witness. Despite their newfound optimism over the future of Christian faith, they are not necessarily as optimistic about the outcomes of their struggles. Rather, they have simply let go of their fear, along with their anger toward their opposition, drawn instead by a sense of joy and compassion.

We found some of these Christians associated with the so-called Emergent Church movement, a movement fueled largely by twenty-somethings who grew up as evangelicals yet for whom major tenets of evangelical faith such as biblical literalism no longer make sense. They've left their churches behind but haven't left the faith. Now they gather in small "house churches" and "cohorts" and discussion groups to find community and spiritual nurture.

Yet we also encountered these Christians among the traditionally liberal, mainline denominations, such as those in Dayton, Saint Louis, and Higgins, Texas.[6] These people tend to be older than the Emergent crowd, yet like them, these mainliners are forming house churches and fellowship groups to engage their faith, and their doubts, in ways they believe more traditional churches are too timid to do.

Although Christians orbiting around the influence of Easter Sunday differ significantly from each other politically or theologically when a single issue is all that is in focus, they are a remarkably cohesive group from a "bird's eye" view. These awe-filled Christians tend to be joyfully and unapologetically Christian, yet they appreciate other faith traditions as well, refusing to deny the legitimacy of other paths God may create for humanity. They tend to treat Scripture as authoritative, though they do not read it literally. They also tend to value prayer, reflection, and community dialogue, as well as care for the poor, more highly than their peers.

These Christians tend to find God's glory reflected in all of Creation, including the earth and its ecosystems, the sacred and secular, the Christian and non-Christian. They value scientific ways of knowing in addition to mystical or spiritual ones. In fact, many do not tend to draw clear lines of distinction between such matters. Typically, too, they are not nearly as concerned with sexual orientation. Many, though not all, support the full equality of lesbian, gay, bisexual, and transgendered people. A surprising number *are* lesbian, gay, bisexual, or transgendered. Most are also quick to affirm the separation of church and state, believing that religion is strongest when it is practiced freely.

Finally, as noted earlier, doubt has played a significant role. Periods of significant doubt seem to act as threshold experiences, moving people from the orbit of Good Friday to Holy Saturday and from Holy Saturday to Easter Sunday.[7]

Three Circles, One Faith

I've asked myself why all this stereotype-defying activity is happening within grassroots Christianity. Why are Christians of widely divergent theological beliefs and political orientations tending to act on their convictions in similar ways even as they may seek to achieve different ends? Our experiences on the walk suggest that it is because the forces of anger, angst, and awe currently exert a stronger influence on Christians than political or theological labels like "liberal," "moderate," and "conservative" do. A shift is taking place in the tectonic plates of Christianity, a shift that is likely to be counted in centuries, not election cycles. The faith itself is changing. Easter Sunday is upon us. We may only be at the earliest twilight hours of this new day, and the sacred energies of Good Friday and Holy Saturday are sure to continue to exert their influence, but just as surely as the sun rises on the horizon, there is a new Christian faith emerging at the grass roots in America. It is time to join hands and hearts with awe-filled evangelicals and mainliners, Republicans and Democrats, who live in red states and blue states, urban jungles and the rural countryside. It is time to clear away our egos, stereotypes, and easy certainties. We are being called to move beyond our anger and angst to become nothing less than the early church of the twenty-first century.

Supporters at CrossWalk America's end-of-walk press conference
at Foundry United Methodist Church, Washington, D.C.

13

A LETTER FROM GOD

I STOOD ON THE STEPS of the Lincoln Memorial in Washington, D.C., two steps to the left of where Martin Luther King Jr. stood when he delivered his "I Have a Dream" speech on August 28, 1963. Bright sunlight bathed my face as I surveyed the crowd, an incredible half million strong! They had driven, bused, and flown in from around the country to join CrossWalk America walkers and leaders, as well as leaders from our partner organizations, to celebrate the symbolic nailing of the Phoenix Affirmations to the "doorway of America" and the rebirth of inclusive, compassionate Christian faith. As I gazed out into the exuberant crowd, I was surprisingly at ease. I didn't feel a bit nervous, nor did I feel any surge of ego. The crowd wasn't cheering for us, after all; the people were cheering for God. They were cheering for themselves and their revitalized *relationship* with God.

"Excuse me, sir" I heard someone say. "Can you tell me where the Vietnam Memorial is located?"

My daydream came to an abrupt halt as I muttered directions to the inquirer. It was April 2005, and we were still a year away from the start of the walk. I was indeed in Washington, D.C.—to raise awareness and support.

As I looked back over the mall area—this time seeing it for the virtually empty space it really was—I began to pray, asking God to turn the daydream into reality. As I prayed, I was struck by a sense that someone was standing at the base of the stairs looking up at me. No one was actually there, but I could almost picture him in my mind's eye. It was Jesus. I asked myself why I would be thinking of Jesus standing there at the bottom of the stairs. A question intruded on my thoughts: "When you arrive in Washington, D.C., a year and a half from now, will you and the walkers have brought Jesus with you?"

"Absolutely!" I responded in my mind. "No matter what happens, no matter what we have to sacrifice, we will make sure that we bear Jesus to D.C. If he doesn't show up here on September 3 next year, all our efforts will have been in vain. If we accomplish nothing else, we will bear Jesus with us to D.C."

A year before we began the walk, it was easy, even fun, to envision a sea of people joining us (and Jesus) there at the Lincoln Memorial. Yet when I began talking with people in D.C. who were familiar with national movements, both secular and religious, their response was nearly unanimous.

"Do you realize how much money it will take to ensure that a half million people join you here? You'll need to amass enormous funds for media and Internet presence. Probably direct mail, too." Organizers looked at our initial projected budget of $400,000 and advised us to at least triple that amount.

I had to laugh. Back in Phoenix, that same $400,000 budget struck church people as being astronomically high. They couldn't possibly hold enough bake sales to fund it! Yet in D.C. those acquainted with waging national campaigns thought it was absurdly low. "To get the big donors, you have to have a big budget. They'll never want to give to such a small event."

To make a very long and rather painful story short, our budget rose quickly to $1.2 million once we accounted for all the additional publicity and support that people in D.C. thought we would need. As might be expected, this new figure made it even harder to inspire church folk—our base—to give sacrificially. Even if a family were to give ten thousand dollars, it would be just a drop in this gigantic bucket. We would still have to raise $1.19 million! On the other hand, while major donors were not the slightest bit fazed by the price tag, they wanted to know our track record for success and our long-term plans. We could show them plenty of plans for the future, but as for a track record, we had none.

After our last serious hope for a major donation fell through in December 2005, just five months before the walk was to begin, we came to the stark realization that unless money were to suddenly fall from the sky, our walk was not going to happen without a drastic reformulation of the budget.

For a little while, we considered calling off the walk and going with a much cheaper and more flexible road trip involving short two- to three-mile walks in and around major cities. Some CrossWalk America board members sat in on the logistics team members' meeting one evening, letting them know that there might be a drastic change of plan and asking for their feedback at a special meeting a few days later. The logistics team had been working for a year, many hours each week, planning the route, researching supplies, and contacting churches to host us. When we broke the news to the logistics planners, we were essentially telling them that most of their hard work might need to be scrapped. The news could potentially cause irreparable damage to both relationships and team spirit.

At the follow-up meeting, however, each of the team members spoke eloquently, explaining that their function was not ultimately to plan a cross-country walk but to get the word out about the Phoenix Affirmations and the faith that stirred in their hearts. "If there's a better way for us to accomplish this goal, I'm in," the logistics team leader, Donna Murphy, said, summing up the feeling of the group. I was awed. Such displays of selfless commitment are rare in our world. To me, the reaction of the logistics team alone made all our efforts up to that point worthwhile.

After a good deal of prayer and conversation at all levels of the organization, we decided to go ahead with the walk, but with a much smaller budget. Even though everyone was willing to let go of the idea on a rational level, we continued to feel called to the walk. We decided to trust our sense of calling.

Off We Go . . .

The walk launched as planned on Easter Sunday, April 16, 2006, with a "bare bones" budget of $280,000, even lower than our original figure yet still enough to hire documentary filmmakers to accompany us each day of the journey as well as money to hire PR and Internet professionals. Although each of these professionals worked for a fraction of the going rate, we realized that we would not have anywhere near the "firepower" to draw a large crowd to the Lincoln Memorial short of divine intervention on the order of Moses parting the Red Sea!

Over the course of our journey, we were hosted by a hundred and fifty churches, seminaries, and other organizations. We stayed in more than two hundred homes. We met face to face with over eleven thousand people, hearing their stories, telling ours, praying, and of course, eating with them! We delivered close to a hundred sermons and presentations. Our home page and blog site on the Internet logged approximately 150,000 unique visitors who spent several minutes each. We posted over two hundred entries on our blog as people from around the world tracked our progress. Individuals and church groups from as far away as Great Britain, who wore pedometers to count steps taken in support of the Phoenix Affirmations as part of our "Walk Wherever You Are" program, logged over forty million steps on our Web site. A special walk was held in Seattle in support of CrossWalk America involving more than two hundred people. Earlier in the year, a Seattle church had done a bike ride from Seattle to Phoenix to raise awareness.[1]

We received consistent local publicity in each state. Articles also appeared in sixty different blogs, and we were interviewed for a handful of major radio shows and national magazines. The walk was featured once on PBS.[2] Ten partner organizations supported our journey as well. They included the Center for Progressive Christianity, No Longer Silent: Clergy for Justice, Pacific School of Religion, Protestants for the Common Good, the Human Rights Campaign, Faith in America, the Still Speaking Initiative of the United Church of Christ, Living the Questions, Mitchell Gold + Bob Williams, and the Beatitudes Society. This latter organization mailed two thousand copies of *The Phoenix Affirmations: A New Vision for the Future of Christian Faith* to Christian leaders across the United States. National figures in the progressive Christian movement, including Dr. James Forbes, Bishop John Shelby Spong, Bishop Carlton Pearson, Dr. Robin Meyers, and Dr. Tony Robinson, all supported us strongly and publicly.

Although the walk never received our hoped-for seven minutes on *60 Minutes* or two minutes on *Good Morning, America* or even thirty seconds on CNN, we felt satisfied by how far the word did in fact travel. As of this writing, traffic to the CrossWalk America Web site and blog has continued to increase, signaling continuing, substantial interest in the movement.

Our journey ended on September 3 with a one-mile walk from Meridian Park in downtown Washington, D.C., to the historic Foundry United Methodist Church a few blocks from the White House, where our final press conference and celebration event was held.

Instead of 500,000 participants, we were delighted that three hundred or so joined us for the final walk and celebration. Most of these were not locals but people who had driven or flown from a significant distance to participate. One couple, for instance, who had walked with us originally near Albuquerque, New Mexico, joined us again in Saint Louis and yet again in D.C. Before the walk, they had never heard of CrossWalk America or the Phoenix Affirmations.[3] A seventy-something gentleman from Sedona, Arizona, who had joined us for the first mile of the walk in

Phoenix, rejoined us in D.C. to walk the final mile. In both places he made his way forward with the assistance of a wheeled walker! "You've renewed my hope in the future of Christian faith," he told us. "I *had* to walk."[4]

We were pleased, as well, to be joined by Bishop John Shelby Spong and his wife, Christine. They not only walked the final mile but also joined us the day before for our last full day of walking. Bishop Spong, who served as one of the two keynote speakers at our final celebration, published three separate articles about CrossWalk America and the Phoenix Affirmations. In one, which appeared after our final event, Spong concluded:

> Will the image of Christianity in America be changed by this wild imaginative act? Only time will tell. However, if nothing else happens except that a group of people found in Christianity in the year 2006 the power to motivate them to walk across America, to bear witness to what Christianity can be, it will be enough for me. For that means that this venerable faith tradition, to which I am so deeply committed, still has within its ranks those who can reform it and renew it to live in another century. I rejoice in that.[5]

In addition to Spong, Bishop Carlton Pearson supported us as our other keynote speaker. Pearson, who once led a thriving Pentecostal church in Tulsa, Oklahoma, gradually came to believe that salvation in Jesus Christ is extended to the whole world, not just believers. After he started preaching and teaching this theology, he was attacked on all sides by his peers. In one year, membership at his church went from five thousand to just two hundred! Although he has since built the congregation back to over a thousand, Pearson says of his ordeal, "We lost everything to find it all." Pearson has been featured on NPR's *This American Life* and on *Dateline NBC*.

Revelation on the Steps

The day after our final celebration, still high on all the emotion that went with it, I made my way once again to the steps of the Lincoln Memorial. While I was completely satisfied—even overjoyed—by the crowd who showed up on September 3 and the publicity generated over the course of the walk, I found myself drawn to those steps. I wanted to ask God for an honest answer to the question I felt had originally been posed to me about bearing Jesus to Washington, D.C.

I felt substantially at ease over this question. I felt we had remained true to Jesus and his message to the best of our ability. Still, I needed to hear *God's* answer, not mine. To this end, I meditated for quite some time, working to become inwardly open enough to hearing God that I could freely listen for, and accept, whatever answer came to me—even a devastating one.

I then posed the question: "God, did we do it? Did we, in fact, bear Jesus with us to Washington, D.C., on this walk?"

Within seconds I felt a strong tug of intuition. The thought that arose from the depths of my soul startled me.

"No," intuition said. "You *did not* bear Jesus with you on your walk to D.C." Yet this word was followed immediately by another.

"*You* did not bear *Jesus* here. *Jesus* bore *you.*"

In an instant, all the volunteers who had worked so diligently over the previous two years raced through my mind; all the churches who had supported us; each of the core walkers (Rebecca, Brad, Meighan, Katrina, Merrill); our guest walker, Mark; our RV driver, Ray; our filmmakers Scott and Chris. I thought of the people along the way who had supported us with everything from meals to money and most especially their hearts. I thought of those who had challenged us to see them as they really are rather than as stereotypes. I thought of our families who had perhaps borne the greatest sacrifice of all, doing without their loved ones not only during the walk but also for the year and a half of preparation. I thought of our home churches and all the people who were thrilled to be asked to radically step up their level of discipleship in order to help change the face of Christianity in our country into a more inclusive, compassionate one. I thought, too, of all the twists and turns we'd made before and during the walk in light of changing situations and new information. And finally, I thought of how all of us involved with CrossWalk America had learned to trust in God working among, between, around, and through us more than we ever have in our lives.

"Yes, God," I said, tears running down my face. "Jesus really did bear us to this place. Thank you."

AFFIRMATION 12

[Christian love of self includes]
Acting on the faith that we are born with a meaning
and purpose, a vocation and ministry that serve to
strengthen and extend God's realm of love.

Priesthood of All Believers

Have you ever noticed how some people, rich or poor, tend to act richly toward life and some people act like they are working off a debt they can't quite pay? Some people's lives are full of examples of sincere generosity and abundant pleasure, while others act as if they are driven by a memory of loss and dutiful rigor.

The difference between one kind of person and another may be explained, in part, by genetics and by various life circumstances. Some people suffer early childhood traumas that convince them that they are unworthy of love and spend the rest of their lives wrestling with a sense that they never quite measure up and act accordingly. Others have enjoyed the benefit of repeated generosity and affirmation of their worth and reflect this in their dealings with others. However, at a deeper level, a less obvious factor is often involved: faith.

If you are one of the nine in every ten people in America who identifies as Christian, chances are that your response to life has as much or more to do with what you understand about Jesus and his path than about any other single factor, whether you regularly attend church or not and whether you read the Bible or not. Let me take you through a brief exercise to explain what I mean. The exercise has nothing overtly to do with Jesus or religion, but I'll follow it up with a couple of real-life examples to flesh out the implications for Christian faith.

Imagine one day you're sorting through your mail and come across an envelope addressed to you with a return address from a bank you've never heard of: Bank of the Path. At first you assume it's yet another piece of junk mail, but the fact that the envelope has come with a first-class stamp affixed and is hand-addressed to you persuades you to open it.

Inside, you find a note and a check. As any red-blooded American would do, you take out the check first. Much to your shock and bewilderment, the check is made out to you in the amount of a million dollars!

Immediately you suspect a gimmick. You look for any fine print indicating that this is a loan amount should you cash the check. There is none. So you pull out the note. The note reads as follows:

> Dear (your name),
>
> We are pleased to inform you that you were a named inheritor of a very large estate. While we are not at liberty to disclose either the identity of the deceased or the amount of the full estate, we have been authorized to share with you a few details.

First, we can tell you that the estate was quite large. Second, you are but one recipient among innumerable others, each of whom is receiving a million dollars. Third, you may or may not have known the deceased personally. If we disclosed his or her name to you, it may not even ring a distant bell. Fourth, you are receiving this check not due to anything you've done or not done but solely due to the generosity of the giver. There are no strings attached to this money. You may use it however you please. Finally, although it was not specified in the will, we hope you will offer a prayer of thanks on this person's behalf.

That's it. Now, assuming you deposited the check and it proved to be valid, I invite you to consider what your frame of mind and general demeanor would be like over the next, say, ten years. I'm not asking how you'd spend the money. Nor am I using this exercise to suggest that money makes all the difference. (Remember, it's not just money you've received anyway. You've been *gifted*—gifted with something quite extraordinary and the result of pure and astounding grace.)

Would you look at your present life any differently—your vocation, your relationships with others, your family life—and would you strive to adjust things in any way?

Would you foresee yourself smiling more often?

Would you be more jovial, laughing more readily than you do now?

Would you radiate more of a sense of ease and peace amid life's twists and turns? Would you be more confident?

Would you forgive any debts of others, financial or otherwise?

Would you have more compassion for those in need?

Would you be more generous with others?

Would you be more thankful?

Would you expect to have any more zeal for doing good in the world?

If you were to meet in the coming year other people who received this same inheritance, can you see yourself pooling a portion of your windfall with them to make an even larger difference in the world?

In general, how would you feel about your life?

Now, set these thoughts aside for a moment as you consider a very different scenario:

Imagine you come across the same envelope from Bank of the Path, but inside you find not a check for a million dollars but a bill for this amount. The note enclosed with the bill states that the amount due is your portion of a very large debt owed by many people that was incurred before you were born and is legitimately owed by you and all the others.

Assume that you are persuaded beyond all reasonable doubt that you do, in fact, owe this money and that the amount comes due precisely ten years from today.

Imagine that the letter closes with the following statement:

> Your debt is being held by an unusually generous individual. While we cannot disclose the identity of the person in question, we have been authorized to inform you that should you live a life worthy of your debt being canceled *in this individual's estimation,* it will be canceled in full ten years from today.
>
> If, however, you have not been deemed worthy of the debt's cancellation, the amount will be due in full. In ten years, if we have not received payment in full and you are deemed unworthy of debt cancellation, we regret to inform you that we will foreclose on any assets you have to repay it.

Consider what your general demeanor toward life might be in the next ten years:

Would you smile more often, or would your demeanor betray more anxiety?

Would you laugh more readily than before, or would you be more serious?

How would you handle life's twists and turns—with more grace or less?

Would you forgive the debts of others or seek to collect them?

Would you be more at ease or more nervous about who may be looking at and evaluating your behavior?

Would you start making regular payments to the bank, or would you try to act in such a way as to convince whoever may be watching that you are in fact worthy? And if you chose this latter path, would you act in a truly "worthy" manner? Could you be sure that your actions are in fact worthy? How genuine could you be under this kind of pressure?

Would you wonder about who else owes this debt? Would you seek out these others, trying to discern together the principles by which the holder of your debt might be persuaded to cancel it?

In short, would you be more or less optimistic about the quality of your life in the coming ten years?

Comparing your feelings about these two letters, which one would you rather receive? I suspect that the answer is so obvious that it isn't worth asking.

Except that the answer does, in fact, matter. Although the letters may be entirely fictitious, chances are that your day-to-day behavior reflects tendencies that mirror at least partially the response a person would make if one of these letters were tucked in his or her pocket or purse.

Let me explain by sharing the stories of a couple people I know, Sue and Nathan. These two are actually not individuals but composites of real people who shared their lives and stories with us over the course of the walk.

Sue's Story

Sue grew up in a Christian home. Though she hasn't been to church in years, her understanding of Jesus and her way of living in the world are very much colored by what she learned in Sunday school and by her experience of her faith community as a young adult.

In church Sue learned about Adam and Eve. Her church taught her that this original couple lived in a paradise called Eden at the beginning of the world, which they believed existed six thousand years ago. In Eden, Adam and Eve lived without sin or blemish. But all that changed one day. Even though God had given them everything they could have ever wanted, Adam and Eve turned their backs on God by eating fruit from a tree God had specifically commanded them not to partake of.

Sue's church taught her that that since God had given this original couple everything out of infinite love and generosity, their turning their back on God's command constituted an equally infinite offense. Being mere human beings, not gods, there was no way they could ever redeem such an affront to God's honor. God subjected Adam and Eve to death, which had not entered the world until they sinned.

To Sue, death is God's judgment on sin. And because their offense against God was infinite, not even earthly death could pay God back for what they had done. Therefore, God created hell as a place where they would be punished for eternity.

Since we are the offspring of Adam and Eve, we have inherited their debt with equal prospects of paying it off in this life without a savior. Happily, though, God is kind and generous. God eventually established a way we could all be redeemed. God sent Jesus.

Sue's church teaches that Jesus was born of a virgin and thus was conceived without incurring "original sin," which is passed on through sexual procreation. She learned that Jesus lived without sin or blemish, like Adam and Eve did in their original state. He was the Son of God, not the son of Joseph.

When Jesus was crucified, Sue learned, his death on the cross was therefore not that of an ordinary mortal. Rather, since Jesus lived without having ever sinned, he was not subject to death like other humans. He lived like the original Adam and Eve were *supposed* to live but did not.

In accepting death on a cross, Jesus took the judgment we deserved upon himself, like an innocent bystander in a courtroom who comes forward to accept punishment on behalf of a convicted criminal. Anyone who truly believes in Jesus—that he is God's Son and our Savior—is redeemed from God's judgment. When God looks at a believer, God sees not our sin but Christ's purity and obedience. We are saved from everlasting punishment. When believers die, they enter heaven to live with God.

When Sue first came to understand her relationship to the original Adam and Eve, she felt like someone who had just received the invoice from Bank of the Path.

"I was staggered by the debt I owed God. And I was frightened because I knew I am as big a sinner as anyone. I'm not perfect. I knew that without help I would suffer the same fate as they did."

When Sue learned about Jesus, however, she experienced this revelation like one might experience reading the accompanying letter from Bank of the Path. She was greatly relieved and discovered that God is generous and could bail her out if she believed.

Yet it eventually dawned on Sue that she was not out of the woods.

"I began to wonder if I was a true enough believer to satisfy God. Everyone has doubts once in a while, and I seem to be cursed with more than most people—at least most people who went to my church. I wondered what my fate would be if I died and God saw into my heart and didn't find enough faith. Would God send me to hell?"

Sue's church provided an answer, which initially gave her hope. They told her that believers act differently from nonbelievers. They told her what "true believers" did and did not do. She figured that as long as she acted like a true believer, she would have enough faith to satisfy God.

Over the years, Sue tried as hard as she could to conform to the dictates of her church. She read her Bible and prayed daily, attended worship each week, and taught Sunday school. Still, she could not break the feeling that she might not measure up to the standard of belief she was supposed to have. She said that she still had doubts and that the more she doubted, the worse it got. She became convinced that she might never have enough faith to get into heaven.

Consequently, Sue took on more roles in her church. She volunteered for mission projects and worked occasionally in a homeless shelter supported by her church. She tried to convert some of her friends to Christianity.

"I figured that if I could bring others into belief and save them from hell, maybe God would conclude that I had enough belief myself."

Increasingly, however, Sue became discouraged. No matter what she did, she could not shake the feeling that she might not be good enough. She kept thinking, "What if there's a ten percent chance that I don't believe fully enough? What if there's just five percent or one percent? Eternity is a long time to suffer. Yet no matter what I do, I just can't be positive that I'll go to heaven."

The members of Sue's faith community offered little to allay her concerns. According to Sue, they all insisted that they were perfectly confident they'd not only be going to heaven but would be wearing crowns of righteousness. But Sue knew some of them well and was unconvinced that they acted like true believers. This only made her more scared. "What if even if you're a hundred percent convinced you have enough faith, you still might not make it?"

One Sunday, beset with anxiety, Sue stayed home from church. The next Sunday she did not return. Nor did she go the next Sunday or the one after that. Eventually, Sue resigned herself to the fact that there was nothing she could do to convince herself or God that she believed in Jesus with perfect sincerity.

"I decided at that point to quietly slip away. I didn't want my lack of belief to affect others, especially the children. I figured that if I caused someone else to slip away, I'd be a goner for sure."

Now Sue is part of the spiritually homeless in America—the six in every ten people who affirm that they are Christian when asked but do not actively participate in any faith community.

"Sometimes I feel guilty about my choice not to attend church, but mostly I've resigned myself to simply live life as best I can and deal with the consequences later. I hope one day to meet Jesus, but I'm not sure what he'll have to say when I do. Will I be a sheep or a goat? Will I be welcomed with open arms or tossed into a lake of fire? I really don't like to think about that."

Nathan's Story

Nathan's story is quite different from Sue's. Nathan did not grow up in a church environment, but he actively participates in one now. There he has learned the same stories that Sue did, but his faith community finds different meaning in them.

"I was taught that the story of Adam and Eve isn't about actual human beings who lived long ago but about *us*. The story is a metaphor that reveals deep things about our relationship with God, each other, and God's Creation."

Nathan's church teaches that we are eternal beings, created out of the very breath of God, yet are also capable of turning our backs on our divine origin and making choices that harm us. God imposed death on Adam and Eve not as punishment but as *protection*.

"At first this didn't make sense to me," says Nathan. "How could death be anything but a curse? But then I realized that if we really have eternal souls, as the Bible teaches, then without death our mistakes could live on with us for eternity. Death ensures that no matter how far we stray from God's path, our decisions have an absolute end point. In eternity, God has the final word, not us."

Nathan's church maintains that just as we may freely choose to turn from God in this life, so God has the ultimate freedom to reject our rejection. Just as God did not give up on Adam and Eve after they turned their backs on God but rather protected and preserved them for life and relationship outside of Eden, so God acts toward all God's creations. Death may be the end of our mortal lives, but it is far from the end of our relationship with God or of God's love and grace.

Nathan maintains that this assumption isn't made on the basis of Adam and Eve alone. Jesus' life, death, and resurrection makes this point even more clearly.

According to Nathan's community, Jesus came not to save us from hell after we die so that we can go to heaven but to save us from dying in this world without ever having really lived.

Nathan says that his church takes seriously Jesus' first public words in the Gospel of Mark, where he announces, "the kingdom of heaven is already here, wake up, change your whole way of thinking, and believe the *good news*!"[6] When you think about it, these must have been pretty shocking words to Jesus' audience. They probably would have responded, "What in the world do you mean? Look at all the pain and struggle we live with! The Romans are on our backs, most of us are poor and living on the edge of existence, the world is full of war and strife, murder and hatred, and you mean to tell us that heaven has already arrived?" Nathan laughed. "If crack had been a drug in Jesus' day, they surely would have thought he'd been smoking it."

Yet Nathan's community finds in Jesus' life, teachings, and actions a God who has indeed made heaven available in the here-and-now. Likely they would agree with the words of the nineteenth-century poet Elizabeth Barrett Browning:

Earth's crammed with heaven.
And every common bush aflame with God.
But only he who sees takes off his shoes.
The rest sit round it and pluck blackberries.[7]

Nathan observes that Jesus once said that the two greatest commandments are to love God with all your heart, mind, soul, and strength and
to love your neighbor as yourself. Then he says that "on these two commandments hang all the law and the prophets" (Matthew 22:40). In other
words, everything hangs on three great loves—love of God, neighbor, and
self. When you look at Jesus' life and teaching, you discover someone
who's walking a path and living as if heaven is here right now. The key to
his experience of heaven is his experience of God's love and grace, which
he receives and reflects outwardly as love for God, love for his neighbor,
and love for himself.

Through Jesus' life, the blind—the spiritually and physically blind—
are given sight. The lame are healed. The outcast is brought into God's
inner circle. Strangers become friends, enemies are reconciled, the poor
are fed, the proud are humbled, the grieving are consoled, the greedy become generous, the despairing are given hope. Every life Jesus touches
receives the touch of eternity. People either accept it and grow or recoil in
disbelief. Either way they are shown a love that will not quit on them.

When asked how he and his faith community know that God will not
quit on the disbelievers, Nathan talks about a cross and an empty tomb.

"The cross shows us that not only heaven is found in this realm but
so is hell. It was not the Jews or Romans who killed Jesus; it was humanity. And it wasn't only Jesus who died there but all of us. Jesus' words on
the cross, 'My God, my God, why have you forsaken me?' echo the countless cries of people throughout the ages who have experienced humanity
at its worst.

"Yet in the cross we also know that God understands and experiences
our pain. It reveals that deep in God's own heart, God knows pain akin
to that of a parent whose only child has been murdered. The cross also
reveals that God's response is not vengeance but fierce grace.

"Jesus prays, 'Father, forgive them, for they know not what they do.'
He knows he can trust this grace. And on Easter Sunday, the empty tomb
confirms it." Nathan believes that we come to know in the fullest sense
that God is capable of taking our pain and despair and also our disobe-
dience and sin and transforming them. We don't have the final answer;
God does. In God's freedom, God rejects our rejection not only of God

but of our neighbor and even of ourselves. The empty tomb shows that there is nothing in all of life and not even death itself that can separate us from God's love. All things become new."

When asked how his beliefs affect his day-to-day life, Nathan is quick to respond.

"I've had certain experiences in my life when I've felt that God had given me a glimpse of love that exceeds anything I could possibly conceive. In those brief moments it was as if time stood still and I was standing in the presence of eternity. I felt a profound sense of giftedness. I was overcome with awe and wonder. But I've also asked myself, 'Are these experiences real, or are they the result of an overly active imagination?' After all, I'm a product of the modern age! But if the cross and empty tomb have anything to do with reality, then they suggest that there is substance behind my experiences. I can trust them. And because I can trust them, I can live them. Little by little, in my own flawed and imperfect way, I seek to reflect God's love for me by loving God, my neighbor, and myself."

Faith in Action

Sue's and Nathan's beliefs about God and God's work in Jesus profoundly shape who they are and how they respond to the world. Sue and the (former) faith community in which her beliefs were forged live with a nagging sense that God may be gracious and loving, but only when certain conditions are met. Given the consequences of failing to meet these conditions, their lives reflect the anxiety and self-loathing that any rational person who held similar beliefs might feel.

By contrast, Nathan and his community live with a strong sense that there is nothing they can do that will keep God's love away from them—ever. Rather than taking this belief as license to sin without fear of consequences, as some Christians claim would happen if God is truly this gracious, Nathan and his community are inspired to act on the faith that each person is born with a meaning and purpose—a vocation and ministry that serve to strengthen and extend God's realm of love. The Phoenix Affirmations were originally written to reflect the faith and life of communities like Nathan's. They represent an attempt to distill the essence of what it means to live in light of amazing grace. No attempt has been made to claim that the Affirmations define what it means to be a Christian, nor is there any expectation that they will serve as a final word to stand for all time, even for those who endorse them. However, the

Phoenix Affirmations do represent a decision for many of us Christians
to be silent no longer about our particular faith and experience. They
reflect a commitment to embody faith in action.

In a sense, one can picture the Phoenix Affirmations as a letter received
from God in the mail. Rather than being enclosed with a million-dollar
check or invoice, the letter simply embraces a life—a life lived in the
awareness that God's heavenly realm can be found in the here-and-now
and that we are loved—loved beyond our wildest imagination.

While walking through Indianapolis, I preached a sermon in which I
paraphrased the Phoenix Affirmations in the form of a "letter from God."
I later posted the letter on CrossWalk America's blog, and it was passed
around from friend to friend and posted on other Internet blogs. A multimedia compilation based on this letter was shown at our final event in
Washington, D.C. I offer the letter to you here as a way of closing our
journey together.

A LETTER FROM GOD
(BASED ON THE PHOENIX AFFIRMATIONS)

Dear Friend,

I have given you a world where those who call on me by different
names still discover the same Me you know in Christ. I have given you
a world where flawed human beings may become my greatest followers and where my voice continues to whisper in people's hearts
throughout the ages (not having ceased to speak two thousand years
ago). I give you a world where my glory can be found in the sacred
and the secular, the Christian and the non-Christian, the human and
the non-human. I give you a world of extraordinary beauty—where
beauty itself may serve as a pathway of relationship with Me.

I give you a world where no matter who you are or what your path
has been, you are inherently valuable; where you possess a dignity and
worth that no one can take away; where the poor and denigrated, the
oppressed and afflicted are my best friends; where religion is best when
it is not forced upon anyone and where human beings may live in the
freedom to worship Me in whatever ways my Spirit guides them. I give
you a world where the power of love far exceeds that of your most
potent of weapons; where it is possible for even the bitterest of enemies to be reconciled.

I give you a soul that is loved beyond your wildest imagination and
a life in which you don't have to sacrifice your mind to live by your
heart. I give you a life that may be lived creatively; where rest, recre-

ation, and just plain fun are as valuable as your vocation. I give you a world where all people's lives—including your own—have a meaning and purpose, a vocation and ministry that is as high as that of any prophet, priest, or king.

This is the world I have given you. All I ask in return is that you accept this world as your own and spread the good news that this gift has been given to all people.

ASPHALT
JESUS

FINDING A NEW CHRISTIAN FAITH
ALONG THE HIGHWAYS OF AMERICA

Discussion Guide and Questions

C. Howie Howard

LAST SUMMER, Eric Elnes's journey with CrossWalk America passed through Kansas City. My church hosted members of the team, enjoyed their company and that of new friends in the community, and immersed ourselves in the Phoenix Affirmations, which continue to shape the ways we practice love of God, neighbor, and self. We've had conversations over a great many questions; we've felt a bit of anger at times when certain expectations or assumptions were challenged; mostly, we have grown in awe of the love of God we know in Christ. Though *Asphalt Jesus* and the Phoenix Affirmations abound with material for reflection, Eric's metaphors of "Good Friday," "Holy Saturday," and "Easter Sunday" orientations, introduced in Chapter Twelve of *Asphalt Jesus,* are particularly useful in helping us understand our life together. Affirming their essential sacredness and interrelationship, this framework suggests a set of overarching questions or areas of interest for readers of *Asphalt Jesus:*

> Good Friday: "In what areas of my life (or my faith) do I feel like long-held assumptions or beliefs are being threatened?"
>
> Holy Saturday: "What doubts to I wrestle with in respect to my faith?"
>
> Easter Sunday: "What, if anything, inspires me with a sense of hope for the future of Christian faith (or of *my* faith)?

Jesus challenged his followers with parables that subverted their expectations and drew attention to directions in which he was pushing them to grow. In like manner, parts of *Asphalt Jesus* stretch us, and paying careful attention to those areas of Good Friday heat will encourage growth. The transformation of Christianity in America toward a more compassionate and inclusive faith will naturally raise more questions than answers as we wonder together what that vision looks like in concrete terms and how we can take steps toward it. Finally, one of the great discoveries of the walk was that there are Christians in every corner of this country longing for the kind of Easter Sunday faith articulated in the Phoenix Affirmations. Those areas of common concern and common call when we say, "I'm not alone, and I'm not crazy!" indicate the Spirit's movement and give us direction for common action.

The questions presented here frequently focus on stories: Eric's story, Gospel stories, and *your* story. The ability to both affirm and challenge us gives stories real, transformative power. Trading stories and listening to storytellers is so thoroughly natural and meaningful to us, we often forget the vital role they play in our lives and culture. I love that the passion story is directly implied by Eric's image of three sacred energies. In many ways, as my friend Jody would say, "the church is simply the community that is gathered around Jesus' story."

This guide is written to stimulate both private journaling and group conversation and also to spark your own stories and reflections. I wish I could be with you, not only to hear your responses but also to find out what new questions our conversations would raise. Let me encourage you to go ahead and explore when tangents and side paths present themselves, especially when the questions draw out experiences and hopes from your own life.

Chapter One: The Idea That Wouldn't Go Away: Listening to God

Eric begins by sharing the story of how the Phoenix Affirmations and the walk from Phoenix, Arizona, to Washington, D.C., began as an idea that simply wouldn't go away. Following a period of active resistance and even after enlisting the help of others, Eric surrenders to the walk and takes the first steps along this new path. His experience is an example of the discipline of discernment—listening for God—and is the basis for further reflections on prayer.

QUESTIONS

1. Eric's experience of resistance followed by surrender became a marker of God's voice in his life. Have you ever seen that pattern in your own life? Or has there been an idea that became less insistent with time, fading away? Does this story help you recognize your own inner "still, small voice"? What might hold you back from attending to it?

2. When it becomes clear that the idea of the walk will not leave Eric alone, he carefully invites others to test it along with him. Whom do you include in your process of discernment? What roles do they play?

3. Woven throughout the chapter is the idea of the connection between God's voice and our deepest inner voice. How are these voices the same voice? Are they also different?

4. A distinction is made between selfishness (acting with regard for oneself exclusively) and self-interest (as one-third of Jesus' great commandment, along with loving God and neighbor); in this way Eric suggests that God's purposes are in concert with our true self-interest. Where do God's purposes and your own interests intersect? Is there an activity that fully, joyfully engages you and also works toward God's purposes? What role does that play in your weekly practice of faith?

5. For many Christians, it is a new idea to think of prayer as primarily a *listening* experience. What was your initial reaction? How does the recipe for "basic prayer" compare with your own practice? If you have integrated a significant time for listening into your prayer life, what is happening?

6. Eric mentions several voices at our "inner table" that most Christians recognize: conscience, the pragmatist, the free child, Jesus. Do you recognize other regulars at your particular table? (For example, as a result of my travels, in certain contexts I always hear the voice of an African mother.) Jesus' voice can be distinct, or it can be in harmony with another; how do you pick it out from the chorus?

7. Asking if an action "looks like Jesus" inspires a greater sensitivity to context than asking "What would Jesus do?" Let's explore this for a moment. What do you believe Jesus' actions would have looked like to an observer? What about his followers or people he talked to? In your experience of reading the Gospels, do they all paint the same picture of Jesus' actions? What is constant, and what varies? Why are the variations important?

8. Eric quotes Bruce Van Blair on the inner voice of Jesus: "This voice thinks differently from the others—and concludes from beyond your capacity to understand. It is quiet-like—peace with power—and it says very beautiful and sometimes very strange things." Have you ever experienced this inner voice? Did you recognize it as Jesus' voice at the time or later, or do you at all? Looking forward, how will you prepare to attend to Jesus' voice when it appears?

Chapter Two: Phoenix Rising

The Phoenix Affirmations condensed nineteen pages of theology into a dynamic statement of twelve principles that fits on a single page. Eric's spiritual experience with a friend moves him to a place where he considers everything in light of "the standard of God's unconditional love." The Three Great Loves of Jesus' great commandment—love of God, neighbor, and self—outline a pattern of relationship that many people are willing to give their life for. The Phoenix Affirmations are not a new creed or a way to define who is or is not "Christian"; they are "simply principles by which some people have chosen to live and love in a manner that to them 'looks like Jesus.'"

QUESTIONS

1. Eric "lost" his wrestling match of discernment regarding the walk (though in a role reversal from the Jacob story in Genesis 32:23–33, perhaps God simply hung on to Eric's ankle until sunrise!). Have you ever experienced God in this kind of adversarial partnership? How did the match go? Whether you won, lost, or wrestled to a draw, what happened next?

2. Eric's spiritual experience receives different receptions in different churches. His mainline congregation doesn't seem to have the vocabulary or background to understand it, and the fundamentalist community elevates his experience to the exclusion of others'. How would your faith community respond to someone with a similar story? Are you aware of particularly helpful or harmful ways of communication between "mystical explosion" and "slow and gradual" people?

3. "When you step out in faith in the name of loving God, neighbor, and self, you do not walk alone" is a theme that emerges throughout this journey. Yet it is often a surprise; we *thought* we were alone! Why did people of such a related spirit become disconnected from each other to the point of feeling like an "only one"? How can you keep and strengthen those connections once you have discovered them? In what new directions can we grow this web of not walking alone?

4. Eric uses the image of the seemingly dead ocotillo shrub to describe many churches in America. Does the image ring true to your experience? If your faith or faith community feels like an ocotillo, what is the "water" you're waiting for? What do you and your community need in order to flourish?

5. People who seek "primarily to meet [their] own needs through helping others" are of special value to a faith community. Do you know anyone who seems to live at this intersection of personal desires and others' needs? How would you describe them and their role in the

community? Is there a way that you practice this principle or a way you would like to try?

6. Let's revisit the "loving God" part of Jesus' great commandment. When individuals love God, what impact does that have on their life, their actions, their way of being? I've found it helpful to think of loving God as "loving the things that God loves." (I encountered this idea through Marcus Borg.) What does God love? Why do you think so? Who might agree or disagree with your understanding of what God loves?

Chapter Three: Hellfire, Damnation, and Garbage Dumps

Two radio interviews in the opening days of the CrossWalkers' journey reveal that the most controversial part of the Phoenix Affirmations is its attitude toward salvation. Eric's trading of Bible quotes with the hosts show that Scripture includes multiple voices on the subject, which are set in the context of Scripture as a whole. "Fire" is understood to be an image the Gospels use to describe purification more than punishment. Belief in "hell" as eternal punishment begins to look like risk avoidance, where living by God's radical grace becomes truly risky.

QUESTIONS

1. If you had caught one of the radio interviews on the air, how would you have responded? Is there a question or a comment you might have phoned in to the station? If you had the opportunity to do an on-air interview with Eric, what questions would you have asked? Imagine where the discussion might have led.

2. "Scripture speaks with more than one voice with respect to salvation." Is there a particular voice you've heard in your own life? One you've heard through others' teaching or through your own experience of Scripture?

3. Eric asks his fellow walkers to consider that the Phoenix Affirmations may be wrong about God's grace, that there is a chance that people who don't believe in Jesus in just the right way will "burn in hell for eternity." He describes how living in light of the "worst-case scenario" leads people to a vision of Christianity that elevates conversion over everything else. What are the risks of living "as if all were loved beyond what we can know"? What makes this leap of faith so difficult? (Or if it's easy for you, what is your secret?) Though it is hard, what makes it *possible*?

4. Eric revises Romans 2:24, replacing *Jews* with *Christians* to make
   a point: "It's because of you Christians that the outsiders are down
   on God." What truth is contained in this insight? How have
   Christians turned non-Christians off on God? What do you think
   attracted people to Jesus' own group of followers or to early
   Christian communities? Are there any implications for your
   church, community, or individual Christian practice today?

5. Imagine a fourth servant in Jesus' parable. This servant is also
   entrusted with some money to tend while the master is away; he
   invests the money, but the investments turn out badly, and when
   the master returns, the servant has less than he was given. How
   would the master respond to this servant? What would the master
   say? If love is indeed a risky investment, what happens after you
   suffer losses?

Chapter Four: Jesus First Baptist Church

Without a preplanned speaking engagement, Eric, Meighan, Scott, and
Chris visit Jesus First Baptist Church in Eagar, Arizona. The CrossWalkers
introduce themselves and the Phoenix Affirmations unapologetically and
are also interested to hear the witness of Jesus First Baptist and find common ground. Through worship, Christ shows up unexpectedly within the
diverse gathering of fundamentalists and CrossWalkers. Eric reflects on
Affirmation 1, focusing on the relationship of openness between authentic Christianity and "other paths that God may provide" and the Christ
understood in Christian tradition to be cosmically present.

QUESTIONS

1. "It has been a long time since I've worshiped in a fundamentalist
   church, and I'd like to hear what the people have to say." Have you
   ever worshiped with a faith community far outside your own tradition? What was your experience? Would you do it again? Might a
   person even make a regular practice of worshiping outside his or
   her own community? What would be the purpose?

2. American flags are prominently displayed on Jesus First's billboard
   and building. What is the church communicating through the use of
   this image? How does it relate to the separation of church and state?
   Many churches also have an American flag somewhere in their sanctuary; what does it mean to have that image in a worship space?
   Why is it important to some people? Might it be offensive to others?

3. "What can I affirm here?" Eric asks during Bible study at Jesus First Baptist Church. "Nothing." When you find yourself in this position, unable to affirm any part of another's spiritual experience, how can you respond in love? Later, Eric thinks, "I do believe what your heart is trying to convey." How would you describe the truth in the Bible study leader's words?

4. "Son, at the base of the cross, it's *all* level ground," says Pastor Rhodes. Imagine yourself at the place he describes. Who else do you see?

5. Have you had any experience of the Jesus who is confounding, who shows up unexpectedly? Can you share that story? What were your expectations—and what allowed Jesus to show up in spite of them?

6. William Sloane Coffin says, "The Church cannot forget Jesus . . . and frequently fears that his message will be rediscovered." What is this message that the church might fear? Why would it seem threatening? What happens when the message is rediscovered?

7. "The Path of Christ, therefore, transcends Christianity just as much as it transcends Buddhism, Taoism, Hinduism, or Islam." What in this statement challenges you? What can you affirm? Taken seriously, what does this mean for those of us on a Jesus-following path? On another path?

Chapter Five: The Trickster Shows Up—Again!

The CrossWalkers' reception in Clovis defies their expectations. Given the cold shoulder by the Clovis Christian Ministerial Alliance president, Eric and company are received warmly by a small church outside the alliance and then by the local media, the mayor, and many residents of Clovis. "Common ground" keeps appearing, mostly by finding it in unexpected places with unexpected people. Standing with outcast and oppressed people, and that doing so is inherently disruptive, is the subject of Eric's further reflections.

QUESTIONS

1. God the Trickster shows up throughout Scripture; Eric mentions Isaac's birth and binding stories, the naming of Peter, and the whole story of the poor Savior Jesus as examples of God's Trickster spirit at work. What are some other stories of God the Trickster from Christian tradition? From other traditions? How did God the

Trickster break into this story of Eric's? Do you have a personal story of God the Trickster?

2. "We'll keep offering back love and joy no matter what we get from them" is Eric and Rebecca's operating philosophy as they walk into an interview with KIJN "Jesus Radio" in Farwell, Texas. How does Eric's take on salvation (in Chapter Three) make him more free to offer others love and joy, regardless of what's thrown at him? Think about situations in which it's easy for you to offer your love and joy to others and ones where it's a struggle; why is it that way? After hearing the story of CrossWalk's reception in Clovis, can you imagine new ways of being in the midst of those harder situations?

3. The negative response from the Ministerial Alliance directly contrasts with Father Chavez's "You're walking for Jesus. That's all I need to know." Describe your understanding of hospitality, from a personal and a scriptural perspective. If Christians are called to be a hospitable people, how does that look in terms of everyday posture and action?

4. The CrossWalkers' time in Clovis parallels several of Jesus' parables and experiences with the Temple authorities in Jerusalem. In addition to turning expectations upside down, all these stories include an element of subversion—that standing with the outcast is necessarily a critique of the status quo. How is that critique made concrete during CrossWalk's journey through Clovis? How do the walkers positively embody a different posture and pattern of relationships?

5. Affirmation 6's call to stand with outcast and oppressed people includes the wrenching "with or without the support of others." It is a direct and personal call. What was your initial response to Affirmation 6? What does it imply about Christians' work and their way of being in the world currently?

6. This chapter explodes the myth of the existence of a monolithic Middle America. What elements of this myth were confronted and discarded? Decide if you would consider yourself a Middle American or not; how did you approach this chapter in light of your own identity? Were any of your expectations challenged?

7. "Many people are more loyal to Jesus than they are to their preconceived notions about Jesus." Do you feel that this describes you? The people in your church? Christians in general? If you take Eric's insight seriously, how will it affect your conversations with other, perhaps very different, Christians?

Chapter Six: Asphalt Jesus

Next on the walk is Hereford, Texas, where the travelers are hosted by the nondenominational Fellowship of Believers congregation. It is a conservative church that strongly affirms others' freedom and regularly seeks out voices beyond their own tradition and expectations. Between barbecue and worship, the groups find plenty of common ground and engage in fruitful conversations about their differences. Eric's reflections on Affirmation 8 and the Golden Rule illustrate how the Three Great Loves of Jesus' great commandment are woven together.

QUESTIONS

1. Pastor Tracy Dunn-Noland says, "Frankly, my congregation can get along with pretty much *anybody* so long as they order *steak!*" What does this say about common ground and where it can be found? Do you have a story about eating with someone very different from you? How were you affected by sharing that meal? Why is the table such an enduring place of meaning and sharing?

2. Merrill Davison notes the difference in travel time between driving and walking eight hundred miles: two days compared to five weeks. How would the story be different if the CrossWalkers had simply driven to Hereford to listen and talk about the Phoenix Affirmations? What have they—and their hosts—gained through walking? Knowing that most of us will not walk across America, what do you gain through their stories?

3. At the barbecue, a man says he reads the Bible "pretty much like everyone else." Who does he mean by "everyone else," and how does "everyone else" read the Bible? (He says "simply," and his wife says "literally"—would you agree?) Describe how you read the Bible.

4. In the middle of a conversation, Eric realizes that the frequent claim others make to be "in the middle" theologically means more than he first thought, including that most people feel that their own point of view is balanced. Given our natural tendency to tip the balance of our perceptions toward our own biases, how should this broad claim be understood? Describe the "middle" that is so widely claimed. Is this middle a true position of humble moderation? Is it different from the status quo?

5. "I think that's how change works, one relationship at a time," says Tracy. When she became an ordained minister, her brother

examined and changed his posture toward women pastors. What relationships have changed you over time? How have you been an agent for change in a relationship with someone else? Are there relationships you're a part of now that have unrealized potential for growth and transformation?

6. The phrase "including those who consider us their enemies" stands out in Affirmation 8, framing Jesus' call to love our enemies in a striking way. In truth, whom do you consider your enemies, in both individual and communal senses? Who considers you an enemy? How would shifting posture from "our enemies" to "those who consider us their enemies" affect your daily life? The life of your faith community? Our individual and communal relationships with those self-declared "enemies"?

7. Karen Armstrong asserts that we naturally seek ecstasy, the experience of being outside one's ego, and will find it in at least one of its transient or lasting forms. Do you achieve a "high" of one kind or another? Religion promises a path toward a more lasting ecstasy; what do nonreligious philosophies have to say about this more lasting form? What does consumerism say? What role do transient ecstatic experiences play in religious practice?

8. A major theme of Chapters Five and Six is expressed in the story of Eric's dad defending the rights of the socialist "party guy." They may not share any political common ground, but at a deeper level, their rights are intertwined. Have you ever stood with someone you didn't agree with? (If you don't have a personal story, imagine yourself in Eric's dad's position.) How did the experience affect you?

Chapter Seven: Faith in Podunk

Eric recounts a few of the many instances when the CrossWalkers found support and connections while journeying through metaphorical "Podunk, USA." The crew is hosted by Doris and Robert Akers, true Texans with some truly unexpected connections to progressive Christianity. Conversations with Pastor Jene Miller offer a glimpse "into the future of Christian faith at the grass roots." Affirmation 11 affects Christians' use of time, perceptions, and soulfulness in light of love of self.

QUESTIONS

1. Scott asks, "Who is Jesus, for you?" Does your response correspond more closely with the Jesus of history or the Christ of present

experience? If you are inclined toward one direction, try leaning in the other and answer again.

2. Jene says, "The institution of the church may be dying, but the church is more alive now than ever. . . . Collapse is actually waking the church up." How would you assess his observation? How does Jene's observation make you feel?

3. Jene asks, "What are we here for?" What purposes might you work toward as a twenty-first-century American Christian?

4. Do rigid systems "need to die and become new again"? What purposeful place could death, or chaos, have within a healthy and creative whole?

5. Is there a place or community where you can "ask any question, express any doubt, explore any aspect of faith or life," and be taken seriously? If not, imagine what such a community looks like to you. What prevents you from experiencing it? If so, describe it in as much detail as you can. Why does it seem so paradoxically risky to create a community that includes such a safe place? What could happen when your questions, doubts, and explorations are unleashed?

6. Eric reflects on the way that slowing down to walking speed changed his perspective. "Patterns emerge that both confirm and challenge your perceptions of reality." What are the patterns Eric describes? What does it mean that you can "change the world by noticing it"?

Chapter Eight: Silence of the (Christian) Lambs

Eric begins by talking about the six out of ten Americans he describes as "spiritually homeless," finding that these people have not been exposed to the kind of faith they yearn for. In Columbia, Missouri, Eric and Rebecca are hosted by Dean, Jason, and Eric, who speak authentically about their bad experiences with Christians. At the pub they share several stories that highlight the silence of progressive Christians when faced with the less than loving actions of others. Eric speaks about the importance of being authentic toward all people (Affirmation 5), emphasizing LGBT people but not excluding others.

QUESTIONS

1. Have you ever been "spiritually homeless"? What pushes a person away from a faith community or keeps a person away? What did Jesus say about his experience or idea of a spiritual home?

2. Jason says, "What really gets me is not the funeral protesters but all the other Christians who stand silently by and let them do it." We have all been silent at times when we could have spoken out. In light of Jason's statement, what can you do next in this area as an individual and as part of a community?

3. The guys say some interesting things about Jed, the "campus evangelist," at the pub: "I respect Jed's passion," "You know he's personally committed to saving you from something he considers horrible," "Jed doesn't use his beliefs to try to take away our rights." What is the common thread here? How do they feel differently about Jed's message and Jed as a person? How do these statements compare with Jason's feelings toward more progressive but silent Christians?

4. Eric recalls a conversation with a pastor in Kansas about churches and church leaders losing their fear of their own intolerant members and thereby growing in spirit and numbers. Are you aware of any fear dynamics in your faith community? How are shared fears made manifest, directly or indirectly? Within a community of faith, how much intolerance should be tolerated?

5. Reconciling "the rejection and punishment of homosexuals with the love of Christ" (William Sloane Coffin) is a problem for Christians, but LGBT people are not the only ones who have been rejected and punished. Are there other outcast or oppressed people who are of special concern to you? How can Christians begin replacing rejection and punishment toward those we have hurt with Christ's love? What concrete ways of being will embody that love?

Chapter Nine: A Little Light That Shined

The walkers continue to Fulton, Missouri, where members of Saint Alban's Episcopal Church share their town's story. Three Christians protested the public high school's production of *Grease,* so the school canceled the next play, *The Crucible*; Saint Alban's responded by hosting a reading of the play. Eric's thoughts turn from the separation of church and state back to different concepts of salvation, with Christian dominionists' desire to save others from eternal torture as the motivation for their work to unseparate church and state.

QUESTIONS

1. At Saint Alban's, laypeople lead worship except for once every month. What impact do you think that has on the life of their faith

community? On the experience of its members? What do the people of Saint Alban's gain through this arrangement? What is lost?

2. Eric says that Saint Alban's story may seem "to some . . . a courageous but not particularly noteworthy way of shedding the light of Christ in a darkened world." Is there an expectation that everything worth doing is "noteworthy"? Or is sharing Christ's light inherently noteworthy and world-changing? What place do small, routine, or mundane ways of being have in terms of shedding the light of Christ?

3. Why do some people fear certain stories (such as, in this instance, *The Crucible*)? What are we afraid might happen? Is telling the story likely to result in making the feared thing happen? What does this say about the power of stories?

4. Have you ever considered that the separation of church and state can be implied by the Golden Rule, by loving our neighbors as ourselves? The historical Jesus wouldn't share our concept of the separation of church and state, but is it something that "looks like Jesus" (Chapter One)?

5. "The bottom line," Eric writes, is that people become Christians "because they meet people who, in their mind, have found a more compelling path than the one they're on." What implications are there in this insight for the practice of evangelism? Do you know any stories that embody this pattern? What is compelling about the Christian path? What repels?

Chapter Ten: Art and Soul

At Christ Church Cathedral in Saint Louis, CrossWalk America draws protesters who seemed to erroneously conflate Affirmation 11 with a particular position on abortion. Christ Cathedral spends extra energy to make worship a place where differences, art, joy, and creativity are welcomed and celebrated, most notably in the Art and Soul Café. Eric describes the orthodox reforms of King Josiah in ancient Israel and the unintended results of ultraorthodoxy. He wonders what import this story may have for Christian rituals and worship practices today.

QUESTIONS

1. Why can tolerance seem threatening? What is an intolerant person afraid of losing or afraid might happen next? Is tolerance a potential cause of harm? A protester wore a T-shirt saying "JESUS WAS

INTOLERANT"—what are the assumptions behind this statement? What emotions does it raise for you? How do you respond to the assertion that Jesus was intolerant?

2. Lydia Ruffin claims that everyone can be creative. Do you agree? How does your creativity find an outlet? How does creativity find expression in your faith community? How do you respond when your practice of worship includes an unanticipated change or surprise?

3. Many Art and Soul Café participants found a simple dance of everyday movements transformative. Think of a simple, transformative event from your own life, and write down or share that story. Did it occur in the context of worship? When experiences of transformation happen outside of "church," how can those experiences affect church life?

4. "People are so used to being observers in church, not participators. When they participate, they tell us, 'I didn't know I felt this way about such-and-such,' or 'I didn't know this emotion was going to come forward,' or 'This got me in touch with something that was kind of out of reach for a while.'" When do you feel that you are deeply participating in church? What feelings do you associate with being a church "observer"? A "participator"? How might all forms of worship, from fully traditional to the Art and Soul Café, move more toward a spirit of participation?

5. What does the story of King Josiah and Jeremiah mean for Christians today? What might Jeremiah say if he were here?

6. "It is not mistakes that kill worship or faith. God is gracious. What kills worship is lack of authenticity." How does Eric's observation compare with your experience? What makes worship real for you? Does this insight challenge or stretch your own practice of worship? That of your faith community? If a commitment to authenticity were taken seriously, what, if anything, would change in your worship?

Chapter Eleven: "Perfesser Creek-Water"

Eric tells Mark Creek-Water's story in which he journeys with the Cross-Walkers from Phoenix to Washington, D.C. Mark's presence initially tested the walk's commitment to share the journey with anyone who wanted to join, but he rapidly became family. The "Perfesser's" eye for the sacred in nature, his generosity, and his rigorous practice of conservation all stretch the team in sometimes difficult but ultimately rewarding ways. Links between the environment as Creation, the Genesis 1 Creation story, and Christ are described and illustrated through Eric's discussion of Affirmation 3.

QUESTIONS

1. The sacredness of creeks and sycamores is readily apparent to Mark along the walk. Some of us have vivid experiences of the holiness of nature; reflect on such a time, re-creating it through all of your senses in a journal entry or story. Some of us also neglect to incorporate nature into our regular pattern of worship; how might you do so more intentionally?

2. Mark practices a way of life that goes beyond what most Christians will follow. Though the rest of the CrossWalkers don't join in all of Mark's disciplines, he has a true impact on the journey and on the people who know him. What role do people like Mark play in moving the whole group forward?

3. Mark has connected with a sense of abundance that inspires his generosity. What can you learn from his example? For those of us who aren't planning to become voluntarily houseless, how can we still be touched or transformed by Mark's story?

4. Eric's interpretation of the Genesis 1 Creation story provides a long-term story arc in which God actively seeks to "give up direct control in favor of investing others with the power to accomplish God's objectives." How does that story continue today? People give up control in a different sense through technology. What role does technology play as we work toward God's purposes?

5. Eric describes five roles God plays in Creation in addition to "commander in chief": empowerer, relationship builder, artist, organizer, and loving parent. How do you experience God in each of these roles? By giving up direct control, God creates space in which the freedom for us to cocreate becomes possible. In which roles are you a cocreator? What do you help create?

Chapter Twelve: Faithful Doubting

Crossing the border between Indiana and Ohio, the CrossWalkers meet Joe over his offer of ice water. At Cross Creek Community Church in Dayton, Ohio, the group encounters the radical hospitality the church is known for. Listening to members' stories, Eric discerns a theme shared by many of the people met on the walk: learning to trust in one's doubts. While preparing to preach in Columbus, Ohio, he finds the metaphorical image of Good Friday, Holy Saturday, and Easter Sunday Christians. Replacing the "liberal-conservative" axis, this image provides a framework for affirming real common ground and understanding our relationships, our differences, and the veiled unity of Christians who have discovered Easter Sunday.

QUESTIONS

1. The chapter begins with Joe and his ice water, and he doesn't reappear after talking with Meighan and leaving for town. Why is Joe's small gesture of hospitality an important part of this chapter's big-picture story?

2. Like Debbie, have you ever felt challenged to accept *either* science or the Bible but not both? How was that challenge presented to you? What assumptions is this either-or perspective based on? When did you encounter an alternative point of view? (It could be right now, in this book!) What roles do science and the Bible play in your worldview? What is their relationship?

3. We've seen that chaos can be understood to have a place in Creation (Chapter Seven); does doubt have a role in faith? If so, what is doubt's role in your faith?

4. Part of Don's story that goes untold is that he had some "reservations about 'progressive' Christians." What might a few of those reservations be? Do you share any of Don's reservations? Don also says "Hallelujah!" to being freed from some of his childhood beliefs. How have your beliefs changed since childhood or young adulthood? Do you respond with "Hallelujah!" or with something else?

5. As descriptors of grassroots Christianity, the Good Friday, Holy Saturday, and Easter Sunday metaphors illustrate a model that is an interdependent whole. Contrast this with a more typical two-pole axis model, such as "liberal-conservative." How has widespread acceptance of the axial model affected our ability to find common ground? To discuss differences? To solve problems?

6. Eric invites progressive Christians to think of themselves as "the early church of the twenty-first century." What makes this time unique and new? Recognizing both the near impossibility and the implicit hope of making broad predictions, describe your vision of what Christianity could be in five hundred years.

Chapter Thirteen: A Letter from God

More than a year before the walk is to begin, Eric decides that "if we accomplish nothing else, we will bear Jesus with us to D.C." Plans shift, but the CrossWalk team remains true to its call, relying on the participation and support of thousands of volunteers. Eric draws two composite character sketches, of Sue and Nathan, to illustrate some important differences the CrossWalkers encountered on their journey. After the walk, Eric asks a daring question of God and discerns a surprising answer. The chapter concludes with "a letter from God," based on the insight that we are all loved beyond our wildest imagination.

QUESTIONS

1. "Will the image of Christianity in America be changed by this wild, imaginative act?" asks John Shelby Spong. Answer for yourself: Has your image of American Christianity changed? Have you? How?

2. Eric touches on the significance of early childhood experiences before moving on to the role of faith in forming a person's worldview. What events from your childhood influenced your faith's development? As you have grown, what from your childhood faith can you affirm? What has been challenged and perhaps changed?

3. "I was staggered by the debt I owed God. . . . I began to wonder if I was a true enough believer to satisfy God," says the character Sue. Is perfect, sincere belief the purpose God calls Christians toward? When Sue wonders, "Will I be a sheep or a goat?" she assumes that a person is necessarily one hundred percent one or the other. What would Jesus say to a person who is metaphorically part sheep and part goat?

4. "The cross also reveals that God's response is not vengeance but fierce grace," Nathan says. Describe how God's grace could be "fierce." If God's example as parent of a murdered child is grace, what does that mean for Christians' response to violence?

5. Name some of the many conditions that Christians have attempted to place on God's grace and love.

6. Respond to the "letter from God" in thought, writing, conversation, or action.

NOTES

CHAPTER ONE: THE IDEA THAT WOULDN'T GO AWAY:
LISTENING TO GOD

1 Parker Palmer, *A Hidden Wholeness: The Journey Toward an Undivided Life* (San Francisco: Jossey-Bass, 2004), pp. 58–59.

2 Bruce Van Blair, personal correspondence.

3 Some people are uncomfortable with the notion that God desires whatever favors our true self-interest or benefit, arguing that God wants us to be less selfish, not more. But be aware that selfishness and true self-interest are very different things. Selfishness is acting on one's personal needs and desires without considering those of others or God's will. As human beings created by God, we are intrinsically connected to both God and neighbor. True self-interest therefore cannot be separated from love of God and neighbor. In this sense, Jesus could be said to be the most self-interested individual who ever lived, living into his fullest self-identity even as he willingly gave his life for others. You will see more on this in Chapter Two.

4 Someone once observed that when we do get to the edge of a precipice to which God has led us, we leap and either discover there is something solid below us that we did not see before or develop wings to fly.

CHAPTER TWO: PHOENIX RISING

1 Mark and Luke add "all your strength" as well.

CHAPTER THREE: HELLFIRE, DAMNATION, AND GARBAGE DUMPS

1 They also objected to our claim that Christian love of God includes walking fully in the path of Jesus without denying the legitimacy of other paths God may create (Affirmation 1). I'll have more to say about Affirmation 1 in Chapter Four.

2   Incidentally, Petty is not the one who sings this song on Dutko's show. I can only guess how he or his management must have responded if Dutko had solicited the rights to use his voice!

3   Fire, in fact, is a major metaphor for the Holy Spirit in Scripture. Isaiah refers to God's Spirit as a "refiner's fire" that burns away alloys, leaving behind only the precious metal (Isaiah 48:10). The disciples are said to have received "tongues of fire" when the Holy Spirit descended upon them at Pentecost (Acts 2:3).

4   Eugene H. Peterson, *The Message: The Bible in Contemporary Language* (Colorado Springs, Colo.: Navpress, 2002). Line from Scripture is Romans 2:24.

CHAPTER FOUR: JESUS FIRST BAPTIST CHURCH

1   *Newsweek*/Beliefnet Poll, "Where We Stand on Faith," *Newsweek,* August 29, 2005, pp. 48–49. Complete poll results may be found at http://www.beliefnet.com/story/173/story_17353_1.html.

2   A *koan* is a short paradoxical, seemingly meaningless, or whimsical statement or story used in Zen Buddhism for meditation and spiritual awakening.

3   Incidentally, we found plenty of evidence on the walk to suggest that fundamentalist Christians are not nearly as homogeneous on the subject of homosexuality as it might seem. Many have faced difficult questions about the beliefs espoused by their leaders when they have discovered that a family member or friend is gay—or when they discovered that they themselves were!

4   Carlton Pearson, from an interview conducted for the CrossWalk America film *Asphalt Gospel.*

5   William Sloane Coffin, *Credo* (Louisville, Ky.: Westminster/John Knox, 2004), p. 138.

6   Eric Elnes, *The Phoenix Affirmations: A New Vision for the Future of Christianity* (San Francisco: Jossey-Bass, 2006), pp. 4–5.

7   In modern times, we are so used to assuming that Israelite faith was monotheistic that we often read direct references to other gods without noticing their import, or we think, "The author really doesn't mean it." The Psalms contain a number of such passages. For instance, Psalm 82:1 intones, "God has taken his place in the divine council; in the midst of the gods he holds judgment." Likewise, Psalm 95:3 asserts, "For the LORD is a great God, and a great King above all gods." What these and similar passages make clear is that Yahweh is not assumed to be merely one god among many, nor did the Israelites believe that other gods could circumvent Yahweh's will.

For an Israelite to worship any other god but Yahweh, therefore, was considered at best foolhardy and at worst blasphemous. Consider all the invective against Israelites who worship the Canaanite god Baal. Whether or not Baal's path could be considered a "true" one with respect to his own followers, it was certainly understood to be a false one for Israel, who had chosen, and been chosen by, Yahweh as its God. As Psalm 97:7 claims with respect to Israelites who worship other gods, "All worshipers of images are put to shame, those who make their boast in worthless idols; all gods bow down before him [Yahweh]."

8 See also Deuteronomy 4:19, where Yahweh is said to have allotted the sun, the moon, and the stars, "all the host of heaven" (which were thought to be gods) to "all the peoples everywhere under heaven." Compare Deuteronomy 29:25–26. For an interesting passage about Yahweh in the Divine Council, see Psalm 82. Some scholars believe that this passage marks the transition from monolatry to outright monotheism, at least within one segment of Yahwistic faith.

9 Some older translations do not read "according to the number of the gods" but "according to the number of the sons of Israel." The difference is due to an ancient copyist's error or, more likely, a deliberate change made by the copyist to conform the text to his monotheistic theology. How this error or fabrication was discovered and confirmed by scholars is a long, complex story, but essentially it was due to the discovery of the Dead Sea Scrolls in the twentieth century. These scrolls gave scholars access to copies of certain biblical texts that are far older than the ones previously used for translation. Scholars had already suspected the translation "according to the sons of Israel" to be incorrect due to a difference found in an ancient Greek translation of the Old Testament known as the Septuagint. The Dead Sea Scrolls provided strong confirmation of their suspicions.

CHAPTER FIVE: THE TRICKSTER SHOWS UP—AGAIN!

1 K. L. Nichols, "Introduction to Native American Tricksters," June 25, 2002, http://members.cox.net/academia/coyote.html.

CHAPTER SIX: ASPHALT JESUS

1 All quotes from Tracy Dunn-Noland's blog are reprinted with her kind permission.

2 Karen Armstrong, "Compassion's Fruit," *AARP Magazine,* March-April 2005, p. 64.

3 Ibid.

4 Ibid.

CHAPTER SEVEN: FAITH IN PODUNK

1 Wayne Muller, *Sabbath: Restoring the Sacred Rhythm of Rest* (New York: Bantam Books, 2000), p. 70.

CHAPTER EIGHT: SILENCE OF THE (CHRISTIAN) LAMBS

1 According to a poll conducted by *Newsweek* and Beliefnet, responses vary between 7.7 and 9.1 in 10, depending on the age group being asked. The average is 8.5. "Where We Stand on Faith," *Newsweek,* August 29, 2005, pp. 48–49. Full poll results can be found at http://www.beliefnet.com/story/ 173/story_17353_1.html. A more recent survey conducted in 2006 by Baylor University reported that 8.2 in 10 identify themselves as Catholic or Protestant. However, this figure does not include those affiliated with smaller Christian groups such as the Eastern, Russian, and Greek Orthodox churches, Christian Science, or the Church of Jesus Christ of Latter-Day Saints (Mormon). It also does not include those unaffiliated with organized religion who nevertheless state a belief in Jesus as "the son of God." *American Piety in the 21st Century: Selected Findings from the Baylor University Survey* (Waco, Tex.: Baylor University, September, 2006); see esp. pp. 7–14. This report can be found at http://www.baylor.edu/content/services/ document.php/33304.pdf.

2 William Sloane Coffin, "An Open Letter to the Roman Catholic Bishops of America," presented November 14, 2000. The text can be found at http:// catholicnewtimes.org/index.php?module=articles&func=display&ptid=1&a id=1007.

CHAPTER NINE: A LITTLE LIGHT THAT SHINED

1 Nancy Gilbert and Torii Davis are real names. Rob Erikson is an assumed identity. Our conversation, however, is real and accurate.

2 Tony Campolo, speaking at the Harry Emerson Fosdick Preaching Convocation, Riverside Church, New York City, October 24, 2006.

3 D. James Kennedy, in materials handed out to participants at a national conference sponsored by the Center for Reclaiming America, February 18–19, 2005, Coral Ridge Presbyterian Church. Reported in the *Christian Science Monitor,* March 16, 2005.

4 Bruce Van Blair, "Faith of Our Fathers?" Unpublished sermon, June 19, 2005.

CHAPTER TEN: ART AND SOUL

1 The full version of Affirmation 11 states, in part, that Christian love of self includes "caring for our bodies" and that we have moved away from Christ's path "when we have denigrated or abused our bodies, or those of others, or denied the rights and responsibilities of others to make decisions about how they care for the bodies God gave them." Phoenix Affirmations, version 3.8.

2 She made this statement when the protesters showed up later in the morning at the Metropolitan Community Church of Saint Louis where walker Brad Wishon was preaching. No one could figure out why antiabortion protesters were showing up outside a predominantly gay church, abortion not exactly being an issue among homosexuals!

3 J. Maxwell Miller and John Hayes, *A History of Ancient Israel and Judah*, 2nd ed. (Louisville, Ky.: Westminster/John Knox, 2006). Another commentary, a bit more dated but accessible to a lay audience, is John Bright, *A History of Israel*, 4th ed. (Louisville, Ky.: Westminster/John Knox, 2000).

4 Note that in Luke 19, Jesus quotes Jeremiah when he turns over the tables of the money changer in the Temple, accusing the religious authorities of turning the Temple into a "den of robbers."

CHAPTER ELEVEN: "PERFESSER CREEK-WATER"

1 Mark Beliles and Stephen McDowell, *America's Providential History,* cited in Glenn Scherer, "Radical Christian-Right Views Sway Politicians and Threaten Environment," *Our Toxic Times,* February 2005, pp. 5, 25.

2 Cited in ibid., p. 3. It is important to note that James Watt disputed having made that statement to Congress. The quote was made widely known by Bill Moyers, who cited an article in an online environmental journal called *Grist*. The author of the article cited a book by Austin Miles called *Setting the Captives Free*. This is the earliest reference to the quote that anyone knows of. And, while the quote is there in Miles's book, he never says Watt said it before Congress. *Grist* researched the whole thing and eventually pulled the quote and apologized to Watt, as has Moyers. *Grist's* article, along with the retraction of that portion, is found at http://www.grist.org/news/maindish/2004/10/27/scherer=christian/#correction.

3 When I refer to "Genesis 1," I am actually referring to Genesis from 1:1 to the first half of 2:4, which is a complete literary unit, written by the same author. For simplicity, I simply refer to the unit as "Genesis 1."

4 This translation is more grammatically close to the underlying Hebrew than a common version, which reads, "In the beginning, when God created the heavens and the earth, the earth was a formless void and darkness covered the face of the deep, while the Spirit of God swept over the face of the waters. Then God said, 'Let there be light.'"

5 I originally gleaned this insight from the German biblical theologian Michael Welker in "What Is Creation? Rereading Genesis 1 and 2," *Theology Today*, 1991, *48*, 69.

6 A social system is already suggested in the Genesis 1 account in the seven instances God evaluates Creation, calling it "good" and finally "very good" (positing value is a social construct); in the three instances God gives names to Creation (again, a product of a social order); and in the case where God announces that the stars are to serve as "signs and for seasons and for days and years" (in other words, they mark the social calendar for humans).

7 For a full listing of these correspondences, see my article "Creation and Tabernacle: The Priestly Writer's 'Environmentalism,'" in *Horizons in Biblical Theology*, 1994, *16*, 144–155.

8 The divisions are Exodus 25:1, 30:1, 30:17, 30:22, 30:34, 31:1, and 31:12. With the exception of Exodus 30:1, each is marked by the phrase "Yahweh said to Moses," much as the Creation account in Genesis is marked by the phrase "Yahweh said."

9 Of particular interest here is the fact that the Priestly Writer uses the expression "Spirit of God" (*ruach elohim*) to describe the power with which God invests Bezalel. Although this term appears a number of times in the Old Testament, it is used in only two contexts by the Priestly Writer: the Creation account in Genesis and the Tabernacle creation account in Exodus. For more on the Priestly Writer's intriguing use of the expression "Spirit of God," see the article cited in note 7.

10 I've always wondered why more stewardship sermons aren't preached on this passage!

11 For more on this particular understanding of God's power and its implications for worship, see Chapter 4 in *The Phoenix Affirmations*.

12 The Synoptic Gospels are Matthew, Mark, and Luke.

CHAPTER TWELVE: FAITHFUL DOUBTING

1   National Oceanic and Atmospheric Administration, "Summer's Peak Has Arrived," *NOAA News Online,* August 1, 2006, http://www.noaanews .noaa.gov/stories2006/s2674.htm.

2   "Living the Questions" is a video-based curriculum designed by two United Methodist pastors as "a progressive alternative for Christian invitation, initiation, and spiritual formation." We discovered the curriculum being used and discussed by a number of churches during our walk. For more information, go to http://www.livingthequestions.com.

3   After reading my characterizations of these three energies, you may wish to explore other related metaphors, like Palm Sunday energy or Maundy Thursday or Pentecost energies!

4   Rod Parsley and Russell Johnson, quoted in Frances FitzGerald, "Holy Toledo," *New Yorker,* July 31, 2006, pp. 29, 30.

5   Curiously, members of certain churches would regularly approach us quietly offering support while describing themselves as the "only ones" in their church who would likely resonate with the Phoenix Affirmations. Yet others in these same congregations would do likewise, apparently unaware that they were *not* alone in their beliefs.

6   We also found them in Amarillo, Texas; Wichita, Kansas; Mount Airy, Maryland; and a younger version in Kansas City, Missouri.

7   Good Friday–oriented Christians lose their certainty about who is responsible for the loss of "their Jesus." Doubt may even move them to let go of their certainties about who Jesus is for them. Similarly, when Holy Saturday–oriented Christians lose their fear of doubt, learning to follow where it leads, they often discover God in surprising places.

CHAPTER THIRTEEN: A LETTER FROM GOD

1   University Congregational United Church of Christ, the home church of Meighan Pritchard.

2   *Bob Abernethy's Religion and Ethics Newsweekly,* April 23, 2006.

3   Bob and Mary Marshall, of Santa Fe, New Mexico. When Bob could not join us in Saint Louis, their son flew in from Rochester, New York, to walk with Mary.

4   Dr. Wilbur Wheaton, former president of Ottawa University.

5 All three articles appeared in *A New Christianity for a New World,* an e-mail newsletter that is read by over one hundred thousand people. The article cited appeared in the September 16, 2006, issue.

6 The Greek word *metanoia,* often translated here as "repent," literally means to change one's way of life based on a complete change of thought.

7 Elizabeth Barrett Browning, "Aurora Leigh," bk. 7.

CROSSWALK AMERICA

CROSSWALK AMERICA (http://www.CrossWalkAmerica.org) is a nonprofit organization committed to changing the face of Christianity in America to a more compassionate, inclusive one. It seeks to establish common ground between people of differing beliefs as a way of exploring and engaging differences more productively. In 2006, CrossWalk America hosted a walk across the United States as its first major step toward promoting the Phoenix Affirmations, twelve principles of Christian faith based on Jesus' core values of love of God, neighbor, and self. CrossWalk America's ongoing work includes creating a nationwide network of individuals and organizations interested in the Phoenix Affirmations and their implications for Christian life; commissioning a film based on the walk, titled *The Asphalt Gospel;* providing educational materials that help laypeople articulate their beliefs more clearly and effectively; and creating Webcast audio and video media that promote Christian compassion and inclusiveness.

THE AUTHOR AND THE
CORE WALK TEAM

The Author

ERIC ELNES is a biblical scholar with a Ph.D. in biblical studies from Princeton Theological Seminary. He is the senior pastor of Scottsdale Congregational United Church of Christ (www.artinworship.com) in Scottsdale, Arizona, and director of the Ocotillo Institute for Exploring Spirituality, the Arts, and Christian Worship. A Seattle native, Eric currently lives in Scottsdale, Arizona, with his wife, Melanie, and daughters, Arianna and Maren. Before and during the walk, Eric served as co-president of CrossWalk America and currently writes a weekly blog column (http://blog.crosswalkamerica.org) and leads its Webcast video initiative.

The Core Walk Team

REBECCA GLENN quit her job in the information technology field, which she served for more than twenty years in positions including consultant, vice president of information technology for an insurance company, and chief information officer for a global semiconductor manufacturer. Rebecca is an active member of Scottsdale Congregational United Church of Christ. Rebecca lives in her native Phoenix, Arizona, with husband, Tom, and son, Weston. Her daughter, Katrina Glenn, was a member of the core walk team, and her father, Ray Gentry, drove the RV support vehicle. Before and during the walk, Rebecca served as co-president of CrossWalk America and currently serves as its executive director.

BRAD WISHON has been an ordained minister for more than twenty years. Born and raised in Saint Louis, Missouri, where he also served as pastor of the Metropolitan Community Church of Greater Saint Louis, Brad currently serves as senior pastor of Gentle Shepherd Metropolitan Community Church in Phoenix, Arizona. Brad is working toward a doctorate in theology and has been a key spokesperson for a number of organizations working for lesbian, gay, bisexual, and transgender (LGBT) equality. Before and during the walk, Brad also served as vice president of CrossWalk America. He currently serves the organization as chairman of the board.

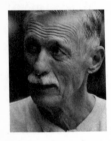

MERRILL DAVISON, who retired from General Dynamics in 2005, was serving in a volunteer capacity as a community developer for Asbury United Methodist Church, in Phoenix, Arizona, until taking a leave of absence to join the walk. Merrill enjoys hiking, riding his motorcycle, and spending time with his grandchildren. Before the walk, Merrill served on the CrossWalk America Logistics Team, transitioning to become on-site public relations coordinator during the walk. Merrill currently serves the organization as a blogger and general volunteer.

MEIGHAN PRITCHARD is an active member of University Congregational United Church of Christ in Seattle, Washington, where she directed the handbell choir for fifteen years. A Yale graduate, Meighan quit her job as education and chorale coordinator for the Seattle Symphony to participate in the walk. She lives in her native Seattle with three cats and a big organic garden. During the walk, Meighan served as on-site logistics coordinator and played hammered dulcimer at events. She currently serves the organization as a blogger and general volunteer.